RAGGED REVOLUTIONARIES

RAGGED REVOLUTIONARIES

The Lumpenproletariat and African American Marxism
in Depression-Era Literature

NATHANIEL MILLS

University of Massachusetts Press
Amherst and Boston

Copyright © 2017 by University of Massachusetts Press
All rights reserved
Printed in the United States of America
ISBN 978-1-62534-279-9 (paper); 278-2 (hardcover)
Designed by Sally Nichols
Set in Adobe Minion Pro
Printed and bound by Maple Press, Inc.

Cover design by Sally Nichols
Cover art: Charles Wilbert White (1918–1979), *Untitled (Fight for Freedom)*, 1945. Tempera on board, 24 x 18 in. (67 x 45.7 cm). Montclair Art Museum. Museum purchase; prior gifts of Mr. and Mrs. Warren F. Van Thunen, the Estate of Francis Herbert Peaty, Mrs. Siegrfried Peierls, and Acquisition Fund, 1996.30.

Excerpts from Richard Wright's letter of c. 1940 to Mike Gold and from *Black Hope*: Copyright © 2017 The Estate of Richard Wright. Reprinted by permission of John Hawkins & Associates, Inc., and the Estate of Richard Wright.

Quotations from Margaret Walker's personal papers and letters to Richard Wright are used by permission of the Margaret Walker Center, Jackson State University.

Quotations from Ralph Ellison's unpublished manuscripts and letters are used by permission of the Ralph and Fanny Ellison Charitable Trust.

Quotations from Stanley Edgar Hyman's letter of 1942 to Ralph Ellison are used by permission of Phoebe Pettingell.

Material from chapter 3 was previously published in "Ralph Ellison's Marxism: The Lumpenproletariat, the Folk, and the Revolution," *African American Review* 47, no. 4 (Winter 2014): 537–54. Copyright © 2015 The Johns Hopkins University Press and St. Louis University.

Library of Congress Cataloging-in-Publication Data

Names: Mills, Nathaniel, 1982– author.
Title: Ragged revolutionaries : the lumpenproletariat and African American Marxism in Depression-era literature / Nathaniel Mills.
Description: Amherst : University of Massachusetts Press, 2017. | Includes bibliographical references and index.
Identifiers: LCCN 2016059943| ISBN 9781625342799 (pbk. : alk. paper) | ISBN 9781625342782 (hardcover : alk. paper)
Subjects: LCSH: American literature—African American authors—History and criticism. | American literature—20th century—History and criticism. | Communism and literature—United States—History—20th century. | Socialism and literature—United States—History—20th century. | Marginality, Social in literature.
Classification: LCC PS153.N5 M557 2017 | DDC 810.9/896073—dc23
LC record available at https://lccn.loc.gov/2016059943

British Library Cataloguing-in-Publication Data
A catalog record for this book is available from the British Library.

For my parents, Michael Mills and Mary Zita Reedy

CONTENTS

Preface ix

Introduction. Communists, Writers, and Other Outsiders 1

1. The Ragged Proletariat: Itineraries for a Transient Concept 20
2. Richard Wright and the Lumpenproletarian Desire for Revolution 49
3. From Oklahoma City to Tuskegee, from Harlem to Dayton: The Sites, Levels, and Travels of Ralph Ellison's Marxism 94
4. Prostitutes, Delinquents, and Folk Heroes: Margaret Walker's Lumpenproletariat 136

Conclusion. Afterlives of the Depression Lumpenproletariat 170

Notes 181

Index 199

PREFACE

During the years I was researching and writing this book, struggles against economic, racial, and gender oppression achieved a new level of visibility in the national news, social media discussions, and everyday political debates. First, the Occupy Wall Street movement brought national attention to the structural inequalities of capitalism and finance. Trayvon Martin was killed in Florida. Michael Brown was killed in Ferguson, Missouri, triggering mass protests against racist policing and ultimately helping make visible the frequency of police brutality nationwide. Many more African American individuals lost their lives at the hands of the police, overwhelming us with evidence and examples of the violent racism of the state. In response, the Black Lives Matter movement has highlighted the prevalence of racial oppression in an era of American history that, not many years ago, had been dubbed "postracial." At the same time, the social recognition and legal protection of gender and sexual equality has been a major site of national struggle: efforts to restrict the reproductive rights of women, to deny constitutional rights to gays and lesbians, and to dehumanize transgender subjects, have been asserted and contested. As I write now, the 2016 presidential election has introduced both reactionary and socialist rhetoric into the mainstream of American politics. This election season has furnished complicated, and at times farcical, demonstrations of how white privilege and xenophobia can both obstruct and be intertwined with commitments to economic justice or working-class interests.

In short, as I've been writing about the African American Depression-era literary left, contemporary events have foregrounded present concerns that also weighed on radical writers in the 1930s: the complexity of American social relations and the brutality underwriting capitalism, white supremacy, and patriarchy. The anticapitalist and antiracist activism that, in both moments, attempts to counteract that brutality, speaks to the perpetual desire for and necessity of revolution. In no small part, this book grew out of the conviction that Marxism, for all of its European and nineteenth-century limitations, can, when appropriated and reworked, teach us about racial, economic, and gender oppression in America—both in the 1930s and now—and how to overcome it.

The general origins of that conviction go back to my academic training in Marxist theory, but the specific moment I now recognize as galvanizing the theoretical and political assumptions informing this book came when, as an undergraduate at Syracuse University, I read Ralph Ellison's 1977 essay "The Little Man at Chehaw Station" in an American literature class. In this piece, Ellison depicts American life as full of unexpected opportunities that complicate the distribution of cultural expertise according to racial, class, and gender rule. For example, African American workers can have advanced knowledge of classical opera; or Hazel Harrison, Ellison's music teacher at Tuskegee, can be at once marginalized as an African American woman in the Jim Crow South and privileged as an associate and peer of multiple European composers and musicians. There's a crucial lesson here for anyone thinking about power and resistance in America: namely, that the disenfranchised possess resources for both cultural creativity and personal self-invention. This point obviously has political ramifications. Working as an activist on the Depression-era left, the young Ellison encounters workers with advanced knowledge of classical opera. The fact that they appreciate high culture while being racially and economically exploited challenges Ellison's orthodox Marxist assumptions about race and class.

Reading Ellison's essay was a watershed moment in my intellectual development. At the time, I was committed to Marxism as the best discourse for understanding power and exploitation, oppression and transformation. I was initially tempted to disregard Ellison's essay as a patriotic defense of the status quo, but the lesson it offered soon seemed one that radical and Marxist intellectuals should embrace and consider rather than dismiss as "liberalism" or Cold War apologetics. Ellison's insistence that the form of American life equipped the marginalized with the possibility of resisting the full extent of their marginalization came to be, for me, a generative starting point for research. A Marxist understanding of American conditions, I decided, should be one that is informed and strengthened by the claims Ellison puts forth in the essay.

While studying the literary and political radicalism of the Great Depression, I came to feel that the writers of the Depression left who best grasped the basic insights described in "The Little Man at Chehaw Station" were certain African American Communists, including the young Ellison himself, whose entryway into Marxism during the 1930s was not the proletariat, but the transients, criminals, underworld operators, and outlaws of modern society. Marxism has a specific designation for such types: the *lumpenproletariat,* or "proletariat in rags." This book explores the strange fact that, for twentieth-century black writers and activists, this clunky German term and minor Marxist concept actually named Marxism's ability to spark revolutionary consciousness in the United States. The social outsiders of the lumpenproletariat inspired committed Depression-era African American writers to confront a complication later suggested by Ellison's essay: it's ignorant to assert that the marginalized are mere victims unable to work against their marginalization, and that doesn't change the fact that it's equally ignorant to mistake the inventiveness and resourcefulness of the marginalized as a sign that structural oppression and exclusion don't exist or are ultimately ineffective. How the young Ellison, along with his comrades Richard Wright and Margaret Walker, wrote about that complication led me on a journey of archival discovery and critical reading that eventually resulted in this book.

This project was made possible by multiple sources of support and guidance. I'm grateful first and foremost to Alan Wald, under whose mentorship and influence this project was conceived and developed, and whose enthusiasm for the study of the American left has been both instructive and inspiring. Marjorie Levinson, Megan Sweeney, and the late Patricia Yaeger were all instrumental in shaping this book's disciplinary and theoretical interventions. Harvey Teres introduced me to the Depression literary left and thus planted the first seeds of this project. As I researched and wrote this book, the support and critical acumen of Corinne Martin were invaluable. Staff members at the Library of Congress, the Beinecke Library at Yale University, and the Margaret Walker Center at Jackson State University all assisted with my research in the archives. Alice Birney at the Library of Congress, and Robert Luckett and Angela Stewart at the Margaret Walker Center were especially helpful. John Callahan, the literary executor of the Ralph Ellison estate, provided helpful suggestions and permission to quote from the Ellison archive. My ideas were enriched at various points by conversations with Alex Beringer, Anthony Dawahare, Sarah Ehlers, Cheryl Higashida, Lawrence Jackson, Konstantina Karageorgos, Chung-Hao Ku, Megan Levad, Brian Matzke, Timothy Parrish, Paula Rabinowitz, Danielle Spratt, Steven Wexler, and John S. Wright. California State University, Northridge and the University of Minnesota provided support. Amanda Harrison and J. C. Lee were vital allies. My editor, Brian Halley, was both patient and enthusiastic as he helped me navigate the publishing process; his expertise and guidance made this book better than it otherwise would have been. Finally, I'd like to thank various friends and family members, human and feline, for their generosity, assistance, and distraction.

RAGGED REVOLUTIONARIES

INTRODUCTION
COMMUNISTS, WRITERS, AND OTHER OUTSIDERS

In his 1971 lecture "Remembering Richard Wright," Ralph Ellison reflected on the life of the man who was his close friend, mentor, and intellectual partner when both began their careers as writers on the Communist left in the 1930s. Ellison describes Wright's arrival in Chicago in 1927, "the city where after years of Southern Negro migration great jazz was being played and reinvented, where the stockyards and railroads, and the steel mills of Gary, Indiana, were transforming a group of rural, agricultural Americans into city people and into a *lumpenproletariat*, a class over whom we now despair."[1] The minor and relatively arcane Marxist concept of the lumpenproletariat intrudes, rhetorically, on this invocation of modern black history and culture, suggesting that Ellison perceived a connection among Wright, twentieth-century black experience, and Marxism. Another of Wright's close friends and fellow African American Communist writers from the Depression, Margaret Walker, also associated Wright with this peculiar Marxist term. Walker defined Wright's work as deriving "from the world of life and the chaotic, disorganized experiences of . . . the lumpenproletariat." Wright is thus "the first black American to write the novel of social protest and to use the lumpenproletariat of black life."[2]

Ellison and Walker's similar descriptions of Wright as concerned with the black lumpenproletariat deploy the term rather casually, but together they suggest a new way of thinking about African American literary leftism and the role of Marxism in politically committed black writing. Given Wright's well-known alignment with the Communist Party of the United States and investment in Marxism in the 1930s, the appearance in these recollections of the lumpenproletariat ("proletariat in rags") in place of the proletariat is counterintuitive. The lumpenproletariat names that which, for Marxism, doesn't matter or doesn't count. Marx and Engels coined the term to describe socioeconomic outsiders like drifters, transients, prostitutes, criminals, and outlaws. Because such individuals do not participate in industrial production and thus have no class identity or social place, Marx and Engels saw them as irrelevant to their epistemological and political interests. Classical Marxism accordingly dismisses lumpenproletarian persons as degenerates who survive through illicit, disreputable measures on the margins of society and are especially prone to co-option by forces of reaction. The decision of Ellison and Walker to identify the Depression's most famous black Marxist writer with the lumpenproletariat stems from the fact that, during the Depression, they too wrote revolutionary literature that centered not on the heroic working class, but on lumpenproletarian figures. In using the lumpenproletariat to examine Wright, Ellison, and Walker's Depression-era engagements with Marxism, I seek not only to offer a new case study of the conceptual and cultural innovation of the 1930s black Communist literary left, but also to disrupt standing assumptions about the relationship of African American writing and Marxist thought. To do so, I pursue the trace of a long-overlooked trajectory of black radicalism, one that engages Marxism through the odd, minor concept of the lumpenproletariat.

Given that the lumpenproletariat is a pejorative term in the Marxist lexicon, a Marxism that revalues outsiders and situates them at the heart of its epistemological and political efforts must necessarily be a revisionary Marxism, one that finds Marxism's limits in order to push it further outwards. The lumpenproletariat names such a limit. Michael Hardt and Antonio Negri explain that the centrality of the proletariat and economic production to Marxism has caused it to neglect the sociopolitical potential of the global poor. "The poor are thought to be dangerous, either morally dangerous because they are unproductive social parasites—thieves, prostitutes, drug addicts, and the like—or politically dangerous because they are disorganized, unpredictable, and tendentially reactionary." The lumpenproletariat, Marx and Engels's term for the poor as understood in this manner, has not been adequately conceptualized but rather "has functioned at times to demonize the poor as a whole."[3] Brent Hayes Edwards writes that the lumpenproletariat "has always represented a problem area in Marxist theory, for the few intellectuals who have not chosen simply to toss *lumpen* around as a broad term of sectarian denigration."[4] When used dismissively, the term blocks Marxism's access to the socially marginalized, those individuals who survive outside of capitalism's relations of production.

Ragged Revolutionaries: The Lumpenproletariat and African American Marxism in Depression-Era Literature addresses the ways African American authors and activists have rethought classical Marxism's framing of the lumpenproletariat in order to better explicate the socioeconomic and cultural structures of the modern United States. The most familiar articulation of this project occurs in the theoretical work of the Black Panther Party in the 1960s and 1970s. The Panthers used the term lumpenproletariat to refer to the criminalized inner-city black population they saw, in place of the industrial proletariat, as the true vanguard of revolutionary change in postwar America. Panther theorists like Huey Newton, Kathleen Cleaver, and Eldridge Cleaver used Marxism's own dialectical and materialist logic, and borrowed Frantz Fanon's rethinking of the lumpenproletariat in colonial and racial contexts, to argue that the unemployed and criminal segments of the black population were, precisely due to their lack of incorporation in the social order, structurally positioned to overturn it. In contrast to the proletarian rhetoric of more traditional Marxist parties, Panther leaders often romanticized the lumpenproletariat: "O.K. We are Lumpen. Right on," Eldridge Cleaver wrote.[5] Their strategic adoption of the visual styles and personas associated with the African American urban underworld is well known. Amy Ongiri explains that "the Black Panther Party went to great lengths to utilize a dress code that consciously restated their affinity with the young, hip, urban 'brother on the block.'"[6] The party even featured a soul and funk band called the Lumpen that performed at rallies.[7]

But the Panthers' lumpenproletarian orientation was not merely stylistic. Rather, it entailed a complex redefinition of Marxism that, at the same time, operated with fidelity to Marxism's core revolutionary principles. Kathleen Cleaver thus explained that a proper Marxist approach to revolution in the United States involved rethinking the social origins of transformative agency. It required categorizing African Americans who lack any relationship to the means of production and "who leave the vicious system of compulsory mis-education without any marketable skills, little allegiance to anything, and a generalized hostility to everything" as a revolutionary force.[8] A Marxism able to speak to and for African American concerns in postwar America, the Panthers theorized, would have to be reorganized around one of its own most neglected concepts.

Kathleen Cleaver's description of the black lumpenproletariat conjures up, for students and scholars of African American literature, Bigger Thomas, the figure created three decades earlier by Wright in *Native Son* (1940). Bigger is hardly a class-conscious worker, yet had he lived in the postwar era the Panthers would have identified him as the revolutionary agent of their brand of Marxism. And in *Native Son*, Bigger's lumpenproletarian perspectives and experiences catalyze, rather than obstruct, Wright's own application of Marxism to modern African American conditions. In other words, there has been a black tradition of Marxism—one that bridges the Old and New Lefts, Depression-era Communist writers and Civil Rights–era radical activists—in which the type Bigger represents has been positioned not as the deformed product of racial and economic oppression, and not as the underworld scum whose base self-interest threatens revolutionary political organization, but as the bearer of antiracist and anticapitalist possibility.

The Panthers' work on the lumpenproletariat can thus be read as an articulation, in theoretical form, of earlier revisions to Marxism advanced in the literary writings of Wright, Ellison, and Walker during the Depression. Each writer used the lumpenproletariat to analyze the socioeconomic processes that, in Depression America, reduce individuals to social discards. But these writers also envisioned new mechanisms and sources of revolutionary change, change that emerges not from the laboring conditions of the proletariat at the point of production, but from the inventive social and cultural practices of the dispossessed, marginalized, discarded, and outlawed. This anti-orthodox black Marxism emerges in texts like Wright's 1936 poem "Transcontinental" and his novels *Lawd, Today!* (written in the 1930s but published posthumously) and *Native Son;* Ellison's 1930s short fiction and two long unfinished prose works, *Tillman and Tackhead* and *Slick;* Walker's poetry collection

For My People (1942), her unfinished Depression novel *Goose Island,* and certain of her unpublished poems of the 1930s. These works imagine modes of agency and political desire beyond proletarian organization or institutional political leadership. Instead, they draw inspiration from the criminalized underworlds of urban America; economically dislocated hobos and transients riding the rails in the midst of the Depression; black folk heroes and romantic, defiant outlaws; and other socially marginal persons and practices.

This lumpenproletarian black Marxism owes its emergence in the Depression to a variety of historical and cultural factors. The Communist Party and the various social and cultural institutions aligned with the party were formative influences on many African American writers. Even though the literary work of Wright, Ellison, and Walker was relatively unaffected by specific turns in party policy during the period, the party fostered a unique discursive milieu in which matters of Marxist thought, black culture, and literary form could be triangulated. Lawrence Jackson's history of mid-century African American literature demonstrates how the support of party journals, clubs, and organizations facilitated the careers of the generation of black writers to which Wright, Ellison, and Walker belonged.[9] Brian Dolinar argues that the Depression-era party fostered the formation of what he calls the "black cultural front," which "provided a network, both formal and informal, of contacts that helped many black writers and artists advance their careers." Artists associated with the black cultural front were by no means "bound to any supposed 'party line'" and worked in relative autonomy from the party's internal "political twists and turns." They were drawn and inspired instead by "the aggressive stance the Communists took against racism . . . and the belief that a society free from all forms of oppression could exist."[10]

If the party created opportunities for black writers to pursue their craft, it also validated black political traditions and black cultural forms as expressive of revolutionary and progressive political ambitions. In 1928, the international Communist movement adopted the "Black Belt" thesis, proposing that territory in the southeastern United States populated primarily by African Americans constituted an oppressed nation. This complex thesis synthesized racial nationalist, anti-imperialist, and Marxist rhetorics and political strategies, elevating African American struggles, which might otherwise appear to be nationalist rather than

Marxist, to prominence in Communist discourse. Robin D. G. Kelley writes that the thesis "confirmed" that "African Americans had their own unique revolutionary tradition" and "[created] an opening for African Americans to promote race politics in spite of the Party's formal opposition to 'Negro Nationalism.'"[11] As Barbara Foley explains, "the radical working-class movement for the first time in U.S. history moved itself off dead center with regard to the issue of confronting racism" as the party "attracted a significant mass base in black communities."[12] The party valued black expressive forms like music and literature as evidence of the distinct national culture of African Americans, but also as, to quote Foley, "indices to the revolutionary spirit of the black masses . . . that . . . might be effectively mobilized in winning black workers and farmers to the Communist movement."[13] In 1935, in response to the rise of international fascist movements, the party shifted away from the Black Belt thesis toward the Popular Front, a strategy by which the party, in order to build coalitions against fascism, sought to ally itself with American liberalism and to establish the contiguity of revolutionary politics with American democratic political traditions. However, Kelley shows that the party still viewed African American culture as a potent vehicle of political desire by "embracing a broad range of black art and artists as not only inherently progressive but also profoundly American."[14] Questions of race and class, nationalism and internationalism, and the revolutionary content of black culture were thus energized by the party's discourse of African American culture and politics, a discourse that influenced and enabled the work of writers like Wright, Ellison, and Walker.

A salient example of Communist involvement in black political struggles in the 1930s, as well as the intersection of Communist activism with the lumpenproletariat, was the party's role in the Scottsboro incident. In 1931, nine African American transients riding a freight train in Alabama were accused by local authorities of raping two white female drifters who were riding the same train. After trials in Scottsboro, Alabama, eight of the nine young men were sentenced to death. The Communist Party's legal arm, the International Labor Defense, stepped in to spearhead the defendants' appeals while the party turned their ongoing legal struggles into an international antiracist cause. Dolinar writes that "the Communist Party would shape the discourse around what they called a 'legal lynching,' " and dates the rise of the black cultural front in part to the Scottsboro campaign.¹⁵

Scottsboro galvanized African American support for the Communist left, but it also showcased the ways in which the Marxist discourse of the left opened up new avenues for conceptualizing intersectional racial, gender, and economic oppression during the Depression. Cheryl Higashida has shown that black Communist women activists like Louise Thompson challenged the "masculinist terms" of the International Labor Defense's rhetorical strategy, which derogated the two white women involved as merely prostitutes in order to frame resistance to Jim Crow as a cross-racial masculine prerogative. For Higashida, a key text of this revisionary effort is Thompson's report of a 1933 Scottsboro rally in Washington, DC. Thompson emphasized how Ruby Bates, one of the white accusers of the Scottsboro men who subsequently denied the charge and joined the left, marched with one of the mothers of the accused. "The text and image in Thompson's story," Higashida points out, "implied that women were redefining the masculinist terms of worker solidarity and Black militancy."¹⁶ I would add to Higashida's analysis that Thompson's rhetorical maneuver of reframing the prostitute (a figure stigmatized, for very similar reasons, both by patriarchy and by classical Marxist evaluations of the lumpenproletariat) as a positive participant in interracial radical politics indicates how, for black Communists, revisiting the category of the lumpenproletariat could empower individuals Marxism has often disregarded.

John Lennon has argued that the left, in the context of Scottsboro activism, redefined what is perhaps the archetypal Depression-era lumpenproletarian figure: the economically disenfranchised hobo. Lennon shows how the Scottsboro case brought the racial and gender interactions of hobo life into the purview of leftist discourse. The Communist Party spearheaded the legal defenses of the accused and challenged Jim Crow by making "class disenfranchisement the primary issue . . . defending the Scottsboro hobos not as 'boys' but as 'workers,' thereby linking their position as transient laborers to workers of every race."¹⁷ Activists sought to redefine the black male and white female hobos of the case as both victimized by capitalism's racial, gender, and economic manipulations. Lennon's reading of the Scottsboro case suggests how the Communist left presented the transients not in orthodox Marxist terms, as self-interested

[7]

and semi-criminal lumpenproletarians, but as "itinerant workers whose mobility offered possible disruptions to white capitalist society" and who "could become the vanguard of the coming revolution."[18]

The lumpenproletariat as a concept may mark what is excluded from Marxism's theoretical priorities, but Scottsboro suggests that in US cultural contexts it can gesture toward individuals who can access, and/or be strategically depicted as accessing, alternative modes of resistance. The rhetorical efforts documented by Higashida and Lennon indicate that this marginal Marxist concept has the potential to direct Marxism's core epistemological and political commitments within the specific conditions of modern American society. In her unpublished memoirs, Louise Thompson reflected on the epistemological gains inspired by the left's Scottsboro activism, particularly the participation of Ruby Bates. The case's particular features defetishized, for African Americans, the structure of social relations normalized by Jim Crow. "We had always been taught, I mean black people, that the enemy was poor whites, and that they were poor white trash, and that the boss was the good white man," she wrote. Ruby Bates and the other white woman involved were, she continues, enemies because they were white and "known as prostitutes." Thompson suggests that the lumpenproletarian status of the women negated the narrative of white female sanctity that underwrote white racial violence: both of these women were unable, according to patriarchy and capitalism's own estimation of prostitutes, to assume Jim Crow's ideological figure of the pure white woman whose violation legitimated racial violence. If Ruby Bates, a woman from the ranks of the "poor white trash," could address a rally and proclaim that "these black boys didn't do it," then the whole set of mystifications on which white supremacy rested was shaken. Out of this complex set of contradictions among patriarchy, Jim Crow, and capitalism arose the revelation that lynching, legal or extra-legal, was a straightforward mechanism of oppression: "This case, in a sense, exploded that myth about rape and exposed some of the forces that were behind it—that poor whites could be used as the agent to do the lynching, but behind it stood the state, its courts, its police, the whole government, in terms of oppression of the black people."[19] The disruptions posed by members of the lumpenproletariat involved in the Scottsboro affair revealed the terms of a decidedly Marxist critique of Jim Crow, unveiling first the ways in which Jim Crow uses racial difference to divide poor whites from poor blacks, and then the manner in which white supremacy functions as an instrument of state power.

The party's role in the Scottsboro case suggests an insight that Wright, Ellison, and Walker would pursue in their writings of the period and that the Black Panthers would later implement: by using the lumpenproletariat as a starting point for revising and expanding Marxist thought, one can produce a Marxism positioned to speak of and for African Americans. The black Marxism I trace in Wright, Ellison, and Walker's Depression-era work is one in which the lumpenproletarian outcast becomes useful for discerning the essential functions of Marxism, materialist critique and revolutionary change, at work *within* modern African American experience. These writers' use of the lumpenproletariat to reinvent Marxism is a practice that is both epistemologically materialist and culturally African American in its protocols.

For many scholars, however, the notion of a *black* Marxism still presents itself as a contradiction in terms. This tension is due in part to the influence of the cultural nationalist arguments of Harold Cruse and Cedric Robinson that position Marxism as a Western intellectual tradition important to the development of black writers and intellectuals but ultimately alien to African American cultural traditions and sociopolitical needs.[20] The history of the black Communist literary left, however, frequently undermines such arguments. As William Maxwell writes, "reflexively anti-Marxist interpreters of black culture" as well as "race-weary proponents of economic fairness" need to recognize that "many African-American modernists saw working-class interracialism as an arduous necessity, the final, elusive key to redeeming a society disfigured by racial slavery." In terms of literary history, this means that "the history of African-American letters cannot be unraveled from the history of American Communism without damage to both."[21] Since the late 1990s, scholars have worked to recover the history of generative transactions between the organizations, cultural venues, and politics of the US Communist left and African American literary traditions, making the study of the black left and the history of Marxism's general influence on African American writing a vibrant subfield of African American studies.

Ragged Revolutionaries contributes to such efforts to recover the literary and conceptual achievements of the black Communist left and to complicate the assumption that Marxism is an exclusively white or

Eurocentric discourse. My reading of Wright illuminates the theoretical idiosyncrasy and novelty of his Marxism, expanding the relevant philosophical frameworks for discussing Wright's work and challenging the perception that he wrote formulaic protest fiction. My discussion of Ellison complicates dominant readings of him as an apolitical or even conservative writer opposed to black protest by recovering his substantial intellectual and literary commitment to revolutionary political thought in the 1930s, a commitment long overlooked due to the unfinished and unpublished state of much of his Depression-era work. Barbara Foley's groundbreaking 2010 study *Wrestling with the Left: The Making of Ralph Ellison's "Invisible Man"* introduced Ellison's oft-neglected Depression career to scholarship and will hopefully inaugurate new interest in his early leftism.[22] *Ragged Revolutionaries* provides a conceptual outline of Ellison's 1930s Marxism and extended readings of some of his fictional endeavors of the decade. Finally, even more so than that of Ellison, Margaret Walker's Depression-era work has received scant attention. With the exception of *For My People*, her work of this period is unpublished, unfinished, or uncollected. In the Depression, Walker's efforts valuably reworked Marxism in correlation with African American feminist investments and cultural traditions; *Ragged Revolutionaries* asserts that she should be counted as one of the Depression left's most innovative writers.

That the lumpenproletariat would be the key term of an African American Marxism articulated in literary form is perhaps less surprising when one considers the prevalence of lumpenproletarian figures in US and African American cultural production. Besides Bigger Thomas, Huckleberry Finn is perhaps American literature's archetypal lumpenproletarian figure, someone who refuses social incorporation because of the labor it entails and who, as a result, enjoys a freedom and mobility unstructured by relations of production. Ralph Ellison would comment in his 1953 essay "Twentieth-Century Fiction and the Black Mask of Humanity" that Huckleberry's decision to break the law and help Jim escape slavery emerges from the moral and politically progressive vantage point he accesses from being beyond or outside of social relations: "Huck Finn has struggled with the problem posed by the clash between property rights and human rights, between what the community considered to be the proper attitude toward an escaped slave and his knowledge of Jim's humanity, gained through their adventures as fugitives together." If "fugitive" experiences allow Huckleberry to demystify slavery's coding of the black subject as property, they also allow Mark Twain, in the postbellum era, to make a historical materialist connection between slavery and modern capitalism by representing "the clash between the direct, human relationships of the frontier and the abstract, inhuman, market-dominated relationships fostered by the rising middle class—which in Twain's day was already compromising dangerously with the most inhuman aspects of the defeated slave system."[23] Twain used the outsider and outlaw Huckleberry Finn to illustrate the kind of socioeconomic and political insights orthodox Marxism had designated such types as being precisely unable to access.

As discussed in chapter 1, lumpenproletarian figures have performed a range of progressive political functions in modern American literature, where they've appeared as both symptoms of social ills and as bearers of liberatory possibility. In contrast to Twain's romanticization of Huckleberry Finn, in Stephen Crane's *Maggie: A Girl of the Streets* (1893), Maggie's fall into the urban lumpenproletarian underworld documents the gender-specific violence that lumpenproletarian status imposes on women. Her work as a prostitute is defined as not a willful rejection of proper labor, but as a gender-specific mode of capitalist victimization. And in Claude McKay's *Banjo* (1929), the realm of the lumpenproletariat is the ground for the imagining of new modes of black internationalism in the context of the Harlem Renaissance.

The practices of the lumpenproletariat also appear in African American culture and in theorizations of African American expression. Lawrence Levine writes that after 1865 "the enduring plight of black Americans produced a continuing need for a folklore which would permit them to express their hostilities and aspirations and for folk heroes whose exploits would allow them to transcend their situation."[24] Levine argues that modern folk tales of "bad men" outlaw figures like Stagolee suggested that "society had to be unhinged, undone, made over," but the stories did not seek "permanent remedies" from the "asocial, self-centered, and futile figures" of the criminal underclass.[25] If Levine's diagnosis echoes classical Marxist devaluations of the lumpenproletariat, Wright, Ellison, and Walker would refurbish folk legends of heroic outlaws in order to make them express revolutionary desires and remedies. Stagolee, for example, would be embraced as an archetypal political agent by members of the

Black Panther Party and, in the Depression era, imagined by Margaret Walker as the bearer of black revolutionary ambition. Chapter 1 discusses how tactics of transience, mobility, and criminal defiance have been situated by theorists like Cecil Brown and Houston Baker as specifically African American modes of politics and expression. *Ragged Revolutionaries* shows how African American culture offered Wright, Ellison, and Walker resources for reconceptualizing revolution as an outsider's tactic informed by black cultural sensibilities. If classical Marxism provided an epistemology that located the socially incorporated proletariat as structurally and dialectically positioned to achieve revolution, US and African American literary and cultural sensibilities furnished ways of imagining the socially dislocated lumpenproletariat's capacity for revolutionary insight and action.

While lumpenproletarian figures travel across the pages of many left-wing literary works during the Depression, this study focuses on the writings of Wright, Ellison, and Walker for multiple reasons. For one, as chapter 1 discusses in more detail, these three writers differed, in their approach to the lumpenproletariat, from the decade's "bottom dogs" writers. Bottom dogs writers like Edward Dahlberg, Nelson Algren, and others were usually affiliated with the left, and narrated underclass life largely in accord with classical Marxist assumptions about the lumpenproletariat's apolitical or reactionary character. Bottom dogs literature and proletarian literature, the two major genres of 1930s left-wing writing, both tended to align in their denial of revolutionary capacity to the decade's social outcasts. While never losing sight of the obstacles lumpenproletarian life poses to revolutionary consciousness, Wright, Ellison, and Walker nonetheless charted and figured political potential in lumpenproletarian experience, performing literary and epistemological maneuvers with the underclass that the decade's other writers on the left generally did not.

Wright, Ellison, and Walker evinced similar sensibilities in their work in part because close personal and working relationships existed between them. Ellison met Wright in New York in 1937, and the two struck up a friendship marked by shared literary, intellectual, and political interests. Wright's study of modernist writing, his engagement with Marxism, his connections with the cultural networks of the Communist left, and the fact that he was, to quote Lawrence Jackson, "leaning toward a theory that envisioned an American class revolution with a Negro vanguard, a perspective that was heretical to strict Marxists," all captivated Ellison.²⁶ The captivation was mutual. Wright's biographer Hazel Rowley notes that by the end of 1937, Ellison was Wright's "closest friend in New York" and "unlike Wright's more doctrinaire Communist friends, Ellison had an open, inventive mind." Wright and Ellison discussed Communist politics and Marxist theory alongside modern philosophy and African American culture, and Wright encouraged Ellison to take the first steps of his literary career, pressing him to write his first book review and first short story.²⁷ Wright's *Native Son,* an ambitious rendering of black lumpenproletarian interiority, was admired by Ellison, who upon its publication defended its political and representational merits against criticisms from others in the Communist Party. The first short story Ellison wrote, at Wright's encouragement, was "Hymie's Bull," a narrative of Depression-era freight-hopping hobos that poses a revolutionary challenge to capitalism and racial oppression.

In later years, Ellison charged that their similar concerns led to some jealousy on Wright's part and a rift between the two. Ellison recollected how he had shown Wright the manuscript for what was likely *Tillman and Tackhead,* a narrative about lumpenproletarian themes he began in the 1930s but never finished. Wright accused him of copying his own work, to which Ellison replied: "Okay, but what do you expect? I thought I was taking your advice."²⁸ This episode indicates how, during the 1930s, the two were very much on the same page in their approach to the lumpenproletariat, black life, and Marxism. In the postwar period, their friendship waned and their interests diverged, and Ellison accepted his canonization as an aesthetically sophisticated alternative to the allegedly blunt and didactic Wright.²⁹ Nonetheless, Ellison continued to cite the importance of his early friendship with Wright. In "Remembering Richard Wright," he discussed having read *Native Son* as Wright composed it. He had long ago moved away from the laudatory opinion of the novel he held in 1940, but the novel still marked a landmark moment for him. "After all, how many of you have had the unexpected privilege of reading a powerful novel as it was literally ripped off the typewriter?" he asked. "Such opportunities are rare, and being young, I was impressed beyond all critical words. I am still impressed."³⁰

Margaret Walker was also close with Wright, whom she met in Chicago in 1936. Walker had already begun writing prior to knowing

Wright. "He had a lot of influence on me, but it wasn't on my writing," she later explained. "It concerned social perspective—Marxism and the problems of black people in this country."[31] Such interests inspired her to join the Communist Party and to participate in a range of leftist political and cultural activities.[32] Walker and Wright discussed politics and literature, and Walker helped with the creation of *Native Son* by collecting newspaper clippings about Robert Nixon, an African American man who had murdered a white woman in 1938 and whose story and trial inspired Wright's depiction of Bigger Thomas.[33] Walker later claimed that her research was so vital that Abe Aaron, a Chicago writer and close friend of Wright's, told Wright that he should dedicate the novel to Walker.[34] Walker also discussed her own in-progress Depression novel with Wright. *Goose Island,* which deals in part with the Chicago lumpenproletariat, was never finished, but Walker would later suggest that scenes in *Native Son* were inspired by or borrowed from her novel.[35] In its similarity to Ellison's allegation that Wright felt Ellison was emulating his work too closely, this charge suggests the confluence of Wright and Walker's aesthetic and political priorities.

Their close friendship and working relationship were soon complicated by personal attachments. "I was in love with him, and he knew it," she reflected, but her feelings were not returned.[36] Wright and Walker eventually fell out in 1939, but her admiration for his work led her to compose a biography, published in 1988, of the writer she still considered "an intellectual giant of his times" and "a writer of great power and great passion." In a move that reflects their formerly aligned interests, Walker's biography is able to identify the lumpenproletariat as a characteristic focus of Wright's work.[37] Walker and Ellison had a more limited relationship. Walker met Ellison through Wright at the Communist-backed League of American Writers Congress in New York in 1939. While in New York, Walker read portions of *Goose Island* to Ellison, and he shared his work with her, over dinner and conversation.[38] Wright's status as one of the most successful Communist writers of the period made him able to introduce Walker and Ellison to the discourses and networks of the literary left. But these three authors are best understood as a cohort of equals bound by revolutionary political commitments, a creative and expansive approach to Marxist theory, and an interest in the figurative significances of the socially dislocated. In the midst of the Depression, Wright, Walker, and Ellison bounced ideas off of each other, compared notes on their readings, and explored the implications of Marxism for the social and economic circumstances around them.

In *Ragged Revolutionaries*, I make reference to a range of works from Western Marxism and continental philosophy in order to delineate and explore the theoretical interventions of these writers. In the chapters that follow, the conceptual inventories of figures like Jean-Paul Sartre, Hannah Arendt, Louis Althusser, Antonio Gramsci, and Fredric Jameson are employed neither to validate Wright, Ellison, and Walker's work, nor to indicate that these writers are to be esteemed to the extent that their ideas conform to European philosophical achievements. Rather, my intention is to situate Wright, Ellison, and Walker as participants in some of the conversations that animated Western Marxist and continental philosophical projects. If concerns like the subjective dynamics of revolutionary consciousness, the nature of political action, the structure of social form, the relation of cultural practices to economic relations, and Marxist formulations of class identity all constitute pressing research projects for modern thought, then Wright, Ellison, and Walker's 1930s writings should be understood as pursuing those projects from the standpoint of black culture, history, and political need. Interlocutors from European philosophy, along with those from the Black Panther Party, provide a useful vocabulary for identifying the epistemological efforts advanced through fiction and poetry by Wright, Ellison, and Walker.

Of course, this method challenges the perception that Western Marxism and European philosophy are culturally and historically alien to African American literary study. However, this distinction of European intellectual projects from black expressive efforts is not one that Wright, Ellison, or Walker made. A definitive feature of their efforts to represent African American life and culture was the conviction that Western philosophical methods—Marxism, but also Freudianism and existentialism—could, when used self-reflexively, offer access to the psychological and material reality of black life. This was an assumption that guided their work during their time on the 1930s left and afterwards.

Thus, Walker would credit Marxist habits of totalization for enabling her to grasp the underlying socioeconomic dynamics of juvenile delinquency in Goose Island, the Chicago slum that served as the setting for her unfinished novel. Her major work after the Depression, her 1966 novel *Jubilee*, was influenced by Georg Lukács's historical materialist theorization of historical fiction in *The Historical Novel* (1937). Walker credited Lukács for providing the "philosophy and point of view" that enabled her to use the form of the novel to rewrite the history of the Civil War and Reconstruction from the perspective of African Americans.[39] As Ellison was writing his 1930s novel *Slick*, which he never finished, he consulted William H. Sheldon's *Psychology and the Promethean Will* (1936), a theory of human psychology articulated in Western cultural terms, to help him tell the narrative of how his African American protagonist attains a revolutionary consciousness. Later, in 1948, he composed an essay on psychiatrist Fredric Wertham's Lafargue Psychiatric Clinic, which treated African American patients from its location in a church basement in Harlem. In "Harlem is Nowhere," Ellison praises the Clinic for providing materialist, philosophical, and psychological explication to Harlem residents of the ways their culture, social situation, and individuality have been shaped by modernity, with the result that "the grandchildren of those who possessed no written literature examine their lives through the eyes of Freud and Marx, Kierkegaard and Kafka, Malraux and Sartre."[40]

Wright's broad interests in European thought are familiar and have already been referenced. He would eventually meet Sartre and Arendt in the mid-1940s, and after he moved to Paris in 1947, he would connect with French intellectual circles. But when he met Sartre and Arendt, he came to them as an equal, as *Native Son* had already explored many of the same existential and political concerns of their own work. C. L. R. James recollected one visit to Wright in which Wright gestured toward his numerous volumes of Kierkegaard, telling James: "Everything that he writes in those books, I knew before I had them." James explains that "he was telling me . . . that he was a black man in the United States and that gave him an insight into what today is the universal opinion and attitude of the modern personality."[41] Wright here explicates what my study takes as a guiding assumption: that the social, political, cultural, and philosophical themes of Wright, Ellison, and Walker's writings did not simply anticipate or align with Western theorists who then retroactively validate those writings. Rather, these authors' experiences and priorities enabled them to pursue many of the same objects of inquiry—class struggle, social form, subject formation, the psyche, the agential self, and so forth—as Western Marxism and continental philosophy.

Ragged Revolutionaries opens by making a case for the general purchase of the lumpenproletariat within literary studies. The multiple ambiguities of the term in Marx inspired the conceptual revisions to Marxism performed by the Black Panther Party theorists. Simultaneously, the conceptual mobility of the lumpenproletariat is manifested in modern literature, where the lumpenproletariat's figurative "raggedness" characterizes both the destitution and the freedom of the socially marginalized. Multiple literary works express the political, racial, and gender dynamics of exclusion through creative significations on the trope of the rag. The history of the production of paper from rags makes this trope either indicative of reduction to discardable refuse or, through the incipient form of paper, generative of new possibilities. Thus, figures of the lumpenproletariat appear in American literature, especially during the Great Depression, to enact figurative and creative explorations of marginality and resistance, exclusion and deprivation.

Wright began his career fascinated with the political possibilities of African American social displacement. Marxism associates the dispossession of the lumpenproletariat with its reactionary tendencies, but Wright, attuned to the emancipatory potentials of flight and migration in modern black experience, reimagines dislocation as enabling revolutionary agency. He rethinks dislocation in various 1930s works, but the full extent of his reorientation of Marxism around the black lumpenproletariat comes in *Native Son*. Bigger Thomas is African American literature's archetypal lumpenproletarian individual, but he is not the self-interested enemy of revolution that orthodox Marxism would hold him to be. Despite the critical tradition of reading Bigger as a depraved product of environmental limitations, Wright's protagonist is actually imbued with a positive and creative human spirit. Specifically, the desire that animates his psyche and his criminal acts—a desire to be located within a social order that will recognize his subjectivity, that will permit him the opportunity to reveal his humanity through his actions—is characterized by Wright as the desire for antiracist and anticapitalist change itself. *Native Son* thus defines the black lumpenproletarian individual as the agent of revolution.

Despite his later reputation as a Cold War conservative, Ellison's 1930s Marxism was remarkable in its theoretical novelty, reach, and sophistication. In the 1930s, Ellison theorized the nature of American society as a fluid and shifting landscape offering possibilities for disrupting relationships of power and exploitation. The symbolic agent of those possibilities in Ellison's fiction is what I call the lumpen-folk figure, a character who combines the inventive practices of the lumpenproletariat with an essential capacity for revolutionary action derived, by Ellison, from Communist framings of African American folk authenticity. Ellison holds that revolutionary institutions must be able to recognize and politically educate the various forms of possibility enacted by such figures. He works through these social, political, and institutional themes in multiple short stories from the period, as well as in two unfinished longer works: *Slick,* a novel about the political education of a black lumpenproletarian character who anticipates Bigger Thomas, and *Tillman and Tackhead,* which enacts a symbolic analysis of Jim Crow's social and psychological workings while locating the origins of antiracist and anticapitalist resistance in lumpenproletarian practices of crime and transience.

Walker's fiction and poetry of the period challenge the classical Marxist assumption that lumpenproletarian individuals are willfully outside of and thus not victims of capitalist exploitation. By charting material connections between the lumpenproletariat and capitalist relations of production, Walker represents the emergence of radical antiracist and anticapitalist consciousness from out of the experiences of the underclass. In her unpublished poetry and her unfinished novel, *Goose Island,* urban lumpenproletarians—juvenile delinquents, gangsters, prostitutes—access modes of revolutionary knowledge and possibility unavailable to the socially incorporated working class. Unlike Wright and Ellison, Walker underscores the situation of lumpenproletarian women and thus offers a more expansive theorization of gender and sexuality as sites of identity and struggle; her portraits of the underclass thus enact intersectional critiques of the gender, sexual, and racial functioning of American capitalism. Walker also composed ballads that narrate the criminal accomplishments of mythic black men and women. These ballads transform the African American folk outlaw into an agent of resistance to Jim Crow, capitalist labor practices, and patriarchal gender and sexual norms. Collected in her first published volume of poetry, *For My People,* these poems demonstrate the resourcefulness of African American folklore as a lexicon that redefines criminal acts as expressing transformative sociopolitical meanings.

In the wake of the great recession, economic and racial modes of oppression and violence have garnered a new social visibility and a concurrent set of responses, from economic justice movements like Occupy Wall Street, to the uprising against police racism in Ferguson, Missouri, to the emergence of the Black Lives Matter movement. As they did during the Depression, antiracist and anticapitalist sentiments and activism have entered the mainstream of US sociopolitical discourse. In this climate, there is value in returning to the 1930s, when similar concerns led black writers to take Marxism—that old-fashioned nineteenth-century European materialism—and reinvent it for African American historical experience, cultural traditions, and political desires. Residing in manuscript archives, occluded by standing narratives of Wright, Ellison, and Walker's literary and political reputations, and obscured by Marxism's traditional theoretical focus on labor and the proletariat, this black lumpenproletarian Marxism has long been hidden from view. *Ragged Revolutionaries* is a reminder that, at this current juncture, the annals of twentieth-century African American literary history can furnish valuable epistemological resources for politics. Wright, Ellison, and Walker's 1930s work should impress upon us that we can create new ways of approaching the very systems that turn people into discards—racism, capitalism, and patriarchy, but also orthodox tendencies in Marxism—by transforming what's been ignored, discarded, and scorned into new catalysts of political and theoretical invention.

1

THE RAGGED PROLETARIAT
Itineraries for a Transient Concept

What would a theoretical and literary critical methodology of the lumpenproletariat look like? Wright, Ellison, and Walker's writings of the 1930s provide an occasion for outlining the protocols of such a methodology. Their work with the lumpenproletariat helpfully foregrounds broader discourses such as classical Marxist formulations of the lumpenproletariat, the Black Panther Party's revisions of Marxism, the literary history of rags and paper as tropes for representing social marginality, the leftist literary climate of the 1930s, and forms of African American cultural practice.

Although classical Marxism sees nothing of value in the lumpenproletariat, the appropriations of the concept performed by the literature of Wright, Ellison, and Walker and later codified in the theory of the Black Panthers are best understood as revisions and expansions, not rejections, of Marxism. The deconstructions black writers and activists have performed with the concept are in fact suggested by Marx and Engels's own texts, when those texts are read against the grain. By resituating this marginal Marxist concept at the center of their own Marxism, these writers enact a conceptual inversion licensed, paradoxically, by the rhetoric and logics of classical Marxism. The black Marxism schematized by this study is thus not the one famously outlined by Cedric Robinson: namely, a generative contradiction between Marxism's radicalism and Eurocentrism that leads the black writer out of Marxism and toward a distinctly black cultural radicalism.¹ Rather, it's a practice of deconstructing Marxism that is, like all deconstructions, an accurate and faithful reading. Grasping the Marxist credentials of literary and sociopolitical texts organized not around the proletariat but its "ragged" counterpart first requires close examination of how the term appears in Marx and Engels's writings.

MARXISM AND THE LUMPENPROLETARIAT

Marx and Engels coined the term *lumpenproletariat,* but they didn't explicitly theorize it. As Robert Bussard notes, they "expected their readers to understand its connotations" even though it never attains a "consistent and clearly reasoned definition" in their work.² Generally, the term refers to social types who subsist without waged labor and by extension lack class identity, dwelling on the margins and in the interstices of capitalist social formations. These types often resort to criminal or other illicit survival practices. In an exhaustive survey of the term in Marx and Engels's writings, Hal Draper concludes that

> the lumpen-class is the catch-all for those who fall out, or drop out, of the existing social structure so that they are no longer functionally an integral part of society. To survive at all, in the interstices of the same society, they must adopt a parasitic mode of existence. The tendency toward illegality simply arises from the scarcity of other choices.³

Rather than carefully theorize the lumpenproletariat, Marx and Engels tend to load it with moralistic scorn. Their callousness is surprising, given the frequent desperation of individuals who must survive without a wage. Unlike the proletarian worker, whose place within production provides her or him with a wage (however inadequate) and sustaining social institutions (labor unions, political parties, etc.), the lumpenproletarian individual must make do with nothing. But while the term suggests, as Draper notes, a causal link between socioeconomic marginalization and criminality, Marx and Engels's rhetoric registers only disgust, and they frequently return to the claim that lumpenproletarian activities—living through criminal pursuits rather than labor, and necessarily putting individual interest above collective collaboration—make this underclass morally and politically suspect.

Thus Dominick LaCapra notes that Marx's "bourgeois, indeed Victorian, sense of propriety" leads him to "[occlude] the problem of the oppression of [the lumpenproletariat] in modern society as well as the need for radical politics to address that oppression and its implications."[4] Marx and Engels intended the German prefix of the term, *lumpen,* to signify not literally, as materially ragged (impoverished by structural disenfranchisement), but connotatively, as criminal, immoral, or knavish.[5] In nineteenth-century English translations of *The Communist Manifesto* (1848), for instance, the term is translated with phrases like "the mob," or "dangerous class."[6] But when Marx and Engels's dismissal of the lumpenproletariat is approached symptomatically, it is clear that it is animated by more than just moral rectitude. The lumpenproletariat names a theoretical challenge that Marx and Engels's texts often use disdain to repress: that modern social structures contain sites of life, practice, difference, and possibility that cannot be incorporated within a production-determined account of social form and class struggle.

The lumpenproletariat is especially salient in Marx's writings on the 1848 revolution in France and the class struggles that rocked the French state until Louis-Napoléon Bonaparte's seizure of power in 1851. In these works, the lumpenproletariat is a political threat to the proletariat. As individuals with no relation to the means of production, they have no class identity and thus no organic political allegiance. This, combined with their desperate self-interest, means that their services can be bought easily by forces of reaction. In *The Communist Manifesto*, the lumpenproletariat "may, here and there, be swept into the movement by a proletarian revolution; its conditions of life, however, prepare it far more for the part of a bribed tool of reactionary intrigue."[7] Marx saw this reactionary tendency as explicating Bonaparte's coup d'état, arguing that Bonaparte, despite representing the interests of no economic class, was able to seize the state by claiming to represent two groups that could not represent themselves as classes: the opportunistic urban lumpenproletariat and the politically naïve, outmoded rural peasantry.[8]

In *The Peasant War in Germany* (1850), Engels indicates that he and Marx saw the lumpenproletariat as a "phenomenon evident in a more or less developed form, in all the phases of society to date." Engels composed this history of the German peasant uprising of 1525 to illuminate the struggles of 1848. In an 1870 preface, he expresses as a law the political danger that was ostensibly only a tendency in *The Communist Manifesto*. Here, the lumpenproletariat is "absolutely venal and absolutely brazen" and "the worst of all possible allies" for the proletariat. He even encourages their destruction as a shrewd political tactic. "If the French workers, in every revolution, inscribed on the houses: *Mort aux voleurs!* Death to thieves! and even shot some, they did it, not out of enthusiasm for property, but because they rightly considered it necessary above all to keep that gang at a distance."[9]

The disgust of even Marx and Engels's casual references to the lumpenproletariat—"passively rotting mass," "scum," "offal,"[10]—exceeds explication by a tendency toward political reaction. Gertrude Himmelfarb thus links Marx and Engels's revulsion to the consequences the lumpenproletariat poses for Marxist thought itself. "Even more than the counter-revolutionary tendency of the lumpenproletariat," she writes, "it was the lack of any 'social' character, any productive function . . . that aroused Marx's contempt. . . . The lumpenproletariat, having no relationship to the means of production, was, in effect, a non-class. Thus it had no historical function, no role in the class struggle, no legitimate place in society, no redemptive role in history. Even when it was reactionary, it was so by accident, so to speak, 'bribed' to be the tool of reaction." The lumpenproletariat is thus what is irrelevant to Marx, "not real human beings but gross matter."[11]

Marx's disgust can be further explicated by considering his singular use of the term to describe the dominance of the French "finance aristocracy" during the 1830–1848 reign of Louis Philippe I:

> the same prostitution, the same shameless cheating, the same mania to get rich was repeated in every sphere . . . to get rich not by production, but by pocketing the already available wealth of others. In particular there broke out, at the top of bourgeois society, an unbridled display of unhealthy and dissolute appetites, which clashed every moment with the bourgeois laws themselves. . . . The finance aristocracy . . . is nothing but the *resurrection of the lumpenproletariat at the top of bourgeois society.*[12]

Since financiers speculate on the value produced by the economic rather than producing anything of value themselves, they are no different than lumpenproletarian swindlers, hustlers, or confidence men. Peter Hayes thus claims that Marx understood the lumpenproletariat, in part, as a behavioral condition that could characterize both underworld criminals

[23]

and financiers: "they did not want to work, they were thieving, and given these propensities they followed their immediate material interests without scruple."[13]

This would seem to imply that the marginality of the lumpenproletariat derives from an inherent, morally wayward refusal of labor and class identity. However, as we saw in *The Communist Manifesto* and as Draper's definition makes clear, the term can also acknowledge the structural causation of socioeconomic exclusion and political reaction. The latter, for example, was utilized by Leon Trotsky in his diagnosis of fascism as a mobilization of "the crazed petty bourgeoisie and the bands of declassed and demoralized lumpenproletariat—all the countless human beings whom finance capital itself has brought to desperation and frenzy."[14] The tension between these multiple significances of the lumpenproletariat's raggedness—material victimization or inherent debasement, structural delimitation or willed moral and political dissolution—is never wholly resolved in Marx. It's unclear often whether the lumpenproletariat is defined by instinctual criminality or economically determined desperation, whether it is a "social scum" or an immiserated stratum produced by capitalism, and this fundamental uncertainty can initiate deconstructive and appropriative readings.

Marx seems to acknowledge the structurally determined conditions that make the lumpenproletariat amenable to criminal *recruitment* at the same time that he suggests the lumpenproletariat is *essentially* criminal. Describing how the bourgeois provisional government, established by the revolution of 1848, recruited a militia to keep the Parisian proletariat in check, Marx explains that the ranks of these "Mobile Guards"

> belonged for the most part to the *lumpenproletariat*, which, in all big towns form a mass strictly differentiated from the industrial proletariat, a recruiting ground for thieves and criminals of all kinds, living on the crumbs of society, people without a definite trade, vagabonds, *gens sans feu et sans aveu*, with differences according to the degree of civilization of the nation to which they belong, but never renouncing their *lazzaroni* character.[15]

His lumpenproletarian individuals are, on the one hand, desperate because economically excluded. Lacking specific skills that might locate them within the waged proletariat, they must scramble for "crumbs" and are thus prone to becoming criminals. But on the other hand, they are *already* disreputable and criminal by nature since they are "*sans feu et sans aveu*" and "*lazzaroni* [in] character." The former phrase, literally denoting those "without fire or confession," connotes both material and discursive homelessness: those without hearth and home, without faith or sociopolitical consciousness. Marx's use of this colorful phrase poses conceptual problems: do lumpenproletarian individuals lack the latter because they lack the former, or are both lacks simultaneous? In other words, does economic dislocation (homelessness) lead to a deformation of consciousness and character (faithlessness), or is the lumpenproletariat always-already so deformed? In the nineteenth century, the Italian term *lazzarone*, referring to the underclass of Naples, often functioned as a pejorative synonym for any unemployed, impoverished, and/or criminal urban groups. More evocative than precise, Marx's use of *lazzarone* indicates the difficulty of defining the lumpenproletariat through means other than rhetorical association. One might conclude that Marx's reliance on French and Italian terms that resist translation suggests the conceptual or theoretical "foreignness" of the lumpenproletariat as that which cannot be empirically or paradigmatically categorized because it names that which resists categorization.[16]

Marx struggles with that resistance in *The Eighteenth Brumaire* (1852) when describing the lumpenproletarian elements mobilized by Louis-Napoléon Bonaparte. Marx does not theorize the term, but spins an open-ended catalogue of figures the term could reference in an attempt to conjure a definition through association and synecdoche:

> Alongside decayed *roués* with dubious means of subsistence and of dubious origin, alongside ruined and adventurous offshoots of the bourgeoisie, were vagabonds, discharged soldiers, discharged jailbirds, escaped galley-slaves, swindlers, mountebanks, *lazzaroni,* pickpockets, tricksters, gamblers, *maquereaus,* brothel keepers, porters, *literati,* organ-grinders, rag-pickers, knife-grinders, tinkers, beggars—in short the whole indefinite, disintegrated mass thrown hither and thither, which the French term *la bohème.*[17]

Though not Marx's intention, this passage refers less to any discernable demographic than to the virtually limitless possibility of modern social modes and places of being, a limitlessness that Marx's concluding "in short" reveals as ultimately defying encapsulation. Peter Stallybrass reads this passage as evidence of Marx's participation in a nineteenth-century bourgeois discourse that struggled to describe and make sense of urban poverty, which appeared as a spectacle so heterogeneous as to unsettle "the process of social differentiation" and "the distinctions between classes."[18] Marx's catalogue suggests that modern urban life retains a density and diversity and should trouble Marxism to the extent that it exceeds explication by theoretical mechanisms of labor, production, class, and class struggle.

In *Capital* (1867), Marx mentions the lumpenproletariat in his description of the relative surplus population. This population is an extension of the working class, a reserve pool of labor including those unable to work and temporarily unemployed, which functions to keep down wages by keeping the available supply of labor power high. Marx delineates the "lowest sediment" of this population as that which "dwells in . . . pauperism." This level includes three groups: those unable to find work, "orphans and pauper children," and "the demoralized, the ragged, and those unable to work, . . . the mutilated, the sickly, the widows, etc." These last are framed sympathetically as the human discards of production. By distinction, the lumpenproletariat is something else: Marx carefully distinguishes "vagabonds, criminals, prostitutes, in short the actual lumpenproletariat" from those other, legitimate proletarian victims.[19] The place of the "actual lumpenproletariat" is somewhat uncertain here, both associated with this pauper strata but also not part of it. It's not clear, necessarily, why those that turn to crime and vagabondage would be different, in any terms other than nonmaterialist moralistic ones, from those honorably "ragged" victims who are also perpetually excluded from proletarian labor. However, Marx's implication is familiar: some of the unemployed are "good" members of the proletariat unable to work or find work, while the "bad" lumpenproletariat names those who refuse work and instead pursue illicit and immoral activity.

The referential parameters of the lumpenproletariat, as a term, become vague almost as soon as they're interrogated. Instead, the term signifies symptomatically, marking moments of premature theoretical closure within Marxism. Its definitional instability in fact makes it useful as a device for undoing closure and identifying new routes of conceptual exploration. That instability means that Marx and Engels's texts rely on figurative, nonliteral rhetorical strategies to represent the lumpenproletariat: parsing the significance of the lumpenproletariat often requires reading Marx and Engels in the manner of a literary critic and decoding multiple connotative gestures. Like any literary analysis, such a reading necessarily engages the play of linguistic signification and often yields multivalent or even contradictory meanings. The term, after all, alludes to that which is not fully known and thus not valued—whether materially, ideologically, or theoretically—by either modern capitalism or Marxist theory. Precisely because those outside of capitalist relations of production resist full consideration by Marxist epistemology, Marx and Engels's attempts to make sense of them end up circling in a figurative and associative proliferation. That deferring of exact definition produces confusion, of course, but it also affords access to the possibilities of interpretation and creative revision generated by the free play of textuality.

By reading closely for the lumpenproletariat in Marx and Engels, one can discover new opportunities for deconstruction and theoretical expansion. For instance, before he faced the challenge of explicating 1848, Marx described the same individuals he'd later denounce as "social scum" in a very different manner. In the 1844 *Economic and Philosophical Manuscripts* he critiques bourgeois political economy for studying workers only as producers and neglecting other aspects of their humanity. He then considers other types who, because they do not work, exist beyond the horizon of political economy:

> The swindler, the cheat, the beggar, the unemployed, the starving, the destitute and the criminal working man are *figures* which exist not *for it,* but only for other eyes—for the eyes of doctors, judges, grave-diggers, beadles, etc. Nebulous figures which do not belong within the province of political economy.[20]

The criminal and the destitute are grouped together on materialist grounds, as individuals defined by a lack of participation in production. Beyond the margins of production, they are also beyond the epistemological bounds of political economy, with the result that they remain "nebulous" presences that cannot be subsumed within its ordering of reality. Of course, this situation could equally characterize orthodox Marxism's own dismissal of those who don't work, whose identity is not secured by class status, and who thus lack full conceptual definition within Marxism. Lumpenproletarian figures thus make the outer limits of Marxist epistemology visible: the conceptual nebulousness of the lumpenproletariat reveals Marxism's points of closure and limitation, and the individuals of the underclass manifest the margins, interstices, and underworlds where Marxism does not yet go and which it cannot yet adequately see.

The lumpenproletariat, then, is a mechanism enabling Marxism to reach beyond itself. In the texts of classical Marxism, it suggests possibilities that become thinkable when the limits of Marxist theory become recognized as limitations. So, for example, LaCapra can treat Marx's "polemical animus" toward the lumpenproletariat as a revelation of "the possibility that modern societies did not offer a more or less ready-made group analogous to the classical revolutionary subject."[21] Jacques Rancière can argue that Marx's rhetorical presentation of the lumpenproletariat indexes the impossibility of imposing philosophical paradigms of class and history on heterogeneous social individuals and processes.[22] And Stallybrass can show how the lumpenproletariat reveals the limits of the classical Marxist assumption that "the domain of politics and the state" straightforwardly reflects economic interests.[23]

Marx and Engels's discussions of the lumpenproletariat end up signaling the possibility that those on the margins of socioeconomic structures of production, and on the epistemological horizon of Marxism as the theory of those structures, could be generative of new directions for Marxist theory and practice. The lumpenproletariat ultimately suggests the adaptation of Marxism to a consideration of criminals, vagabonds, drifters, hustlers, "in short" all those with no legible social status. As we'll see, the potential for revision and modification associated with the lumpenproletariat allowed certain African American writers and theorists to think the consequences, for Marxism, of black sociopolitical and cultural particularity.

THE BLACK PANTHERS AND THE LUMPENPROLETARIAT

In the 1960s and 1970s, Black Panther Party theorists sought to apply Marxism to the conditions of the internally colonized African American population, using the concept of the lumpenproletariat to make Marxism speak to and for African Americans. The Panthers followed the example of Frantz Fanon, who employed the lumpenproletariat to think the dynamics of anticolonial struggle in *The Wretched of the Earth* (1961). For Fanon, the colonial context necessitated revising Marxist principles—"slightly stretch[ing]" them—to incorporate the role of racial difference in the power structures of the colony.[24]

Fanon argues that Marx described the lumpenproletariat in a manner that universalized the political orientation of the nineteenth-century European underclass. But in the space of the colony, the lumpenproletariat is a revolutionary rather than reactionary force. For Fanon, the colonial lumpenproletariat is:

> that fraction of the peasantry blocked at the urban periphery, those who still have not found a single bone to gnaw in the colonial system.... It is among these masses, in the people of the shanty towns and in the lumpenproletariat that the insurrection will find its urban spearhead. The lumpenproletariat, this cohort of starving men, divorced from tribe and clan, constitutes one of the most spontaneously and radically revolutionary forces of a colonized people.

Doubly alienated from both the collective culture of the colonized nation and the resources of the colonizer's urban space, Fanon's lumpenproletariat resembles Marx's *gens sans feu et sans aveu*, the materially and psychically homeless. Yet given the racial stratification of the colonial space, the lumpenproletariat finds its material needs—here, entrance into "the enemy citadel at all costs, and if need be, by the most underground channels"— filled not through the bribes of those in power, but by the anticolonial revolution: "the pimps, the hooligans, the unemployed, and the petty criminals... give the liberation struggle all they have got, devoting themselves to the cause like valiant workers. These vagrants, these second-class citizens, find their way back to the nation thanks to their decisive, militant action."[25] Without fundamentally challenging the way Marx defined the lumpenproletariat, Fanon revised Marx's estimate of its social and political character. In Black Panther thinker Kathleen Cleaver's words, Fanon "articulated the colonial question in lucid originality, employing or discarding, refining or broadening, the Marxist-Leninist approach as appropriate to his subject."[26]

Huey Newton developed the lumpenproletarian orientation of the Black Panther Party, but it was arguably Eldridge Cleaver who provided the party's most sustained analysis of the lumpenproletariat. In a 1970 pamphlet, Cleaver writes that Fanon "unearthed the category of the Lumpenproletariat and began to deal with it, recognizing that vast majorities of the colonized people fall into that category." This particular concept is thus suited to Cleaver's aim of repurposing Marxism for mid-century US conditions inflected by racial difference. Cleaver's revisionary

[29]

appropriation of Marxism disassociates the concept of the proletariat from empirical industrial laborers. While expanding the concept's exclusive reference to the working class, Cleaver retains Marxism's abstract-structural designation of the proletariat as the agent of revolutionary change produced by structural conditions of capitalism. In the United States, there exist a white and a black proletariat, each composed of two elements—the working class and the lumpenproletariat. For Cleaver, the working class is the "right wing" of this revolutionary body: reactionary, bought off by capitalism, invested in the status quo, and manipulated by racist ideologies. By contrast, the lumpenproletariat forms its "left wing" and revolutionary vanguard. Industrial workers, Cleaver argues, have become conservative and actively invested in the system; the automation of production has ensured that the working class is dwindling in numbers and that its political outlook has become merely protective of jobs and wages. As a result, the lumpenproletariat, and the black lumpenproletariat in particular, possesses the revolutionary potential of the original Marxist concept of the proletariat.[27]

Cleaver is conscious of both the Marxist lineage of his argument and its challenge to official manifestations of Marxism:

> Some blind so-called Marxist-Leninists accuse the Lumpen of being parasites upon the Working Class. This is a stupid charge derived from reading too many of Marx's footnotes and taking some of his offhand scurrilous remarks for holy writ. In reality, it is accurate to say that the Working Class, particularly the American Working Class, is a parasite upon the heritage of mankind, of which the Lumpen has been totally robbed by the rigged system of Capitalism which in turn, has thrown the majority of mankind upon the junkheap while it buys off a percentage with jobs and security.

Cleaver presents his political theory as a better reading of Marxism. It is not the lumpenproletariat *itself* that is inconsequential or parasitic, but Marx's characterization of it as such, which Cleaver in turn dismisses as the stuff of "footnotes" and "offhand remarks" rather than an essential Marxist principle. Cleaver's redefinition of the lumpenproletariat similarly preserves, while re-evaluating, some of the rhetoric attached to Marx's descriptions. The lumpen are "all those who have no secure relationship or vested interest in the means of production and the institutions of capitalist society, . . . who have never worked and never will," who aren't trained for any employment, "who have been displaced by machines, automation, and cybernation." But the lumpenproletariat also contains "the so-called 'Criminal Element' . . . who don't even want a job, who hate to work and can't relate to punching some pig's time clock, who would rather punch a pig in the mouth and rob him than punch that same pig's time clock and work for him." Echoing Marx's *The Eighteenth Brumaire* catalogue while refusing to make Marx's moralizing distinction between those who can't work and who refuse to work, Cleaver wraps up his definition: "In short, all those who simply have been locked out of the economy and robbed of their rightful social heritage."[28] Given the racial divisions of American history and society, the black lumpenproletariat, the most alienated and disenfranchised segment of the population, seems to Cleaver and the Panthers to be the group most objectively invested in the overthrow of the current order.

Cleaver replaces the proletariat with the lumpenproletariat as the bearer of revolutionary change, and he derives the revolutionary potential of the black lumpenproletariat from Marxism's understanding of the structural causation of transformative agency. Cleaver understands the lumpenproletariat to be a revolutionary force because he sees its marginalization as a denial of its "rightful social heritage." Like the proletariat in *The Communist Manifesto*, it has nothing to lose and a world to win. Industrial workers in the United States, Cleaver argues, no longer occupy that structural role. "Working Class Proletarians are the House Niggers of Capitalism," he declares in a later essay. The workers' political institutions have taken Marxism and made it the "religion of those who had found their plug in the system." Cleaver aims to be more Marxist than the Marxists by reclaiming Marxism from this distortion. Those who lack any stake in the system—the condition of revolutionary action—are today not the workers, he argues, but the castoffs and refuse from an increasingly automated economy. Not that the lumpenproletariat is automatically politically conscious. Cleaver retains the Marxist narrative of the lumpenproletariat's susceptibility to bribery, arguing that the American state uses welfare, a "neo-colonial technique of social control," to contain the lumpenproletariat's political potential by giving it a stake in the present order. But welfare is only a tenuous "plug" in the system. Rather, like *The Communist Manifesto* proletariat, the objective political orientation of the lumpenproletariat—particularly the African American lumpenproletariat—is "against every organized structure that exists in the world today."[29]

Marx saw the self-interested exigencies of lumpenproletarian existence as immanent to capitalism and not conducive to socialism. But in 1972, Cleaver was convinced that the lumpenproletariat was not only structurally positioned to overthrow capitalism, but that lumpenproletarian experience itself is the dialectical anticipation of post-capitalist social life. The "ultimate revolutionary demand," he wrote, is not the demand of the workers for jobs, but of the lumpenproletariat "to be cut in on Consumption in spite of being blocked out of Production. . . . The point is not equality in Production, which is the Marxist view and basic error, but equality in distribution and consumption."[30] In other words, the lumpenproletarian demand is equal access to the means of reproducing life without dependence on labor, a severing of human fulfillment from the injunction to work. In the present, the lumpenproletariat struggles to survive without labor: in the postcapitalist future, existence without labor will be the rule. The future classlessness of socialism, for Cleaver, is best appreciated by attending to the classless existence of today's lumpenproletariat. Cleaver thus develops a lumpenproletarian Marxism within the very conceptual framework of classical Marxist historicism, positioning the lumpenproletariat as the dialectical, even teleological precursor of post-class society.

The Panthers' lumpenproletarian orientation has been criticized on multiple fronts. Contemporary Marxist critiques of Cleaver objected to his revisionary efforts, which they read as antirevolutionary misinterpretations. The black Marxist scholar C. J. Munford argued in 1973 that Cleaver simply hated workers, and that his emphasis on consumption was a "'gimme-gimme' mentality, the ultimate in consumerism which denies the human need for labor."[31] Henry Winston, an African American Communist activist, published an extensive critique of the Panthers in 1971 in *Political Affairs*, the journal of the Communist Party. Winston argued that in forsaking working-class organization, the Panthers handicapped the revolution in the United States. "The Cleaver-Newton theory of the lumpenproletariat as vanguard would mean objective surrender to the ruling class because only the working class can lead the fight against poverty and exploitation."[32] At issue in such critiques, of course, is the legibility of the Panthers' approach to the lumpenproletariat *as* a Marxist one: the weight of Marx's authority and of the proletarianism of classical Marxism make a Marxist revision of the lumpenproletariat simply unthinkable. Even Stokely Carmichael—hardly a dogmatic Marxist—called the Panthers "stupid" for ignoring Marx and Engels's warnings and thinking the lumpenproletariat could be organized politically.[33] Jeffrey O. G. Ogbar and Chris Booker have suggested that the Party's emphasis on recruiting from the lumpenproletariat, and its leaders and members' tendency to posture as lumpenproletarian outlaws, hindered its ability to organize a disciplined mass movement.[34]

Yet such critiques threaten to obscure the work a thinker like Cleaver was able to do with the *concept* of the lumpenproletariat. Surveying a racially polarized nation with an internally colonized black population, an increasingly automated productive economy, and the conservatism or inaction of traditional leftist and working-class institutions, Cleaver used this concept to reorient Marxist discourse accordingly. More important than the question of whether Cleaver's claims were "right," or whether the tactics drawn from them were effective, is the crucial truth about Marxism itself—and about Marxism's identity in American contexts—that Cleaver demonstrates. Cleaver models how an African American Marxist theoretical practice can proceed by self-reflexively revising and adapting Marxist precepts to the contours of black experience and political needs.

Black Panther activist Bobby Seale used the African American folk figure Stagolee—an archetypal pimp, outlaw, and "bad man"—to reimagine Marx's lumpenproletarians as political agents. "I transformed Stagolee . . . into brothers standing on the block and all of the illegitimate activity," he told Cecil Brown. "In effect, they were the lumpen proletariat in a high-tech social order, different from how 'lumpen' had been described historically."[35] Seale foregrounded this revision in his account of his time in the Black Panther Party:

> Marx and Lenin would probably turn over in their graves if they could see the lumpen proletarian Afro-Americans putting together the ideology of the Black Panther Party. Both Marx and Lenin used to say that the lumpen proletariat wouldn't do anything for the revolution. But today, in a modern, highly technological society, with its CIA, FBI, electronic surveillance, and cops armed and equipped for overkill, here are black Americans . . . becoming the vanguard of a revolution, despite all attempts to totally wipe us out.[36]

For Seale, black folk sensibilities enable a strategic rewriting of orthodox Marxism's devaluation of the lumpenproletariat. His gothic metaphor suggests that by making Marx and Lenin "turn over in their graves"—by revising their conclusions about the lumpenproletariat—the Panthers were keeping Marxism *alive*: reinvigorated by particular concerns of African American culture and politics and thus relevant to the specific conditions of revolutionary struggle in postwar US society.

This enactment of fidelity through revision is made possible by Marxism's own epistemological character. Given Marxism's status as the science of material conditions within history, modification is central to its theoretical practice. Kathleen Cleaver acknowledges as much when she writes that "any attempt to apply Marxist-Leninist theories cold from the pages of old books to the hot reality of present day life . . . betrays the essence of the science." To be a proper Marxist, she continues, one must "advance the inherited theories into the future." Ironically, this often puts the proper Marxist at odds with nominally Marxist institutions, including, from her perspective in 1975, the Communist Party of the United States.[37] Louis Althusser explains how a Marxism that fancies it has reached an explanatory endpoint, where its theses and concepts finally make sense of reality and thus need no further adjustment, is a Marxism that has crossed from materialism to idealism, from a contingent project to a static set of absolute truths. "Marx did not 'say everything' . . . because to 'say everything' makes no sense for a scientist: only a religion can pretend to 'say everything.' On the contrary, a scientific theory, by definition, always has *something else* to say." The "central thesis" of Althusser's thought, which he locates as fundamental to Marx and Lenin's as well, is thus "the idea of knowledge as *production*": truth is reached only through the perpetual generation of more and updated knowledge about the world. "*Marxist theory can fall behind history, and even behind itself, if ever it believes that it has arrived,*" he warns.[38] Althusser clarifies what the Panthers' Marxism reveals about Marxism itself: its nature as not an all-encompassing master theory, but as the living, situated crafting of materialist knowledge and revolutionary possibility.

RAGS AND PAPER: THE TROPE OF THE LUMPENPROLETARIAT

If the lumpenproletariat is a generative concept for Marxist theoretical work, it also can enable new critical considerations of literary representations of marginality. The connotations and figurative valences attending the raggedness of the "ragged proletariat" often converge as a trope in modern works that deal with socioeconomic and discursive marginality. Raggedness is a complex and mobile figure, as it can connote both delimitation and potential: a state of being discarded or a state of incipient renewal. In a manner similar to the conceptual ambiguity of the lumpenproletariat in Marxism, raggedness can suggest either hopeless moral and political depravity or openness to progressive organization and definition. Raggedness figures Marxism's characteristic account of the lumpenproletariat as simultaneously exteriorized by and free from the institutions and discourses of capitalist modernity; as immiserated products of an oppressive system that excludes them from ideological legitimacy and material means of survival, and as free agents who create new possibilities from the margins of both capitalist social formations and traditional revolutionary organizations.

The ability of raggedness to trope the conditions of the marginalized derives from the material history of the production of paper from rags, a practice in which excess and refuse are transformed into the potential of blank pages. In Europe, paper was produced from decomposed rags until the end of the eighteenth century, when an increased demand for books and newspapers led papermakers to seek more readily available raw materials.[39] Yet the state of the rag as both an endpoint (something thrown out, discarded, decomposed) and a new beginning (a raw material to be transformed into something else) persists as a useful literary trope for processes of marginalization, exclusion, and resistance. The trope of the rag figures both *realistic* and *romantic* understandings of the socially marginal: it indicates the material devastation and desperation of those reduced to rags, those who must subsist as the castoffs of society. But it also conjures the potential of those who, because exteriorized from means and relations of production, can craft new practices of subsistence and transform the margin into a place of new departures.

Patricia Yaeger identifies this figurative work of the rag in James Agee and Walker Evans's landmark text of Depression-era photojournalism, *Let Us Now Praise Famous Men* (1941). She notes how Agee describes the clothing of poor whites as "surfaces" on which he can, as a writer, "[construct] a dignity for this clothing" and its wearers. However, that dignity is a romantic quality specific to literary form, one "that only *he* can describe; this shirt loses its aesthetic power when he shifts to the

[35]

perspective of the poverty-stricken, class-bound white subjects he wants so desperately . . . to venerate." Elsewhere in the text, rags "suggest a deeper pollution; they describe a world drifting away from the human" and "humanity immersed in dirt: the body in extremis, in crisis."[40] The rag is the sign of bodies that have been discounted, of bodies that can be reimagined through the work of writing, but in a manner necessarily removed from the real cost of that discounting. The rag and its shadow sign, paper, capture the tensions, negotiations, and possibilities emerging from social and discursive exclusion.

In similar ways, the figure of the rag animated a famous debate in the history of Marxist thought. In his study of Baudelaire, Walter Benjamin interprets the figure of the ragpicker as a figure for Baudelaire himself. "The poets find the refuse of society on their streets and derive their heroic subject from this very refuse. . . . Ragpicker and poet: both are concerned with refuse, and both go about their solitary business while other citizens are sleeping."[41] As Michael Jennings notes, the ragpicker is Benjamin's figure for his own archival methodology, one that seeks to produce knowledge from the discarded ephemera of history.[42] In Benjamin's hands, the ragpicker is a romantic figure for the subversive production, under cover of darkness, of new epistemological and political directions from out of the discards of exclusion and expulsion. Theodor Adorno, however, counters with a more sober analysis. He faults Benjamin for overlooking "the capitalist function of the ragpicker—namely, to subject even rubbish to exchange value."[43] Adorno indicates how the ragpicker plays a role in the reproduction of capitalism, and the terms of this debate are the very issues that the figure of the rag incites: Does the ragpicker turn rags into new forms of insight and practice, or simply into more commodities? Do those on the margins of capitalist society access revolutionary potential, or are they deformed by immiseration and false consciousness?

These questions often occur in American literary works that examine social marginality. Huckleberry Finn, for instance, is an outsider whose rags are a sign of both material lack and romantic potential. In *The Adventures of Tom Sawyer* (1876), Mark Twain's titular protagonist famously dreads labor. Huck, the outcast with no familial or social place and thus no obligations, is a hero to boys like Tom and a threat in the eyes of their mothers. "Huckleberry was cordially hated and dreaded by all the mothers of the town, because he was idle, and lawless, and vulgar and bad—and because all their children admired him so, and delighted in his forbidden society, and wished they dared to be like him." He "did not have to go to school or to church, or call any being master or obey anybody." To Tom and his friends, he is a "romantic outcast."[44] Huck's status as a threat (to power) and source of freedom (to those subservient to power) is signified by his ragged appearance:

> Huckleberry was always dressed in the cast-off clothes of full-grown men, and they were in perennial bloom and fluttering with rags. His hat was a vast ruin with a wide crescent lopped out of its brim; his coat, when he wore one, hung nearly to his heels and had the rearward buttons far down the back; but one suspender supported his trousers; the seat of the trousers bagged low and contained nothing; the fringed legs dragged in the dirt when not rolled up.[45]

His clothing is both a literal manifestation of the poverty being an outcast entails and registers the "gaudy" appeal of his condition to socially constrained boys like Tom. Furthermore, by describing his ragged clothes as "in perennial bloom," Twain reimagines them in terms of potentiality and generation. Huck's rags mark his exclusion from the social order. But they also signal his capacity, because of his exclusion, to enact Twain's various moral and sociopolitical critiques of that order (both in *The Adventures of Tom Sawyer* and in the 1884 *Adventures of Huckleberry Finn*). His rags, in other words, become blank paper for the imagination of new critical perspectives.

Not all writers correlate the raggedness of lumpenproletarian marginality with possibility. In *Maggie, A Girl of the Streets* (1893), Stephen Crane highlights the destructiveness of Maggie's recourse to prostitution at the end of the novel. Maggie lives with violent and alcoholic parents, and works in a "collars and cuffs" factory with "twenty girls of various shades of yellow discontent." They produce collars, "the name of whose brand could be noted for its irrelevancy to anything in connection with collars."[46] Her romantic relationship with Pete, an attractive bartender, promises a means of escape from her life and her alienated labor, but it leads instead to her sexual disgrace and banishment from home. Abandoned by Pete and by her family, she turns to prostitution. In her final appearance in the novel, she has become anonymous—referred to only as "the girl"—and walks the street in search of trade. This mobility contrasts sharply with the confined life she led previously, but it contains none of Huckleberry Finn's romantic possibility. Raggedness is aligned instead with the repulsiveness of transient men who prey on the socially outcast and defenseless Maggie: first a "ragged being with shifting, blood-shot eyes," and then a "great figure" wearing "torn and greasy garments" who, it is suggested, violates and murders her.[47] Lacking both class status and social identity, she is vulnerable in an underworld where raggedness, as it did for Marx, connotes only violent depravity. Maggie serves as a resolutely realistic counterpart to the romanticism of Twain's marginal hero. This representation derives from Crane's emphasis of journalistic documentation over figurative license, and also indicates his awareness of the ideological and material violence social exclusion entails for women—violence easily lost in depictions, such as Twain's, where the outsider figure as an unencumbered male individual approximates normative patriarchal constructions of masculine individualism.

Claude McKay's Harlem Renaissance novel *Banjo* (1929) is the only African American text to have been examined specifically through the lens of the lumpenproletariat concept. By selecting the underworld of Marseilles as his focus, McKay continued to challenge Harlem Renaissance preferences for depictions of black life that would affirm normative middle-class standards, an endeavor that had famously prompted W. E. B. Du Bois to denounce McKay's previous novel, *Home to Harlem*, as "filth."[48] In *Banjo*, the lumpenproletariat enacts the novel's sophisticated theorization of black internationalism in the interwar period. Brent Hayes Edwards observes how McKay describes Marseilles's diasporic community of African Americans, Africans, and West Indians as a lumpenproletariat subsisting on the margins of waged labor and proletarian respectability. McKay describes this community as "dumped down in the great Provençal port, bumming a day's work, a meal, a drink, existing from hand to mouth, anyhow any way, between box car, tramp ship, bistro, and bordel."[49] Edwards argues that unlike Marx, McKay sees this marginality as a source of potential, and the novel's drifters embody an alternative internationalism to those of both imperialism and Marxist proletarianism. By highlighting the internal divisions among the black Marseilles lumpenproletariat, McKay also critiques various forms of black internationalism, such as Garveyism. For Edwards, this lumpenproletarian "vagabond internationalism," articulated on the margins of established movements and collective identities, is defined only by internal difference and by the "debate" and "miscommunication" that characterize African diasporic expressive practices—"the Dozens writ large, with Ananse, Frère Lapin, and the Signifying Monkey soused and clamoring for the soapbox."[50]

In an essay echoing Edwards's reading, William Maxwell argues that *Banjo* redefines the transience imposed on people of African descent through slavery and imperialism as an "adversarial" internationalism, thereby reimagining rootlessness as a new source of identity and resistance.[51] McKay employs papers and rags to figure the articulation of this internationalism. A key articulation of this recovery is an episode describing how wandering black sailors who, McKay writes, having "lived their lives in the great careless tradition" and lost their identification papers, are issued new papers "distinguished by the official phrase: Nationality Doubtful."[52] As Maxwell notes, "the move to deprive" these sailors of national identity "paradoxically eases their national wandering."[53] Intended to signify the loss of place and identity, the phrase "Nationality Doubtful" allows McKay to mark an emergent (trans)national identity defined only negatively (or "doubtfully"). McKay deploys tropes of paper and rags in a complex manner here: the "Nationality Doubtful" papers codify these sailors' removal from the nation at the same time that they define a new ground of subjectivity, encapsulating the simultaneous exclusion and freedom of the "great careless tradition" of lumpenproletarian vagabondage.

Yet the papers signify in another symbolic register at the same time. One " 'Nationality Doubtful' man," Taloufa, an African sailor, engages in a fruitless attempt to win the right to enter England, where he had lived "for over forty years," and has accumulated "a pile of foolscap correspondence with the British Home Office." The "way of civilization with the colored man, especially the black" is here signaled by an excess of paper that registers the excessive repressions of national exclusion. Yet the figure of the black vagabond is then rendered as a symptomatic challenge and alternative to Western civilization, as "the red rag to the mighty-bellowing, all-trampling civilized bull."[54] *Banjo* reimagines the papers of that repressive and defined exclusion as "red rag[s]" that incite an unformed, undefined, and revolutionary defiance. This figurative play between paper and rags, contained form and resistant formlessness, synchronizes McKay's complex approach to internationalism and diaspora.

When approached through the trope of raggedness, the lumpenproletariat can function in literary criticism by revealing how writers use literary tools to diagnose and recast marginality and exclusion. Whether thematically or through specific figurations of rags and paper, Wright, Ellison, and Walker's work often reimagines lumpenproletarian existence as one of unstructured potential and transformative agency. At the same, these writers attend to the processes of economic, gender, and racial marginalization that misshape lumpenproletarian life in the Depression United States. Keeping both romantic and realistic poles of the trope of the rag in sight, their writings analyze and indict capitalism, white supremacy, and patriarchy while simultaneously imagining revolutionary solutions and alternatives.

THE PROLETARIAT AND THE LUMPENPROLETARIAT IN DEPRESSION LITERATURE

In the 1930s, Marxism and the lumpenproletariat were thematic and representational concerns of US literature. During the Depression, formal protocols of literary Marxism were developed by writers and critics associated with the proletarian literature movement as well as with the lesser-studied genre of bottom dogs literature. While the focus of each differs—proletarian literature generally considers the collectivization and revolutionary agency of the militant proletariat, while bottom dogs texts map the travels of lumpenproletarian outcasts—both tend to approach their content through the lens of Marxist orthodoxy.

Signature formal maneuvers of the Depression-era proletarian novel—as identified by Walter Rideout's *The Radical Novel in the United States* and codified in Barbara Foley's magisterial *Radical Representations*[55]—involve representing the formation of proletarian class consciousness as well as the development of the revolutionary proletariat from out of the individual experiences of workers. In other words, proletarian literature is not merely a set of empirical representations of working-class identity; rather, it endeavors to depict American working-class experience in light of the specific Marxist concept of the proletariat, the collective subsumption of the singular laboring subject and the structural negation of the capitalist mode of production that the members of the working class must and will become. These novels thus tend to position the emergence of the collective proletariat, as foretold in *The Communist Manifesto,* as both the solution to the alienation of individual working-class characters and the bearer of societal transformation.

Accordingly, the classless lumpenproletariat is frequently an object of suspicion in proletarian literature: they're the types who, because of their vice and political ignorance, resist incorporation into the proletarian collective. The life of the underclass serves as the individualistic, alienated, and self-interested alternative to proletarian collectivism. A clear example of this suspicion comes in Mike Gold's 1930 novel *Jews Without Money*. The text depicts the development of Mikey (based on Gold himself) from a politically unconscious and criminal youth from the Jewish Lower East Side into a committed member of the proletariat. At the end of the novel, Mikey has entered the industrial workforce, but capitalist labor offers him neither security nor identity: "Jobs, jobs. I drifted from one to the other, without plan, without hope. . . . I was nothing, bound for nowhere." Only when he hears from a "man on an East-Side soap-box" that "out of the despair, melancholy and helpless rage of millions, a world movement had been born to abolish poverty" does he overcome alienation and find his true identity and purpose. The conceptual ideal of the proletariat, heralded by a revolutionary activist, presents itself to Mikey as the bearer of the "workers' Revolution"—the "true Messiah" that secularizes and materializes Mikey's longing for "the Jewish Messiah who would redeem the world." The ending line of the novel—"O great Beginning!"—makes clear that his old life, as an individual worker, has ended, and his new life, as part of the proletarian collective, has begun.[56] From within the cultural and historical parameters of Jewish American working-class experience, Gold's ending aestheticizes the ending of *The Communist Manifesto*, in which the formation of the proletariat is both the precondition for and the catalyst of an inevitable negation of capitalism. It also resonates with other proletarian novels that dramatize the classical Marxist emergence of the proletarian collective, such as Robert Cantwell's *The Land of Plenty* (1934), Arnold Armstrong's *Parched Earth* (1934), William Rollins's *The Shadow Before* (1934), and Clara Weatherwax's *Marching! Marching!* (1935).

In this ending, Mikey is also saved from the lumpenproletariat. Gold frequently describes the criminal element of the Lower East Side in tones that echo Marx and Engels's portrait of the lumpenproletariat as scum. "They never worked. They played pool all day, or drank in saloons. Some were cheap pimps, others cheap thieves or gunmen. They fought and quarreled with the world, and with each other." Gold even displays the classical Marxist ambivalence over whether the lumpenproletariat's condition is socially fabricated or inherent: "One hates gangsters, as one must hate all mercenaries. Yet some are unfortunate boys, bad eggs, hatched by the bad world hen." The notorious gangster Louis One Eye terrifies the workers of the neighborhood, but "is under the protection of Tammany Hall": his actions have been co-opted by state forces to keep the working class in check, to stop it from emerging as the proletariat. He is "a monster useful to bosses in strikes, and to politicians on election day." As his moniker suggests, Louis One Eye ("one-I") is an alienated individual, unincorporated into any socioeconomic class and thus merely self-interested and a pliable tool of reaction. Mikey's mother, the novel's personification of proletarian virtue, voices Marx's moral and political disapproval of the lumpenproletariat when she tells a prostitute: "Get a job in a factory, and be a good girl."[57]

At the end of the novel, a desperate Mikey is on the verge of joining the neighborhood gang, which is lead by his old friend "Nigger," a Jewish American youth whose nickname references his dark complexion. While his main pursuits involve "drinking and whoring," Nigger has also been an effective champion and defender of the boys from the neighborhood. Before he became a gangster, Nigger punched a teacher who called Mikey a kike—"It was Justice"—and stood up to a cop who harassed Mikey and his other friends: "He was ready to die for justice. The cop was not as brave."[58] Throughout the novel, Nigger seems to be a potential force for radical resistance. His nickname, when combined with his dedication to confronting anti-Semitism, suggests that his commitment to justice transcends racial or ethnic particularism. But his individualized toughness ultimately leads him only to a lumpenproletarian life of crime. By the end of the novel, he is like Louis One Eye in that he embodies the individualistic urban subject Mikey must reject, regardless of any political potential such individuals might offer, in order to be reborn in the international proletariat.

Bottom dogs fiction of the 1930s tends to be politically aligned with the proletarian literary project but characterized by different representational and thematic procedures. Named by scholars after *Bottom Dogs*, the 1929 debut novel of Edward Dahlberg, bottom dogs texts were generally composed by pro-Communist writers but, to quote Rideout, their political "message tends . . . to be implicit only. For the most part refusing the assistance of slogans, resolutions, and other revolutionary gestures, these novelists ambush the reader from behind a relentlessly objective description of life in the lower depths."[59] Foley suggests that such texts "do not centrally depict the development of a revolutionary working-class identity."[60] Rather than stories of workers forming into a collective proletariat or representations of Communist activism, these novels depict outcasts and criminals who never attain sociopolitical awareness. Their protagonists rarely encounter or comprehend, and often express hostility toward, Marxism and the Communist movement. Classical Marxism's political suspicion of the lumpenproletariat is thus often the starting point, in these works, for analyzing the obstacles American conditions pose to proletarian class struggle and to bottom dogs individuals being "swept into the movement by a proletarian revolution."

Sometimes these authors are implicitly critical of the Communist movement for being unable or unwilling to reach the lumpenproletariat because it is devalued by Marxist orthodoxy. Looking back at the 1930s, Dahlberg would remark that poverty, the condition of the underclass he wrote about, was beyond the horizon of the Communists' focus on labor and production. As such, it only mattered when it was "enjoyed by a drayman, hodcarrier, steamfitter or riveter, a longshoreman, millhand, or steelworker. . . . No matter what hardships the *lumpenproletariat* suffered such people did not count."[61] As what "didn't count," the lumpenproletariat is often framed in bottom dogs novels as a blind spot in need of consideration. However, these texts generally still underscore Marxism's account of the character of lumpenproletarian types, foregrounding the unsavory behaviors and ideological leanings of the underclass as a check against the unexamined surety of Communist prescriptions. Acel, the drifter protagonist of Edward Anderson's *Hungry Men* (1935) declares "there's a million men in this country on the road, and if these men were organized or were prepared to follow some organization, it'd be something." But throughout the novel, Acel and his fellow transients are often unable to recognize Communism as the bearer of their own interests. In fact, Acel is inclined to justify capitalism as a "survival-of-the-fittest law," a reification of the self-interest that is all members of the lumpenproletariat know.[62] Rather than offering positive evocations of proletarianism, bottom dogs texts proceed in a negative manner by diagnosing the limits of revolutionary political efficacy with respect to the lumpenproletariat.

During the 1930s, the Jewish American Communist writer Nelson Algren was the bottom dogs novelist whose treatment of the marginalized and transient was most thoroughly informed by Marxist theory. Algren demonstrates both the orthodox Marxist understanding of the lumpenproletariat and the figurative utility of rags and paper in his 1935 short story "A Lumpen." The story opens with the titular narrator, a transient staying at a local shelter, alighting on the streets of Chicago. He encounters a man "handing out little books" and takes one to study. "Are You the Wreck of a Man, Consultation Free" proves to be the title of this self-help pamphlet. He pores over it seeking an answer to his condition—"readin' it hard like I had buboes and wanted to know from the book where to go"—but ultimately has to throw it away when he reflects that the staff at the shelter wouldn't approve of such reading material. The next day, he encounters an interracial Communist parade. The sight of "niggers ... walkin' with white men, carryin' banners" is illegible to the narrator. One of the signs carries a prominent Communist slogan of the era—"Black and White. Unite and Fight"—but the very concept of interracial cooperation is foreign to him. "Them's mighty cocky niggers," he says to a fellow bystander. His recourse to white racism demonstrates his inability to read the political text before him. "I kept thinking of them Black and White signs all morning," he tells the reader, referring at once to the literal placards of the marchers, the interracial activism of Communism, and his general inability to "read" the various printed solutions—self-help, Communism—available to him. The narrator ends the story having finally found a source of income: he sells copies of Huey Long's newspaper *The American Progress*.[63] As Marx predicted, his "conditions of life" have made him unable to think beyond self-interest and have primed him to become a "bribed tool of reactionary intrigue."

This straightforward illustration of Marx's approach to the lumpenproletariat relies on figures of rags and paper. The protagonist's ragged state—his material lack and the cognitive deformations (political illiteracy, white supremacy) accompanying that lack—is positioned in relation to a range of possible options for transforming his raggedness into something new. Those options are figured as papers: the "Are You the Wreck of a Man, Consultation Free" book, the signs of the Communist marchers, and *The American Progress*. Because of his exteriorized status, the lumpenproletarian figure is capable of being written into a variety of social and political identities and programs—as Marx predicted, however, he is more amenable to reaction than revolution.

Algren's first novel, *Somebody in Boots* (1935), frames its narrative of Depression-era transients with chapter epigraphs quoting *The Communist Manifesto*'s warnings about the lumpenproletariat. As William Solomon explains, *Somebody in Boots* is a "textual experiment designed to examine the validity of Marx's political theory," as articulated in *The Communist Manifesto*, when applied to "conditions in the United States in the 1930s."[64] The novel validates Marx's antagonism toward the lumpenproletariat even as it displays Algren's sensitivity to the material plight and attendant limitations of marginalized individuals. Cass McKay, a homeless drifter, is so deformed by the violence of lumpenproletarian sites (brothels, freight cars, jail cells) that his cognitive abilities and ambitions cannot transcend his conditioning. For a brief period in the novel, he is introduced to the Communist movement in Chicago by a black musician, Dill Doak, who attends Communist rallies when not performing and who possesses a clear Marxist understanding of American capitalism. But the interracialism and collectivism of the movement, and its revolutionary ambitions, find no corollary in Cass's own experiences of a marginal realm where self-preservation trumps all. William Maxwell shows how Cass's underworld of hobos and criminals is one in which white supremacy is violently maintained and normalized. He is thus unable to understand Communism's appeal because the idea of transcending racial difference is, within the bounds of his experience, unintelligible.[65] At the end of the novel, Cass is no better off than at the beginning: he has learned nothing, and he leaves Chicago to rejoin the freight-hopping lumpenproletariat—a form of mobility that, in the novel, offers no hope of personal or political transcendence.[66]

As members of the Depression-era literary left, Wright, Ellison, and Walker were certainly aware of and influenced by the various projects and texts of proletarian and bottom dogs literatures. However, in their own approach to the lumpenproletariat, they often reimagine its socioeconomic exteriority as a source of new resources for revolutionary agency. In effect, Wright, Ellison, and Walker's work extends Dahlberg's observation—that is, to write of the lumpenproletariat is to write about what doesn't count—by asking what Eldridge Cleaver would ask decades later: how can the socioeconomic, racial, cultural, and gender facets of the lumpenproletariat expand the range of what can count for and as progressive radicalism?

MARXISM, LITERATURE, AND BLACK CULTURE

Paul Gilroy remarks that the transatlantic black counterculture he famously theorizes has been somewhat at odds with orthodox Marxism. This is due in part to "the simple fact that in the critical thought of blacks in the West, social self-creation through labour is not the centre-piece of emancipatory hopes. For the descendants of slaves, work signifies only servitude, misery, and subordination." Instead, artistic and cultural practices are the Black Atlantic's "means towards both individual self-fashioning and communal liberation."[67] Gilroy's claim about the ambivalence toward labor in black cultural expression allows us to contextualize the relative lack of empowering portraits of labor in Wright, Ellison, and Walker. In their Depression writings, industrial and agricultural work is more often entrapping than yielding of insight or agency, and the classical Marxist emphasis on labor as the catalyst of proletarianization and revolution is largely absent.

Instead, in their writings revolutionary consciousness and action emerge primarily from and within lumpenproletarian experiences of crime, transgression, and life on the margins. The central archetype of their work could thus be described as the lumpenproletarian *hustler*, a character who gets by outside the law and social identities organized by class, who must invent his or her life and identity on the fly, in various states of transience. As Stuart Hall and others posit in *Policing the Crisis: Mugging, the State, and Law and Order* hustlers, as modern black urban lumpenproletarians, "live by their wits" through "modes of survival alternative to the respectable route of hard labor and low wages."[68] This figure allegorizes politics as a creative mode of *practice* very different from the exploitations of labor.

By "practice," I am referring to Michel de Certeau's sense of the term as an everyday tactic, the creative implementation of resistance that works with and against the structural conditions of a given time and place. Like a drifter on the move or a hobo hopping a freight train, a tactic possesses a "mobility that must accept the chance offerings of the moment, and seize on the wing the possibilities that offer themselves at any given moment."[69]

I see de Certeau's concept of the tactical rendered within African American cultural theory by Houston Baker's figure of the train-hopping blues singer, whose vernacular origins and deconstructionist practice of the blues register the fluid mobility and persistent political commitment of black cultural expression. "Like signification itself, blues are always nomadically wandering. Like the freight-hopping hobo, they are ever on the move, ceaselessly summing novel experience.... Standing at the juncture, or railhead, the singer draws into his repertoire hollers, cries, whoops, and moans of black men and women working in fields without recompense."[70]

The blues and the tactic name what Louis Althusser designates as the properly scientific kind of Marxist materialism: a theoretical practice unconfined by preconceived mandates of orthodoxy or static foundational claims. In order to emphasize the necessity of revision, expansion, and theoretical invention to materialism, he employs a figure who resembles the train-hopping hobo, the archetypal lumpenproletarian of Depression America: "an idealist is a man who knows which station the train leaves from, and also its destination.... The materialist, on the other hand, is a man who gets on to a moving train without knowing either where it is coming from or where it is going."[71] The hobo who rides trains illegally and who is thus both exterior to and free from the structures of society and discourse in a given historical moment embodies the free-ranging experimentation that constitutes Marxism's scientific character.

Cecil Brown's argument about the black cultural legend of Stagolee is relevant here as well. Brown uses Benjamin's ragpicker to delineate a particular characteristic of African American oral traditions and music. As Benjamin's ragpicker "takes the old and discarded and turns it into something new," rap artists have similarly reworked the contradictions of black urban experience:

> The marginal people of a city have to take the scraps and fragments and put them together to make a whole cloth. Rap music takes its name from the verb 'to rap,' which is short for 'rhapsodize,' which in Greek means 'to stitch a song together.' African Americans have a tradition of stitching bits of narrative together.[72]

This practice of black culture is exemplified in the history of the Stagolee legend. A notorious underworld operator, Stagolee enabled black artists to explore the interrelations of masculinity, city life, and social marginalization. Stagolee embodies the experiences of a modern African American "'rag' proletariat," and thus "it is not coincidental that the music that first celebrated the Stagolee ballad was called ragtime."[73] Brown traces how the story of Stagolee has been told by numerous black cultural forms—ballads, the blues and ragtime, toasts, the Black Panther Party's lumpenproletarian rhetoric, and rap music—in order to express black sociopolitical needs in various modern contexts and periods. In other words, Brown suggests that the Stagolee legend, like modern black oral culture itself, is "lumpenproletarian" in form as well as content: it stitches together ragged "scraps and fragments" into the "whole cloth" of politically and socially sustaining narrative. Like Baker, Brown suggests the unexpected resemblance of Althusser's scientific Marxism and African American cultural expression: both are defined by tactical adaptation and revision, and both resemble the practical resourcefulness of lumpenproletarian life rather than the organized, territorialized processes of labor.

Finally, literature itself converges with the tactical nature of Marxism and black culture. De Certeau observes that the working of a tactic is like that of the literary or rhetorical figure. He thus finds "homologies between practical ruses and rhetorical movements" and notes that figures perform "tricks" with language, tricks that defy "the legalities of syntax and 'proper' sense."[74] As an illegitimate or criminal manipulation of linguistic sense, the literary figure resembles the illicit inventiveness of the lumpenproletarian individual: the former is thus a generative resource for thinking through the epistemological and political consequences of the latter. A black Marxism organized around the possibilities of the lumpenproletariat is a Marxism well suited to literary form, and thus unsurprisingly finds expression in the work of three of the Depression-era left's most innovative black writers.

2
RICHARD WRIGHT AND THE LUMPENPROLETARIAN DESIRE FOR REVOLUTION

In his social and existential marginalization, the condition of being *sans feu et sans aveu* that Marx described in *The Class Struggles in France,* Bigger Thomas emerges from *Native Son* (1940) as African American literature's most representative lumpenproletarian character. The condition of Marx's ragged proletariat—"a mass strictly differentiated from the industrial proletariat, a recruiting ground for thieves and criminals of all kinds, living on the crumbs of society, people without a definite trade, vagabonds"[1]—certainly describes Bigger's position in the South Side of Chicago, where, shut out from opportunities for social and personal fulfillment and offered only unrewarding waged labor, he is drawn to criminal enterprises. "I felt that Bigger . . . carried within him the potentialities of either Communism or Fascism," Wright explained in "How 'Bigger' Was Born" (1940), invoking Marx's political estimation of the lumpenproletariat, because alienated from any class interests, as susceptible to either proletarian or reactionary organization but "[prepared] . . . far more for the part of a bribed tool of reactionary intrigue."[2] Bigger Thomas's lumpenproletarian characteristics—political ignorance and criminal tendencies provoked by being external to social, class, or cultural incorporation—are routinely mentioned in descriptions of *Native Son*, even when the concept of the lumpenproletariat is not under discussion. For example, James Smethurst describes the "modernist mold" of character from which Bigger is "cast" as "a person who has fallen out of society, has no roots. . . . He or she is alienated from his or her work; has no god, no traditional values."³

In the 1930s, Wright was a prominent member of Communist left literary circles.⁴ That Wright constructed his first published novel as an examination of the revolutionary potential not of the laboring proletariat but of the urban underclass, dismissed as mere scum by orthodox Marxism, is indicative of how complex was the correlation between revolutionary politics and Marxist vocabularies of class in Depression-era leftist fiction. Cast out from any stable class position, even that of the exploited proletariat, Bigger Thomas allows Wright to relocate revolution to the margins of classical Marxism's dyadic relations of production. *Native Son* offers an incisive portrait of lumpenproletarian subjectivity, characterizing Bigger so as to delineate both the nature of lumpenproletarian desire and the transformative praxis that flows from that desire.

My reading of Bigger's subjectivity departs from the common understanding of him as a deformed product of unjust social conditions whose repulsive actions reflect and retroactively condemn those conditions. In this understanding, Bigger is not a subject but, to cite a phrase from James Baldwin's influential 1951 reading, "a monster created by the American republic."⁵ Readers of *Native Son* who align Bigger with the concept of the lumpenproletariat have borrowed Marx's skepticism about lumpenproletarian political tendencies and, as a result, also posit Bigger's primarily symptomatic function. William Solomon and William Maxwell hold that Bigger embodies obstacles to proletarian politics posed by the reactionary co-option of lumpenproletarian individuals. Solomon identifies Wright's and *Native Son*'s attention to "the hard-to-predict fate" and "ideological swerves of the American lumpenproletariat."⁶ Maxwell argues that "How 'Bigger' Was Born" makes "reference to the ideological ambivalence of Marx and Engels' lumpen" in order to compare Bigger's false consciousness with that of "the lumpen of 1848." Just as Marx and Engels identified the danger posed by the lumpenproletariat to revolutionary workers, Maxwell argues that Wright issues Bigger as a warning to the left: "white radical friends must look squarely at his native son's elastic definition of self-defense and imperative violence, as well as the possibility that the meaning discovered there will not fulfill Marxist forecasts."[7]

I argue that, rather than a reiteration in American contexts of Marxism's suspicion of the lumpenproletariat, Wright's characterization of Bigger revises Marxism's understanding of the dynamics of revolution. As a result, Wright's novel anticipates aspects of Jean-Paul Sartre's, Fredric Jameson's, and Louis Althusser's various efforts to theorize the revolutionary political implications of subjective identity, as well as Hannah Arendt's philosophy of politics as public, active self-revelation. Marx's concept of the lumpenproletariat frames Wright's central concern in *Native Son:* the triangulation, from the perspective of African American political chances, of Bigger's subjectivity with the dynamics of action and the stakes of social recognition.[8]

Bigger is not simply a by-product of US racial and economic relations, but retains a positive psychic interiority that both operates in the midst of and draws resources from his socioeconomic exteriority. In a 1940 letter to Mike Gold, Wright expressed his surprise that "so few" readers seemed to "insist upon the humanity of Bigger, and the entire novel was written to sear that one idea into the reader's mind. Are we going to let what capitalism has done to Bigger make us reject him? Will the drapery of his hate and fear make us afraid to recognize the human impulses, warped to be sure, which surge and dominate him?" For Wright, such recognition was of vital political importance: if the left failed to see the humanity of those outcasts "warped" by capitalism, the fascists would certainly appropriate it.[9] Samuel Sillen recognized Wright's intentions in a 1940 *New Masses* review, describing Bigger as a "positive and creative individual." Furthermore, he linked Bigger's character to a capacity for revolutionary action. "Too much attention has been paid to the unfortunate ways in which society has forced him to express himself," Sillen complains about other critical responses to *Native Son*, "and not enough to the dynamic emotional force which drives him toward an assertion of his will to create a different world for himself. It is only partly true to say that capitalism makes him what he is; it is even more important to insist that capitalism *unmakes* what he is, a sensitive, imaginative, and creative personality." Bigger thus preserves "the deep urge to live and create which no exploitative society can permanently subdue."[10] In an influential scholarly

[51]

reading, Donald Gibson faults those who see Bigger as only a social type rather than as a "particular person" and "a discrete human entity."[11] An accurate understanding of *Native Son* requires a similar excavation of Bigger's complex subjectivity from the weight of naturalist interpretations.

In his 1930s writings, Wright redefines anticapitalist revolution as the product of African American desire for subjective visibility. The invisibility of the black subject is, of course, a recurring theme in African American writing most famously articulated by W. E. B. Du Bois in *The Souls of Black Folk* (1903) as the "veiling" of individual subjectivity by racial difference. This theme leads Wright to rework Marxism for African American concerns. The black lumpenproletarian individual, for Wright, is racially, socially, and economically marginalized. If, in Althusser's well-known theory, subjectivity is the product of institutionally organized activity, the black lumpenproletarian individual is someone whose actions, outside of and thus unnoticed by any institution, fail to garner recognition as those of a subject. What this leads Wright to eventually conclude, in *Native Son*, is that the desire for revolution is the desire for the public affirmation of the self. Given the utter exteriority of individuals like Bigger Thomas—who, as Cedric Robinson writes, possesses "the desperation that was the precondition for the making of total and violent revolutionary commitments"[12]—that desire outpaces, in its potentially transformative power, the class-based motivations of classical Marxism's proletariat. And while the desire for individual recognition may seem a bourgeois or even reactionary motive, Wright's location of its origin in the social invisibility enjoined on African American lumpenproletarians by Jim Crow and capitalism underscores its radical implication: that achieving that desire necessitates a wholesale transformation of American society. Bigger, Wright explains, "felt the *need* for a whole life and *acted* out of that need."[13] Organizing that desire within the Communist movement, the only program that can grant the subjective affirmation Bigger desires, is the task *Native Son* identifies for political strategy.

Wright thus challenges the philosophical concept of identity informing Marx's mistrust of the lumpenproletariat. Nicholas Thoburn argues that in Marx the lumpenproletariat names "a mode of practice oriented toward the bolstering of identity cut off from the flows and relations of the social." Lumpenproletarian life, because marginal to social processes, preserves individual identity in essential terms free from sociohistorical fluctuation. The proletariat, by contrast, is "a non-identitarian mode of practice... immanent to the mutational social relations of capital." Rather than a static and finite identity, the proletariat is the "class of the overcoming of work and its identities" that will emerge out of and negate the range of identities offered by capitalism.¹⁴ In short, the lumpenproletariat signifies the stasis of ahistorical identity, while the proletariat signifies the historical dynamic of becoming and revolution. Accordingly, Thoburn's argument holds that Marxist as well as poststructuralist projects should recognize the concept of the lumpenproletariat as a negation of difference and alterity. Wright's work, especially *Native Son*, suggests an alternative evaluation of the lumpenproletariat's correlation with identity. The *black* lumpenproletarian individual, for whom identity is not fixed but denied, engages in practices of self-creation rather than self-preservation, practices that necessarily impinge on present socioeconomic relations so as to force historical change. Wright's first novel, *Lawd, Today!*, explicitly theorizes the black working class's tendency toward protective forms of political reaction. Wright thus anticipates the Black Panther Party's identification of black lumpenproletarian individuals, rather than the socially and economically incorporated proletariat, as the agents of revolution. In 1972, Eldridge Cleaver described the proletariat as having "[taken] the long march into the system" and "becoming, rapidly, foul, reactionary, and fanged." Wright doesn't see the industrial working class as the enemy of revolution, but like Cleaver he relocates revolutionary capacity to those on the system's margins, who in Cleaver's words "had been left out, unplugged—the Lumpen."¹⁵

My reading of Wright's innovative black Marxism is not merely celebratory. Wright's formulation of revolution as an expression of desire is bound to gendered figurations of social life and politics that lapse into complicity with patriarchal framings of the intersection of gender and race, simultaneously illustrating and deconstructing Wright's project. Hazel Rowley writes that "the question of black manhood" is central to Wright's concerns as a writer: "How can a black man be a man, if every time he manifests his will he is crushed by white oppressors?"¹⁶ In *Lawd, Today!* and *Native Son*, Wright develops a complex answer to that question. Yet Wright's investment in the "question of black manhood" in a project that figures political action as masculine reveals problematic considerations I address in this chapter's coda. As we'll see in chapter 4,

[53]

Margaret Walker's approach to the figure of the lumpenproletarian woman was inspired in part by her recognition of and departure from the gender protocols of Wright's work: "our perspectives were diametrically opposed in this regard," she recollected.[17] Reading for gender in Wright in a way that neither rejects his work outright nor excuses regressive tendencies opens up new perspectives on the triangulation of gender, race, and lumpenproletarian status.

REVOLUTIONIZING THE LUMPENPROLETARIAT IN "TRANSCONTINENTAL" AND *LAWD, TODAY!*

Given the visibility of lumpenproletarian immiseration and dislocation brought on by the mass unemployment of the Depression, and in light of Jim Crow's race-based forms of sociocultural exteriorization, the transience of the lumpenproletariat appealed to Wright as a form of mobility, and mobility functions in his 1930s fiction to counteract intersectional processes of racial, economic, and gender oppression. Rowley writes that trains "thunder through the landscapes of Richard Wright's Southern fiction" and "carry a promise of manhood and, with it, the whisper of liberty."[18] In "Big Boy Leaves Home" (1936), the whistles of passing freights punctuate the story's thematization of lynching as a mechanism whereby white supremacy, economic exploitation, and the emasculation of black masculinity in the South are reproduced. The black male protagonists note the trains are "headin fer up North" where they've been told blacks "got ekual rights."[19] The whistles sound an emancipatory counterpoint that disrupts the narrative's account of an otherwise smooth and untroubled reproduction of Jim Crow. Big Boy and his friends, trespassing on a local white landowner's property and swimming in his pond, are surprised by the landowner's son's fiancée. Seeking retribution for the young men's simultaneous violation of Jim Crow's economic, sexual, and racial taboos, the son shoots two of Big Boy's friends before Big Boy kills him in self-defense. Knowing a lynching is inevitable, Big Boy responds to the summons of the train whistles, stowing away in a delivery truck to make his escape to the North. Given the regional specificity of Jim Crow and its violent strictures on black masculinity, the transient practices entailed by socioeconomic dislocation—hitchhiking, hoping freight trains, and so on—become, for African American men, means of resistance and survival.

Train whistles also feature in the background of "Almos' a Man" (1940). Dave Sanders, a seventeen-year-old black agricultural worker in the South, longs for a gun so he can claim a figurative form of manhood not available to him under the labor conditions of Jim Crow: "Shucks, a man oughta hava little gun aftah he done worked hard all day." He procures a gun, and, while on the job, accidentally shoots a mule belonging to his white employer, Hawkins. As a result, Hawkins intends to increase his exploitation of Dave's labor, taking more wages from him to pay off the mule's value. Since Dave's family will suffer from the loss of the income Dave's wages provide, he is threatened with a beating at home as well. Dave senses the truth allegorized in this turn of events: Jim Crow agricultural production stifles and profitably co-opts black assertions of masculinity. "All he did was work. They treat me lika mule." Fantasizing about using his gun to shoot at Hawkins's house—"Jussa enough t let im know Dave Sanders is a man"—Dave correlates the reclamation of masculinity not with personal revenge, but with systematic antiracist and anticapitalist political action: he desires to shoot Hawkins's house and the institutions it metonymizes, rather than Hawkins himself.[20]

But to have any chance of making such fantasies practical, Dave must escape the South. He hops a freight train that carries him, figuratively, toward revolutionary transformation: "the long rails were glinting in the moonlight, stretching away, away to somewhere, somewhere where he could be a man."[21] For Wright, revolution is both enabled and figured by a mobility determined by the individual disenfranchisement associated with the lumpenproletariat and rendered newly visible by the Great Depression. Wright thus offers a revolutionary implementation of Houston Baker's theory of black expression as structured by the liberating fluidity of the blues: "Even as they speak of paralyzing absence and ineradicable desire, their instrumental rhythms suggest change, movement, action, continuance, unlimited and unending possibility."[22]

Morris Dickstein argues that many Depression writers were drawn to Communism as a result of their fascination with and pity for the victims of the decade's economic crisis, when "many men and even children took to the road simply because there were no jobs, or because their families were disintegrating around them." Wright's friend and fellow Chicago Communist writer, the bottom dogs novelist Nelson Algren, who began to write in the early 1930s after riding freights himself, is Dickstein's model

[55]

of the "empathetic writer" who "was invariably radicalized by what he saw on the road, by his exposure to so many marginal and miserable people."[23] Dickstein helpfully identifies one impetus underwriting Wright's association of revolutionary possibility with socially dislocated individuals. The origin of the Great Migration in the need to escape Jim Crow further explicates Wright's perception of mobility as a liberatory practice of resistance. In *12 Million Black Voices* (1941), Wright's lyrical folk history of the African American people structured around historical materialist categories, he describes how industrialization during World War I led African Americans to defy their feudal white Southern overlords and escape for the North: "If we have no money, we borrow it; if we cannot borrow it, we beg it," and if Northern employers don't arrange transportation, "we walk until we reach a railroad and then we swing onto a freight."[24] In this historical scenario, hopping a freight train is not being socially discarded but seeking out new possibilities: less a reflection of utter immiseration than a willed act of resistance to racial and economic exploitation. Wright's own circumstances also informed his interest in mobility. Only after escaping the South to Chicago could he join the Communist Party and the John Reed Club, becoming at once a radical and a writer and accessing the kind of empowerment Dave Sanders seeks. If Nelson Algren became a writer by taking the measure of Depression-era transience, Wright's own discovery of the lumpenproletariat was informed by the migratory trajectories of African American modernity and yielded not merely sympathy for the those of the lower depths but conviction of their revolutionary potential.

In his 1936 poem "Transcontinental," Wright uses the illicit tactics lumpenproletarian individuals enact as a consequence of socioeconomic exteriorization—hitchhiking, trespassing, robbery—to figure a Soviet-style revolution. The poem opens within the perspective of a transient hitchhiker gazing at a scene of appealing, luxurious, upper-class prosperity and social belonging. The scene is contrasted with the directionless, meaningless, and alienated movement of life on the road, defined by the "ceaseless hiss of passing cars." This criticism of wealth is a distinctly lumpenproletarian one, proceeding from the desire for social inclusion and a fixed place rather than ceaseless, directionless transience. Yet the speaker also reveals the artificiality of upper-class life, comparing it to the worlds depicted "in the movies / On Saturday nights / When we used to get paychecks." Besides aligning the production of mass culture with class rule, these lines suggest that those who still get paychecks—workers able to spend their wages on mass culture's products—cannot perceive the artificial, and thus exploitative, nature of class difference. The lumpenproletariat, which no longer possesses a place in production, can thus question the dynamics of the social order that excludes it. The working-class subject, by contrast, participates, as a producer and consumer, in the reproduction of capitalism: the proletarian "buys in," if only as a passive and exploited spectator, to the construct of class difference. Only when one can no longer go to the movies can one see how the fictive nature of the cinematic text extends *beyond* the theater to the economic stratifications of the social order. Hence, the speaker poses two politically charged queries: "America who built this dream" and "America who owns this wonderland." The discrepancy limned by the questions—that those who labor are alienated from the fruits of their work—is the essence of class exploitation, and its recognition by the lumpenproletarian speaker furnishes the germ of revolutionary consciousness.[25]

The speaker imagines the day when hitchhikers will no longer just watch passing cars, but act. "America is ours / This car is commandeered," the poem declares. "We'll drive and let you be the hitch-hiker." Revolution is imagined as a criminal act: the self-interested, illicit activity of the lumpenproletariat metaphorizes world-historical transformation. For the rest of the poem, the speaker and fellow hijackers travel the country in the stolen car, bringing a radical coalition of African American sharecroppers and urban industrial workers on board. The lumpenproletariat, far from a reactionary enemy or bribed appendage of revolution, is the vanguard or driver of this car, which brings a Soviet America into existence. To signal his revisionary rejection of Marx's political devaluation of the lumpenproletariat, Wright pointedly mentions how "pimps idlers loungers," the rhetorical coordinates of Marx's scorn, are left behind in Wright's new understanding of lumpenproletarian politics.[26]

This origin of revolution in socioeconomic marginality is demonstrated negatively in *Lawd, Today!*. Published posthumously, *Lawd, Today!* has struck readers as atypical for a Communist writer. Rowley describes it as lacking the "revolutionary optimism of 'proletarian literature.'"[27] This perception stems in part from misconceptions of proletarian literature as narrowly didactic and formally simplistic, but *Lawd, Today!* is unusually skeptical of the political capacity of the urban proletariat. In a manner that anticipates Eldridge Cleaver's arguments, the novel illustrates the ideological co-option of the black working class.

Protagonist Jake Jackson works as a sorting clerk in the Chicago post office. Wright himself had worked in the Chicago post office, which was "the best job for black male workers—indeed, the only 'clerical' job available to them" in a segregated economy.[28] The material conditions of Jake's working-class life hinder his ability to act on the vague dissatisfaction he feels with that life. Throughout the novel, he is bothered by a "haunting and hungering sense of incompleteness," an "uneasy emptiness." The ceaseless routine of labor intensifies this unease. As he enters the post office to begin his shift, "he wondered if he would have to go on this way year after year 'til he died. Was this *all?* Deep in him was a dumb yearning for something else." However, all he can envision is "an endless stretch of black postal days," the inability to ever transcend class and racial limitations. Labor is represented as automatized and unable to yield any consciousness but false consciousness: Jake is highly aware of the racial inequity structuring his class status, but his response to that inequity takes the form of racial nationalism rather than materialism. As he slots mail for distribution to various states, the routine of the work leads him to fantasize that he's loading guns on a "black battleship surrounded by black generals" in the middle of a race war. He "[pushes] a letter for Mississippi through the twelveinch guns of the black battleship" and "continued building dreams of a black empire."[29]

Jake's labor thus delimits the consciousness he can access from that labor. His labor's physical resemblance to working the guns of a black ship signals the immanence of the exploitation of labor and racial nationalism and the complicity of the latter with the former: "his left hand drew the letters toward him and his right hand struck them with the dauber. *Boombomp, boombomp, boombomp, boombomp* . . . His mind and body had fallen into the rhythm of the thing."[30] Anthony Dawahare argues that, for Wright, nationalism's connections with capitalism and racism make it "an ideology incapable of self-reflexively addressing the very precondition for its being, that is, a racist class society."[31] But if nationalism is an ideological reflection of capitalism, then it's not the self-interested lumpenproletariat that is most susceptible to reactionary recruitment. Rather, the rhythms of proletarian labor here enact ideological co-option.

Kimberly Drake observes that the working-class Jake is incorporated into socioeconomic networks. He "has accepted a position in society" and is thus, unlike Bigger Thomas, unable to critique or act against the forces structuring society. *Lawd, Today!* depicts Jake's subservient class status through a gendered rhetoric that Wright will deploy again in *Native Son*: the proletarian male subject is emasculated by domestic necessities whose reproduction ensures his submission to racial and class domination. In part this gendered formulation of working-class servitude is continuous with Jake's own violent sexism, an aspect of his character that advances the novel's negative critique of proletarian consciousness by cuing the reader to, as Drake notes, "view with distrust those objects, people, and ideals Jake holds dear."[32] Yet this equation of masculinity with agency and femininity with servitude is pervasive in Wright's Depression-era writing and never escapes its androcentric implications. Jake's sexism is intended by Wright to index his desire to escape the confinements of domestic necessity. As we'll see in *Native Son*, this figurative strategy advances a generative theory of political action that simultaneously excludes women as political actors and occludes spaces of domesticity and labor as sites of political struggle.

In *Lawd, Today!*, the multiple levels of co-option and incorporation attendant on Jake's proletarian status are examined through this gendered binary of freedom and servitude. Much of Jake's anger at his economic limitation manifests itself in violence toward his wife Lil. Lil suffers from medical complications following an abortion Jake tricked her into receiving, and the debt he owes for her treatment binds him to his labor. In one of his few moments of rational calculation, he determines that he would need to work for sixteen years just to pay off that debt alone. "*What in the world can a man do? I'm just like a slave . . .* He owed so many debts he did not know which debt to pay first. . . . His eyes grew misty with tears, tears of hatred for Lil and tears of pity for himself."[33] Lil threatens to lodge a complaint about Jake's abuses with the post office, which would make him lose his position. Lil later does make such a complaint, and Jake is forced to incur another debt, paying a local black businessman to use his influence on Jake's behalf with his employers. This cycle of labor and debt keeps Jake perpetually chained to labor and dependency. Even when Jake tried to halt the reproductive cycle of domestic needs by forcing Lil to have an abortion, his act registered its futility by increasing his indebtedness to Lil's doctor.

Jake's desire to escape the material limitation of working-class life in fact leads him to avow capitalism. Brannon Costello points out that Jake's "master narrative that explains the world to him" is the "American success myth" he discovers in mass culture. Jake idolizes wealthy capitalists, and Costello argues that he desires not a change of the system itself, but "to get enough money so that he can emulate these giants of capitalism that he so admires."[34] Mass culture produces his conformity to an ideological narrative that keeps him bound to labor and debt. Working-class experience, Wright thus suggests, leads the worker to reactionary self-interest and an adherence to capitalist ideology. Jake's fellow postal worker Al tries to sell him on the advantages of joining the National Guard, where one can get paid to put down "the Reds" when they "start something." For Marx, the self-interest of the lumpenproletariat leads it to join the class struggle against the revolutionary proletariat. For Wright, Jake's dependence on labor makes *him* the likely target for reactionary recruitment. The Guard offers the worker both wages and masculinization: "You wouldn't be in all the mess you in now with that dame of yours if you was in the army and knowed how to handle a woman," Al tells Jake.[35] The illusion of control over one's financial resources, circumstances, and dependents appeals to those whose social status is defined as an emasculating submission to all three. It is Wright's proletariat, not the lumpenproletariat, whose "conditions of life . . . prepare it . . . for the part of a bribed tool of reactionary intrigue."[36]

Jake admires lumpenproletarian figures who embody, in his view, the agency of unfettered masculinity. Early in the novel, he praises gangsters: "Jeeesus, it takes nerve to be a gangster! But they have plenty of fun. Always got a flock of gals hanging on their arms. . . . And got money to throw away . . . They don't live long, but I bet they sure have a hell of a sweet time while they do live. Better time than a lot of us who work hard every day for a measly living." Unlike the anonymous worker, whose labor merely reproduces conditions of bare subsistence, the gangster wins notoriety and distinction through criminal actions. The comparative freedom of the lumpenproletarian—who is necessarily male not simply because he has a "flock of gals" but because he isn't bound to domestic needs and duties—frequently attracts Jake and his coworkers' admiration. "Sometimes I feel like being just a hobo," one remarks, rather than a worker who is only "a squirrel turning in a cage."[37]

Even though Jake and his friends regularly make stock anti-

Communist remarks, they nonetheless admire the Soviet revolutionaries Lenin and Trotsky, not for their politics but for their lumpenproletarian-like notoriety and the bold "nerve" of their actions. Late in the novel, they revel in how "Leenine . . . scared the piss out of them rich white folks" and how "Tricksky" was "hardboiled" with "hair all flying" and "eyes that looked like they could see through you." The mention of Trotsky leads one of the group to reference Soviet political discourse:

> "I heard a Jew boy say that guy wanted a revolution that went on always . . ."
> "*Always?*"
> "*Always*, man!"
> "What kind of revolution's that?"
> "Damn if I know."
> "Gawddamn, I'm scared of them kind of folks."

Trotsky's doctrine of permanent revolution is stripped of its political specificity and instead serves as an index of how bad and dangerous the Soviets were. The workers then link this to reports they've heard of how American Communists "sure scared them white folks down South" in their activism around the Scottsboro case. Their potential conversion to the left is underscored by their esteem of Lenin and Trotsky as specifically nonwhite: they imagine that Lenin must have had "some Chink blood in 'im" and that his notoriety is in part a product of his nonwhiteness.[38] Lenin and Trotsky thus become "Leenine" and "Tricksky," outlaws who embody Wright's recasting of revolution as the deeds of infamous individuals who are free men despite being nonwhite, and who thus stand as desirable alternatives to the enforced subservience of Jake and his peers. This revision of revolution proceeds under the contours of false consciousness, inflected as it is by chauvinism and racial essentialism, yet it's a false consciousness that allows the characters to metaphorize, if not cognitively access, both the nature of revolutionary desire and the organic disconnection between working-class experience and political capacity.

If the lumpenproletariat in *Lawd, Today!* exists as a specter of possibility on the margins of black working-class consciousness, *Native Son* examines directly the social and psychological sources of the lumpenproletariat's political potential. Wright announces this goal in "How 'Bigger' Was Born" by aligning Bigger with Lenin, conflating the lumpenproletarian figure with the revolutionary. The Soviet figurations that assign radical agency to the lumpenproletariat in "Transcontinental" and *Lawd, Today!* recur in the essay's catalogue of Bigger Thomas types. Wright first lists black individuals he knew in the South, who responded to the confinements of segregation with "extremity and violence" and enacted a mode of unorganized rebellion against white rule: "The Bigger Thomases were the only Negroes I know of who consistently violated the Jim Crow laws of the South and got away with it," even if they were eventually "shot, hanged, maimed, lynched, and generally hounded until they were either dead or their spirits broken." This criminal defiance was motivated by this type's social marginality and attendant desire for belonging, his alienation "from the religion and the folk culture of his race" and his desire for the "glitter" and promise of mass culture. Furthermore, these individuals were enacting the only political action, however ineffective, that Wright ever witnessed, given that black Southern middle-class "leaders" were complicit with Jim Crow.[39]

Upon moving to Chicago, Wright "made the discovery that Bigger Thomas was not black all the time; he was white, too, and there were literally millions of him, everywhere." This observation leads Wright to theorize Jim Crow as not a regionally peculiar system, but as an "appendage" of the capitalist mode of production itself, a "far vaster and in many respects more ruthless and impersonal commodity-profit machine." Wright's materialist analysis of Jim Crow as a superstructural manifestation of capitalist productive relations defines the stakes of Bigger's rebellion as simultaneously anticapitalist and antiracist. This theoretical move legitimates his surprising identification of Lenin as the next Bigger Thomas type he encountered. "There is in me a memory of reading an interesting pamphlet telling of the friendship of Gorky and Lenin in exile. The booklet told of how Lenin and Gorky were walking down a London street. Lenin turned to Gorky and, pointing, said: 'Here is *their* Big Ben.' 'There is *their* Westminster Abbey.' 'There is *their* library.'" Wright describes Lenin's gesture as "the Bigger Thomas reaction."[40] Lenin's play with the homonyms "their" and "there" identifies the necessary complicity of Western culture with capitalist and imperialist rule. His gesture defines revolution as originating in a state of social disenfranchisement and enacting a desire for the cultural inclusion over which the ruling class exercises a proprietary hold. The motives of the Bigger Thomas type become, through reference to Lenin, motives of anticapitalist praxis, and the lumpenproletarian becomes the revolutionary.

"How 'Bigger' Was Born" warns that Bigger "[carries] within him the potentialities of either Communism or Fascism." Given "the sense of exclusion, the ache for violent action, the emotional and cultural hunger" of the lumpenproletariat, the Bigger Thomas type is definitively positioned against "the *status quo*" and is susceptible to either reactionary or revolutionary alternatives.[41] This formula reiterates Marx's bifurcation of the political tendencies of lumpenproletarian individuals, but not his sense of their motivation. Similarly, early in *Native Son* Bigger feels admiration for the imperialist ventures of fascist Japan and Italy, as well as the anti-Semitic persecutions carried out by Nazi Germany. Such projects strike him as outlets for his "gnawing hunger and restless aspiration," and he longs for a fascist leader who could lead blacks to "act and end fear and shame."[42] For Wright, the lumpenproletariat's susceptibility to reactionary co-option is not motivated by apolitical material self-interest. In both texts, Bigger seeks a larger, protopolitical goal: the destruction of a present that precludes him. The left must then organize the lumpenproletariat not only to keep it from the ranks of reaction, but to educate and harness the transformative force of its aspiration.

Native Son theorizes the "Bigger Thomas reaction," the desire for a new social order that could include and furnish public acknowledgement of oneself as a self, a subject fully recognized and distinguished. The political drama of the novel is expressed in "How 'Bigger' Was Born" as the passage from Bigger to Lenin. *Native Son* narrates the development Bigger undergoes in first seeking to counteract his exclusion from public visibility through ultimately ineffective criminal means, and then finding the Communist Party as the vehicle of the inclusion and recognition he craves. *Native Son* posits that the desire of the black lumpenproletarian individual to be recognized in the public sphere as a distinct subject, because it's a desire that America's racial and economic order by definition cannot realize, is the very impulse of revolution itself.

NATIVE SON AND THE DESIRE FOR SUBJECTIVITY

On the famous first page of *Native Son,* in the wake of the alarm clock's ring, Bigger is revealed in sentences in which he, as the subject of the actions described, is effaced: "A surly grunt sounded above the tinny ring of metal. Naked feet swished dryly across the planks in the wooden floor and the clang ceased abruptly." Bigger then turns on the light, but this act is also rendered passively: "Light flooded the room and revealed a black boy standing in a narrow space."[43] Bigger is the author of both actions—turning off the alarm clock, turning on the light—but his agency remains invisible, unrevealed behind those actions. Wright's syntax indicates how Bigger inhabits a social location, a "narrow space", in which acting does not grant public recognition of his subjectivity. Instead, he is visible to the reader and to the world as only a type from racist discourse, the emasculated "black boy."

In a sequence foreshadowing the novel's extended consideration of Bigger's attempt to demonstrate his subjectivity through violent and criminal action, his killing of the rat is an act that only partially reveals himself as the actor. As the rat tries to escape to its hole that Bigger has blocked with a box, "Bigger aimed and let the skillet fly with a heavy grunt. There was a shattering of wood as the box caved in." The causal connection between throwing the skillet and the rat's death is lost in the space between the two sentences, and his mother declares: "Boy, sometimes I wonder what makes you act like you do."[44] The act's violence and Bigger's pride in accomplishing it prevent him from being legible as a fully human subject. Later, his killing of Mary will be recoded by racist discourse to a similar end. His mother's reprimand thus invokes the novel's central problem: when one's actions do not bring recognition of one's authorship of them, the fact of one's subjectivity or inward identity remains invisible and thus something to "wonder" about.

Sounding like Marx and Engels when they discuss the lumpenproletariat, his mother tells Bigger he's "just a tramp" who refuses to labor because he prioritizes "his own pleasure" with the criminal exploits of "that gang of yours." His mother tells him that they "wouldn't have to live in this garbage dump if you had any manhood in you," and describes his refusal to work as making him visible only as that which doesn't quite count as subjectivity: "the most no-countest man I ever seen in all my life!" But Bigger is aware that slotting himself into proletarian status entails its own anonymity. His mother reminds him that the family will only continue to have food if Bigger takes the job as the Daltons' chauffeur that the relief agency has arranged. But Bigger resists working-class status because of his awareness of how those who do work sacrifice any opportunity for subjective distinction to the cyclical and necessary nature of labor. His girlfriend Bessie Mears "had often described to him when she had come from long hours of hot toil in the white folks' kitchens, a feeling of being forever commanded by others so much that thinking and feeling for one's self was impossible." Bigger chafes against the double bind of his predicament: "Yes, he could take the job at Dalton's and be miserable, or he could refuse it and starve. It maddened him to think that he did not have a wider choice of action."[45] Neither option allows him to assert himself *as* a distinct self.

When Bigger does take the Dalton job, he is not recognized as a subject but as an interchangeable replacement for the family's previous chauffeur, Green. Mrs. Dalton's blindness registers the Daltons' inability to see Bigger as anything other than "the new boy," another no-countest man.[46] He is given Green's old room at the Dalton house, and the suggestion that Bigger is welcomed into the "green room" indicates that he is expected to play an impersonal and prescripted role. The novel is thus forthright in its critique of labor as a necessary yet unrewarding task of domestic sustainability. In the fullest consideration of the role of the domestic and domestic ideology in *Native Son*, Susan Edmunds notes that "Bigger is the only character in Wright's novel who finds no attraction or compensation in the prospect of a domestic fate and who would rather cause and endure terror than submit to one." Edmunds argues that Bigger's lone protest against "domestic compliance" enacts a critique of the New Deal welfare state, which the novel figures as a new mode of racial rule enacted through discourses of domestic and family stability.[47] Beyond its role in the novel's protest of specific Depression-era mechanisms of state control, Bigger's resistance to labor, working-class status, and the domestic advances a general theory of black political action, one that locates the origin of politics in Bigger's desire for public acknowledgement.

He expresses that desire when, before taking the Dalton job, he spots a skywriting plane. Bigger wants to fly a plane himself, but the visibility such an action would bring to his subjectivity of course makes it inaccessible for him. "If you wasn't black and if you had some money and if they'd let you go to that aviation school, you *could* fly a plane," Gus responds, a hypothetical scenario so implausible it causes them to laugh. The plane is inscribing an advertisement for Speed Gasoline, which Bigger knows is not directed at him. " 'Use Speed Gasoline,' Bigger mused. . . . 'God I'd like to fly up there in that sky.' "[48] Bigger is not recognized by the ad's address, and the ad's admonition only prompts him to desire that he could be the subject of the active mobility it suggests.

In his introduction to St. Clair Drake and Horace Cayton's sociological study of African American Chicago, *Black Metropolis* (1945), Wright would revisit the problem he formulates in the opening scenes of *Native Son*. Analyzing the invisibility of urban African Americans segregated from the mainstream of American public life, Wright quotes William James's *The Principles of Psychology* (1890) to explain "what a man would feel if he were completely socially excluded." In James's words:

> No more fiendish punishment could be devised ... than that one should be turned loose in society and remain absolutely unnoticed by all the members thereof. If no one turned round when we entered, answered when we spoke, or minded what we did, but if every person we met 'cut us dead,' and acted as if we were non-existent things, a kind of rage and impotent despair would ere long well up in us, from which the cruelest bodily tortures would be a relief; for these would make us feel that, however bad might be our plight, we had not sunk to such a depth as to be unworthy of attention at all.

What for James is a thought experiment is, for Wright, the condition of the African American individual who, in Wright's words, "has come as near being the victim of a complete rejection as our society has been able to work out."[49] James thus explicates Bigger's rage in *Native Son* as not merely irrational or the result of a deformation by oppression, but as the expression of a desire for recognition.

Bigger and his friend Gus demonstrate the racialized obstacles to self-expression when they "play 'white,'" a game in which they perform white identity by mimicking the speech of generals, political leaders, and capitalists they've encountered in popular culture. Their performance defines whiteness as agency: Bigger's military leader orders Gus's general to send troops into action, Gus's J. P. Morgan orders Bigger to sell stocks of US Steel, and Bigger's president orders Gus's secretary of state to a cabinet meeting to discuss "[doing] something with these black folks." Whiteness is subjectivity, defined here in practical and materialist terms as the ability to act in such a way that you are revealed as the individual author of that action; the identity of J. P. Morgan or the president is the ability to issue commands that affect the lives of others. African Americans, on the other hand, are only material upon which whites act, and blackness, for Bigger and Gus, is played and lived as the inverse of subjectivity. "They don't let us do *nothing*," Bigger complains. "We black and they white. . . . They do things and we can't. It's just like living in jail."[50]

Wright's correlation of subjectivity with practice can thus be explicated by Louis Althusser's well-known theory of the social construction of subjectivity. For Althusser, social institutions organize the everyday acts of individuals in order to achieve the function of ideology: reproducing and naturalizing ruling relations of dominance and exploitation. However, for Althusser, ideology is not a matter of consciousness or beliefs, but is embedded in institutional activity that "*interpellates concrete individuals as concrete subjects.*"[51] Ideology works through the aggregate of activities an individual performs, in a manner that facilitates the functioning of social rule, in order for that individual to "count" as a subject. As Warren Montag explains, Althusser's theory of subjectivity holds that "ideology is immanent in its apparatuses and their practices . . . and is entirely coincident with them."[52] Althusser's well-known drama of interpellation allegorizes this practical fabrication of the subject. In the scenario, an authority figure delivers an impersonal "hail"—"Hey, you there!"—in a street. An individual then "turn[s] round" to respond to the hail, and in the practice of turning, performs the subject position that the institution has defined for it: "By this mere 180-degree physical conversion, he becomes a *subject.*"[53]

Wright conceptualizes the denial of subjectivity to black individuals through an inversion of the model articulated by Althusser. In Bigger and Gus's "playing white" game, they reveal their *non*-subjectivity in that they perform subjectivity as an exclusive practice of whiteness: to be white is to have the ability to act in a way that confirms one as a subject. The "Use Speed Gasoline" advertisement is specifically designed to not "hail" Bigger as its subject. Since racial restrictions prevent Bigger from practicing the mobility it directs, it functions as a noninterpellation that establishes his nonsubjectivity. *Native Son* thus poses the dilemma of the subjective status of an individual who not only cannot do anything to be recognized as a subject but who, furthermore, is specifically constructed, through a process we might term a *negative* or *negating* interpellation, as *not* a subject.

Wright demonstrates negative interpellation when Bigger and Jack go to the movies and watch a double feature. *Trader Horn*, a 1931 film, is

[67]

"shown on the posters in terms of black men and black women dancing against a wild background of barbaric jungle." The film, which fails to hold Bigger and Jack's interest, is a stock colonialist distortion of Africa. The other film, *The Gay Woman* (Wright's invention), is "pictured on the posters in images of white men and women lolling on beaches, swimming, and dancing in night clubs."[54] The resemblance of the posters, which both feature men and women dancing, suggests their common function of naturalizing racial difference as the difference between subjectivity and nonsubjectivity itself, between the subject and the savage. Bigger and Jack enjoy *The Gay Woman* because it offers a comic representation of agency set against sensual pleasure:

> Amid scenes of cocktail drinking, dancing, golfing, swimming, and spinning roulette wheels, a rich young white woman kept clandestine appointments with her lover while her millionaire husband was busy in the offices of a vast paper mill. Several times Bigger nudged Jack in the ribs with his elbow as the giddy young woman duped her husband and kept him from the knowledge of what she was doing.

Bigger's erotic desire for the protagonist's body is cathected with his desire for her craftiness, her ability to act, to arrange subversive pleasures for herself. When Jack comments that "them rich chicks'll do anything," he defines both her sexuality and agency as libidinal objects. However, agency is presented exclusively *as* whiteness. In an illustration of the intersection of economic and racial power, the source of the protagonist's agency is her husband's wealth, which comes from the production of blank (white) paper. Wright's white upper class owns the means of the production of possibility itself, of the ability to be the author of one's own deeds.

The film thus depicts an all-white world removed from the necessity of labor, a world of free pleasure, in which Bigger can find no correlate of himself, in whose terms he cannot be interpellated as a subject. As Jack says: "if them folks saw you they'd run. . . . They'd think a gorilla broke loose from the zoo and put on a tuxedo."[55] Jack here alludes to *Trader Horn*, which refuses to interpellate the black viewer as a subject, instead constructing black identity specifically as nonsubjectivity. *Trader Horn*'s definition of "black men and black women" rests on organic compulsion rather than free agency. Both films, then, address Bigger only as the black other of subjectivity.

Bigger thus imagines himself into the world of *The Gay Woman* in the only way he can, as a servant, a prop or accessory to the actions of whites. *The Gay Woman* provokes his desire for subjective agency, and then compels him to sublimate that desire as objectivity executed in mere adjacency to subjectivity. Until now, Bigger had been resentful of having no outlet for action and being forced to take a servile position with the Daltons out of necessity. After seeing the film, however, he hopes that, as a chauffeur, he might participate as an accessory to the activities of rich whites:

> Maybe Mr. Dalton was a millionaire. Maybe he had a daughter who was a hot kind of girl; maybe she spent lots of money; maybe she'd like to come to the South Side and see the sights sometimes. Or maybe she had a secret sweetheart and only he would know about it because he would have to drive her around; maybe she would give him money not to tell.[56]

In the terrifying, disastrous first night he spends with the Daltons, Bigger ironically realizes this desire to the letter. Mass culture's representation of subjective agency as white incites, in Bigger, a desire for it that can never be achieved without violent punishment. The fear that consumes Bigger when Mary Dalton and Jan Erlone materialize as the "daughter" and "secret sweetheart" of this fantasy and hold out the possibility of its realization is the mechanism through which ruling ideology makes Bigger perpetually desire subjectivity while fearing to demonstrate it through any action. The production of this prohibited desire works to confirm his subordinate status as merely adjacent to subjectivity. The movie theater scene thus dramatizes Wright's sense of the revolutionary import of the desire for subjectivity, a desire that, if acted on, challenges the very ideology of white capitalist rule.

Native Son thus engages in the complex task of theorizing political desire and action within modern African American contexts, and the novel should be recognized as an important contribution to twentieth-century philosophical discourses of politics and subjectivity. Wright's understanding of black politics as driven by the desire for acknowledged subjectivity aligns his work, in some key ways, with the political philosophy of Hannah Arendt. In *The Human Condition* (1958), Arendt develops an idiosyncratic theory of politics grounded in ancient Greek thought and based on an ontological distinction between the activities of labor and action. Her distinction is mapped onto the division of private and public realms, the former of which is associated with domestic obscurity and the latter with political action. To this extent, Arendt and Althusser share a common investment in subjectivity as formed by and around activity, what Althusser terms practice and Arendt the *vita activa*. Labor, for Arendt, is a practice of necessity dictated by the basic needs of the household. A private, cyclical activity that involves reproducing the species, both through childbirth and working to provide food and shelter, labor offers no public acknowledgement or individuation for its doer. Arendt's critique of labor is one Bigger might recognize: "the daily fight in which the human body is engaged to keep the world clean and prevent its decay bears little resemblance to heroic deeds; the endurance it needs to repair every day anew the waste of yesterday is not courage, and what makes the effort painful is not danger but its relentless repetition."[57]

Action, for Arendt, is politics proper, which occurs when individuals, temporarily freed from the necessities of labor, recognize each other as the subjects of free actions that are not determined by necessity. Action is defined by "the disclosure of the agent in the act," and the public realm takes the character of the Greek polis, "the only place where men could show who they really and inexchangeably were." Action is transformative: since it is free from dictates of need, "one deed . . . suffices to change every constellation." And since action occurs among other subjects in a visible public realm, it "always establishes relationships and therefore has an inherent tendency to force open all limitations and cut across all boundaries."[58] The essential unpredictability of action makes it a motive force in human history, while the recognition it grants compensates for the anonymity and repetitive nature of private or domestic life. In its double orientation of conferring subjective visibility and upsetting strictures, Arendt's theory of action closely approximates the action Bigger wants in the opening scenes of *Native Son*. It also illuminates the revolutionary import of this lumpenproletarian figure's self-interested desire.

In *On Revolution* (1963), Arendt emphasizes, in a way that echoes Bigger's perception of the world of *The Gay Woman*, the pleasure of individual action in the polis as "public happiness." That pleasure is the proper motive of revolution, and Arendt uses that motive to distinguish the American Revolution from the French Revolution. The former was motivated by the pleasures of public action, while the violence and excess of the latter stemmed from its mistaken preoccupation with domestic matters of poverty and material need. The French Revolution thus became the model for modern thinkers, particularly Marx, who understood "not freedom but abundance" as "the aim of revolution." Arendt argues that the American Revolution better embodied the classical sense of politics, in that it sought not to address material needs but to constitute a polis. In "the speech-making and decision-taking, the oratory and the business, the thinking and the persuading, and the actual doing" of the revolution itself, its actors discovered the "experience of being free," what John Adams called the "action . . . that constitutes our pleasure." Arendt thus argues that democratic councils, which "make their appearance in every genuine revolution," enact the function of the ancient polis in modern settings (Arendt's historical examples include the Paris Commune during the French Revolution and the factory-organized *soviets* of the Russian Revolution). Removed from the necessities of the daily rounds of private life, these publics harness revolutionary desire by fostering "an enormous appetite for debate, for instruction, for mutual enlightenment and exchange of opinion."[59] Their function is not governance or power but politics: they allow individuals to disclose themselves as subjects through free and recognized action. The desire harnessed by Arendt's conceptualization of revolutionary politics is precisely the desire of Bigger sketched in the opening of *Native Son:* the desire not for money or a job, but for the pleasure of public participation, the liberation of the self from domestic concerns into the world-historical visibility of a polis.

While it may seem unusual for a Communist writer, the significance of happiness and the polis theorized by Arendt very much resembles Wright's sense of political desire in the Depression era. In *12 Million Black Voices,* Wright describes blacks who leave the South during the Great Migration as not primarily seeking prosperity, but as wanting to "fulfill the sense of happiness that sleeps in their hearts." This longed-for fulfillment is stimulated, as it is for Bigger, by modern mass culture, "the movies, magazines, and glimpses of town life." In the cities of the North, "strange moods" overtake this younger generation: "the streets, with their noise and flaring lights, the taverns, the automobiles, and the poolrooms claim them." This generation's strange desires lead, during the Depression, to Communism, but Wright describes the party not according to any ideology or specific interest-based appeal, but as a revolutionary council in Arendt's sense, a

[71]

polis that fosters recognition and self-expression across racial lines: "In many large cities there were sturdy minorities of us, both black and white, who banded together in disciplined, self-conscious groups and created new organs of action and expression." The party's Scottsboro activism is Wright's example of the capacities of these political organs.[60]

This sense of revolution as stemming from a desire for individual recognition might seem incompatible with Marxist thought, but the Marxist purchase of this way of thinking politics can be clarified by Jean-Paul Sartre's understanding of the subjective dynamics of class struggle. In *Search for a Method* (1960), Sartre argues that because Marxism lacks existentialism's concern with "real men in depth," its accounts of revolutionary actions dissolve concrete subjective motives into mere reflections of economic and historical forces.[61] Sartre finds this to be both idealist and reductionist, and holds that Marxism needs existentialism to capture the experiences of individuals in history. As Fredric Jameson explains, Sartre wants to reframe "action not as the *result* of some larger entity (such as class being) which 'manifests itself' through the act in question, but rather as free invention directed toward the future." For Sartre, attending to the subjective motives of certain agents in a historical moment of class struggle allows one to access what Jameson calls "a concrete reexperiencing" of revolutionary action and to correct Marxism's neglect of the subjective dimensions of politics.[62]

Sartre thus theorizes action as a project, a "moving unity of subjectivity and objectivity." One of his examples is the act of a black airplane mechanic who stole a plane in London, flew it to France, and was killed. Even though, subjectively, he "did not want to make a political demonstration" and was only "concerned with his individual destiny," he achieved, objectively, a "particularization of the collective revolt of the colonized" and "an emancipating act." Furthermore, in its very ontology as an action—a refusal to be passive—it is a "choice of a brief, dazzling freedom, of a freedom to die."[63] Sartre's choice of example explicates the objectively revolutionary character of Bigger's desire to fly planes. Like Sartre and Arendt, Wright is committed to the subjective reality of revolutionary action often occluded in classical Marxism. Before Wright knew both Sartre and Arendt, *Native Son* drew on African American history and experience to parallel the interventions of these European philosophers.[64]

LUMPENPROLETARIAN CRIME AND REVOLUTIONARY ACTION

Native Son proposes that acting to compel recognition of oneself as the author of one's acts is, in the racial contexts of US capitalism, revolutionary. A society that can recognize the black individual as a subject rather than an object and that provides opportunities away from the repetitive cycle of anonymizing labor for the individual to define him or herself as a subject is neither racist nor capitalist. Rather, it approximates the famous description of communist society in Marx's *The German Ideology*, where labor no longer delimits the freedom of self-revelation, and one can "hunt in the morning, fish in the afternoon, rear cattle in the evening, criticise after dinner . . . without ever becoming hunter, fisherman, shepherd or critic."[65] Michael Warner describes Arendt's polis similarly, as a "common framework of interaction that is needed to allow both a shared world of equals and the disclosure of unique agency."[66] As we'll see, Bigger's sociopolitical desire in *Native Son* is for a new world in which subjective difference is recognized and validated among equal participants in public life. Because that desire for access to a polis is, Wright holds, both anticapitalist and antiracist, action motivated by it is necessarily *criminal* in its relation to the social order it defies. Criminal activity and revolutionary action are thus correlated in the novel, as Wright assigns transformative potential to the illicit practices, perspectives, and strategies of the lumpenproletarian outlaw.

The opening section of the novel advances Wright's connection of crime to social recognition and transformation. Bigger does encounter one positive interpellative hail in the opening pages, when he sees a poster for State's Attorney Buckley's reelection campaign: "the white face was fleshy but stern; one hand was uplifted and its index finger pointed straight out into the street at each passer-by." The poster reads: "IF YOU BREAK THE LAW, YOU CAN'T WIN!" Bigger is interpellated as a criminal, an identity designed to reproduce the entrapment of the black individual, but which also entails a limited recognition of subjectivity because Buckley's threatened punishment does not entirely efface the limited agency of the law breaker. Bigger does not passively respond to this interpellation. "You crook," he says to Buckley's image. "You let whoever pays *you* off win!"[67] Bigger politicizes the difference between the criminal and law enforcer: to be what the state dubs a "criminal" is simply to lack power, and to be an agent of the law is to be a "crook" with power. The relationship of the law to the outlaw here becomes one between the state and the oppressed, and the outlaw who "can't win," Bigger, becomes, potentially, a political rebel. This moment sets the tone for the rest of the novel, in which criminality provides a rhetoric for subjective definition and revolutionary agency.

Before he becomes enticed by the Dalton job, Bigger initially intends to avoid work by lumpenproletarian means: holding up Blum's Delicatessen with his gang's help. They've robbed black businesses before, but this will be the first time they rob a white-owned establishment. Their motive is more than just pecuniary:

> They felt that it was much easier and safer to rob their own people, for they knew that white policemen never really searched diligently for Negroes who committed crimes against other Negroes. . . . They had the feeling that the robbing of Blum's would be a violation of ultimate taboo; it would be a trespassing into territory where the full wrath of an alien white world would be turned loose upon them; in short, it would be a symbolic challenge of the white world's rule over them; a challenge which they yearned to make, but were afraid to.

Since robbing black businesses doesn't provoke the attention of the law, it doesn't reveal Bigger and his accomplices as the subjects of the crime. Robbing a white store forces the racially structured legal system to "[search] diligently" for the perpetrators, compelling public recognition of their distinction. Through what Sartre would call the "unity" of its subjective motives and objective significances as a project, this crime becomes a political act, an act of which they will be legible as the (vilified) authors, and thus a "challenge" to the production of black invisibility. Because Bigger senses the larger implications of this act, he cannot bring himself to follow through on it. Instead, he distracts the gang from the robbery by physically intimidating Gus with his knife: a substitute, ineffective mode of self-assertion through phallic brutality.[68]

The Gay Woman, when read against the grain, reveals the revolutionary potential of crimes committed against a racist social order. In the film, the protagonist's romantic trysts come to an end when a "wild young man" mistakes one of her lovers for her rich husband and tries to kill him with a bomb. The man is identified as a Communist, but the term means nothing to Bigger and Jack, who, drawing on mass culture, know Communists only as "a race of folks who live in Russia" and who "must be wild." They discuss how "Reds must don't like rich folks," but have no sense of why, because the film's representation of the Communist robs him of any rational motive: his violence and dislike of the rich are simply "wild" compulsions, like those of the dancing Africans in *Trader Horn*.[69] The Communist nonetheless embodies an instructive confluence of crime and revolution. By making him a bomb-thrower rather than a properly Marxist activist, Wright enables this anti-Communist trope to bring anarchism into the narrative purview. The novel thus gestures toward anarchist Mikhail Bakunin's nineteenth-century redefinition of the lumpenproletariat as, given the relative affluence and ideological inculcation of most European nations' proletariats, revolutionary agents. "Marx speaks disdainfully, but quite unjustly, of this *Lumpenproletariat*" Bakunin writes in *Statism and Anarchy* (1873). "For in them, and only in them, and not in the bourgeois strata of workers, are there crystallized the entire intelligence and power of the coming Social Revolution."[70] Furthermore, the film foreshadows Bigger's relations with the Daltons, and the position Bigger will occupy with respect to the Daltons is filled, in the film, by the bomb-thrower. Bigger's later criminal activity (causing Mary's death, disposing of her body, forging a ransom note, hiding out from the manhunt) is foreshadowed on screen and recoded as political resistance. Wright's "wild" bomb-thrower is a symptom of how resistance necessarily appears as crime when (mis)represented by the social order it seeks to destroy.

Bigger will try to seek recognition of his subjectivity through crime, but this requires him to engage in an ideological struggle with white class rule to define his actions as those of a self, and not those of a "wild" monster. Bigger labors to access the political implications of his criminal pursuits and present them as acts publicly disclosing a self. However, the fact that his crimes can easily be represented as confirming racist stereotypes of black male subhumanity frustrates his project. The Communist characters in the novel help move Bigger past this impasse, but the novel's address to the Communist movement involves a reciprocally informative lesson structured around the Communist/criminal figure of *The Gay Woman*. Bigger must recognize the Communist movement as the vehicle of his desire for recognition, while Communism must grasp and harness the revolutionary desire inherent in black criminality.

If Bigger couldn't follow through on the act of robbing Blum's Delicatessen, he finally experiences the self-realization of his agency and attendant subjectivity through another series of actions: causing Mary's death and disposing of her body. On this night, Bigger performs an identity for himself that is objectively inaccurate yet subjectively empowering. Like Sartre, Wright refrains from reducing the lived experience of an action to its objective truth, keeping these two registers distinct so as to identify and excavate the sense of self and agency revealed within the subjective contours of the action. Once Bigger realizes he's accidentally strangled Mary, he conceives of himself as "a murderer, a Negro murderer, a black murderer." There are two errors here. Mary's death was not a murder, and this misrecognized selfhood is heavily coded by racist narratives of black masculinity that typify rather than individuate black male subjects. But this misrecognition provides an identity that he can proceed to *act out*, and for the first time in the novel, he plans and schemes: he begins concocting a slanted version of the events of the night that will implicate Jan; he worries about his fingerprints and creates a narrative to explain their presence in Mary's bedroom; and since Mary intended to travel to Detroit the next morning, he plans to place Mary's body in her trunk and send it to Detroit in advance, thereby delaying the discovery of her death. When he changes his plan and elects to burn the body in the furnace, he briefly considers also throwing the Daltons' cat in the flames before remembering that "Cats can't talk." This comic detail illustrates the excess of tactical calculation involved in his activities.[71] Bigger is now performing the agency that he has been conditioned to see as the exclusive prerogative of whites. In Mary's body Bigger misrecognizes himself as someone who has already *acted*, a murderer, and then continues to play that part through actions that concretize that identity.

Bigger reflects on his newfound selfhood the next morning: "He had murdered and had created a new life for himself. It was something that was all his own, and it was the first time in his life he had had anything that others could not take from him." Mary's death provided a "circumstance to make visible or dramatic his will to kill": it serves as an exterior, practical demonstration of an interior self. Prior to this moment, Bigger's interiority had been that of an unfree object. Gus and Bigger had discussed how "white folks live" in their "stomach[s] ... chest[s] and throat[s]." Then, his interiority consisted of a stifling implantation of white rule, one that compelled him to behave in ways that do not grant subjectivity because they are not reflections of an autonomous self: Bigger feared that "something awful's going to happen to me. . . . It's like I was going to do something I can't help." Now, however, his act has distinguished him as a free agent apart from exterior influences, forming "a barrier of protection between him and a world he feared."⁷² For the rest of the novel, Bigger will refuse to surrender his (mis)identification of himself as a murderer.

Even before Bigger encounters Boris Max, he constructs a political analysis around this self-discovery. The pleasure of action and subjective distinction that he experienced in the wake of Mary's death leads him to articulate such pleasure as a right, the denial of which constitutes the oppressive content of racial and capitalist rule. He thus theorizes the privilege of the white ruling class in terms of that pleasure. In the Dalton house, subjects are distinguished spatially, as "each person lived in one room and had a little world of his own," while in his own apartment, circumstances refuse distinction to African American individuals: "all slept in one room." Later in the novel, Bigger's fantasy of utopian social transformation rearranges this double correlation of privacy and privilege, collectivity and oppression. Bigger envisions postclass and postracial society as one that *universalizes* the Daltons' privilege of subjective distinction. He describes the present as one where the individual is anonymous and invisible, "a black sprawling prison full of tiny black cells in which people lived; . . . no one could go from cell to cell and there were screams and curses and yells of suffering and nobody heard them, for the walls were thick and darkness was everywhere." He instead envisions "a vast crowd of men, white men and black men and all men, and the sun's rays melted away the many differences, the colors, the clothes" in order to bring out "what was common and good." This is not the transcendence of subjective distinction, but the extension of the recognition of that distinction to all, regardless of color or class: "And in that touch, response of recognition, there would be union, identity; there would be a supporting oneness, a wholeness which had been denied him all his life."⁷³ Bigger's vision of postcapitalist society is not one in which individual difference has been negated as a bourgeois construct, but one in which equality grants "recognition" and "identity" to each of its distinct members. The heart of the revolutionary impulse, Wright suggests, is a personal desire for individual significance, for a polis in which everyone's unique humanity is revealed in the light of day.

Bigger may conceive himself as a subject through murder, but in line with Arendt's theory of politics, he also requires public recognition as the subject of that action. Immediately following Mary's death, Bigger yearns for his guilt to be revealed. On the one hand, he feels empowered and safe from the law as long as he manages to "act just like others acted, live like they lived." Society's blindness toward him, its inability to see a black man as subject, will allow him to escape detection. But without revealing his act, he can't be acknowledged as an agent. This problem is dramatized when Bigger writes his ransom note. In *The Gay Woman,* the capitalist controlled the means of authorship by controlling the production of paper; here Bigger appropriates paper, a means of the revelation of the self, to write his own plot, in both the narrative and criminal senses of the term. The catch, of course, is that the note can't disclose himself as Mary's murderer, but must cast suspicion on the Communists as her kidnappers. Hence, he removes all traces of himself from the note, including the singular crime of which he understands himself the author. He prints it in order to "disguise his handwriting," he crosses off his opening "I" and replaces it with "we," and signs not his name, but "Red."[74]

As a result, "there was in him a kind of terrified pride in feeling and thinking that some day he would be able to say publicly that he had done it. . . . He wished that he had the power to say what he had done without fear of being arrested."[75] Bigger's compulsion to be revealed as the criminal manifests itself symptomatically. The morning after Mary's death, he accidentally drops the cash he stole from Mary's purse for his brother Buddy to find. Similarly, Abdul Jan-Mohammed argues that Bigger's reluctance to clean the furnace, a reluctance that leads to the discovery of Mary's remains when the reporters step in to clean it instead, registers his "unconscious desire for recognition."[76] If Mary's death was an accident that paradoxically revealed to him his subjectivity, then these accidents are symptoms of his desire for acknowledgment of that subjectivity. From the moment he started anticipating the police investigation and covering his tracks, Bigger was playing the role of the culprit in a murder-mystery plot he was helping to construct, a plot whose climax necessitates the revelation of himself as its author.[77]

But it's not until close to his capture that he realizes that this criminal mode of self-revelation will not confer recognition. As he rides the streetcar to work the morning after Mary's death, he feels empowered among the white passengers. "Would any of the white faces all about him think that he had killed a rich white girl? No! They might think he would steal a dime, rape a woman, get drunk, or cut somebody; but to kill a millionaire's daughter and burn her body? He smiled a little, feeling a tingling sensation enveloping all his body." Later, again riding a streetcar with whites, he feels the urge to confess his murder of "a rich white girl, a girl whose family was known to all of them." Bigger contrasts killing a "rich white girl" that other whites recognize as a subject to crimes that, because inflicted on blacks unknown and unrecognized, don't receive recognition. He hopes that his crime will distinguish him from the stereotype of the black male thug who steals from other blacks, rapes black women, or fights other black men—all actions that, confined to the bounds of a racist stereotype and committed against individuals whose race denies them the status of subjects, can't reveal subjectivity. What he doesn't anticipate is that the rape of a white woman is the crime he will be (non)recognized as committing. "They'll say you raped her," Bessie reminds Bigger, who then realizes, in a moment of crushing defeat, that "there would be no way to prove that he had not."[78]

For Bigger, the rape of a white woman is not an act of sexual violence, "rape was not what one did to women," but a discursive mechanism of racial rule: "He committed rape every time he looked into a white face."[79] Bigger knows the sociopolitical density of the charge of rape when leveled in these circumstances. Kimberly Drake explains that in white racist ideology, the body of the white woman stands for "the pure spaces of white-dominated middle- and upper-class society; black men who assert their right to enter into this world of social and economic privilege are called rapists." Drake argues that the political valence of the rape charge means that, in *Native Son*, rape is a trope for both "racial oppression and for the protest against it," as the latter is enacted through a "metaphorics of rape or forced entry." She critically diagnoses how that symbolic protest is deconstructed by its displacement of "the complexity of the flesh-and-blood white woman," but Wright also clearly demonstrates the failure of that figuration of rebellion.[80] If Bigger's crime can be recoded as the rape of a white woman, he ceases to be seen as its subject and instead confirms himself as a subhuman that is driven by mere instinct. The recoding of his act as rape enables him to be denied identity and instead slotted into a racist prefabricated stereotype for black men. Later, when he's on the run from the manhunt, he sees the newspaper headline "AUTHORITIES

[79]

HINT SEX CRIMES" and knows that "those words excluded him utterly from the world." In the same paper, he reads that the police suspect Bigger was only Jan's accomplice in Mary's murder, since "the plan of the murder and kidnapping was too elaborate to be the work of a Negro mind." Bigger's futile response, "Jan didn't help me! He didn't have a damn thing to do with it! I—I did it!," signals how racist ideology will not grant him, as a black male rapist, recognition as a doer of deeds.[81]

When Bessie reminds Bigger that he will be accused of rape, Bigger appears to lose the agency he's so recently discovered. He decides he will have to kill Bessie to prevent her from talking to the authorities, but it's "as if the decision were being handed down to him by some logic not his own, over which he had no control, but which he had to obey." It's as if once he realizes that his actions will not distinguish him as a subject, he ceases to *be* a subject. When he sexually assaults Bessie, it is described as an act of bodily compulsion. "The loud demand of the tensity of his own body" renders him "imperiously driven, he rode roughshod over her whimpering protests, feeling acutely sorry for her as he galloped a frenzied horse down a steep hill in the face of a resisting wind." He then kills her after he convinces himself that he really has no choice if he is to escape capture: "Yes. It *must* be this way." Wright's indictment of Bigger's treatment of Bessie is clear, and is structured according to the novel's central theme of subjectivity and its recognition. Bigger's objectification of Bessie as a mere body on which to release his "tensity" anticipates the law's later introduction of Bessie, in court, as a non-person, someone whose rape and murder don't "count" in the public forum. Her body is introduced by State's Attorney Buckley merely as evidence for the charge that Bigger raped Mary, the recognized subject who, because white, *does* count and whose rape and murder are punishable.[82] By perpetuating the dehumanizing logic of racism—by, as Abdul JanMohamed writes, "want[ing] to enslave someone weaker than he precisely in the manner in which he himself has been enslaved"[83]—Bigger voids his own claim to subjectivity. The sequence registers a potent critique of structural racism: Bigger's treatment of Bessie desubjectivizes him by reflecting his internalization of a logic designed precisely to deny subjectivity to black bodies.

Despite the failure of Bigger's efforts to use crime to gain recognition, Wright suggests that lumpenproletarian perspectives and actions provide components of political awareness and revolutionary action not yielded by proletarian experience. As we've seen, working-class status in *Native Son* binds an individual to tasks of labor that don't confer subjective distinction, and that keep the individual from the public realm. Describing Bessie, Bigger notes "the narrow orbit of her life: from her room to the kitchen of the white folks was the farthest she ever moved," and the routine of labor leads only to the desire for self-obliteration: "Most nights she was too tired to go out; she only wanted to get drunk." As he did in *Lawd, Today!,* Wright relies on a metaphorical gendering of the private realm as feminine and thus, by association, passive. Bigger scornfully conflates the two women in his life who value the meager rewards of working-class stability, aligning his mother's religiosity with Bessie's drinking as modes of self-denial: "What his mother had was Bessie's whiskey, and Bessie's whiskey was his mother's religion. He did not want to sit on a bench and sing, or lie in a corner and sleep." Rather, Bigger desires public activity, to "merge himself with others and be a part of this world, to lose himself in it so he could find himself."[84]

Wright complicates this gendering of labor and domesticity when Bigger, on the run and hiding in a vacant apartment, hears two working-class black men, Jack and Jim, discussing him in the next flat. Jack resents that Bigger's actions have caused him to lose his job: "the boss tol' me he didn't wan' me in them streets wid this mob feelin' among the white folks. . . . Yuh see, tha' goddamn nigger Bigger Thomas made me lose mah job. . . . Ef Ah knowed where the black sonofabitch wuz Ah'd call the cops 'n' let 'em come 'n' git 'im!" When Jim states he'd refuse to turn a fellow African American over to the police, Jack responds: "Man, yuh crazy! Don' yuh wan' a home 'n' wife 'n' chillun?"[85] Jack's name underscores his similarity to Jake Jackson, a worker who, anxious to protect a meager stake in the system and reproduce his basic domestic needs, must affirm and defend that system. In *Native Son*, working-class conditions diminish revolutionary capacity.

When Bigger becomes a criminal, he accesses a materialist critique unavailable to the working-class characters. As he hides from the manhunt in an abandoned South Side tenement, he glimpses, in the next building, a couple making love in a cramped apartment in front of their children. "It was familiar; he had seen things like that when he was a little boy sleeping five in a room." Now, however, when he views this situation from the spatial and social margin, he can offer a materialist analysis of it: "Five of 'em sleeping in one room and here's a great big empty building with just me in it." Cramped living conditions are transformed, in his consciousness, from an inevitable reality to a socially and economically determined injustice. As he searches for another vacant apartment, he is aware of how "empty flats were scarce in the Black Belt," and how segregated housing practices enable both the poor maintenance and inflated rents that made domestic life a routine struggle. He draws on his own experience as an outsider displaced from social status to understand the experience of all South Side blacks: the lack of empty flats in which he can hide returns his consciousness to the difficulties black families face in finding suitable housing. "They keep us bottled up here like wild animals, he thought."[86] When Bigger looks on the workings of racial capitalism from without, from the vantage point of the lumpenproletarian, he perceives the injustices that those who must protect their place within the system cannot.

The cognitive empowerment of the lumpenproletarian perspective implies political possibility. At the end of his flight, he is finally apprehended when the police glimpse him on a rooftop. "There he is!" one officer yells. This cry, coming as it does from a cop about a suspect, resembles Althusser's interpellative address, but does not grammatically interpellate Bigger as a subject: it's addressed not to an individual who can then demonstrate subjectivity by responding to it, but to another police officer. Bigger remains merely the object of their exchange. When he hears this cry, he decides to make a run for it, which prompts a second cry: "Stop, *you!*"[87] Challenging his designation as an object by acting in resistance, Bigger forces this however meager recognition of his subjectivity. Despite his ultimate failure to win recognition through Mary's death, crime is still linked, by Wright, to political praxis: both defy the law of an unjust state. Bigger's perspective and actions as a lumpenproletarian figure retain, for Wright, the general forms of both materialist critique and revolutionary action, forms the Communist left must acknowledge and appropriate.

THE COMMUNIST PARTY AS POLIS

Fredric Jameson argues that the two equally real values of the commodity-form (its appearance as an object of exchange and its material truth as a product of labor) allow Marxism to assign reality either to the subjective performance of individual action or to its objective historical determination: "history can be written either subjectively, as the history of class struggle, or objectively, as the development of the economic modes of production . . . : these two formulae are the same, and any statement in one can without loss of meaning be translated into the other." Informed by Sartre's argument that the actions of revolutionaries can't be reduced to reflections of historical shifts, Jameson holds that the conscious motives of subjective political action aren't necessarily misrepresentations of objective historical processes or manifestations of false consciousness, but a potential "[code]" for revolutionary trajectories.[88]

Wright similarly distinguishes and relates Bigger's personal motives and his deeds' objective political significance. When he signs his forged ransom note, he intends only to cast suspicion on Communists, but he does so by claiming to be "Red." In the movie theater scene, he and Jack incorrectly identify Communists as a "race of people," but the error indicates the alignment of African American and Communist political interests. Mikko Tuhkanen points out that Daltonism is a specific form of colorblindness, the inability to distinguish green from red. Since the Daltons' racial blindness manifests itself as the inability to distinguish Bigger from the previous chauffeur, Green, the reference subtly suggests Bigger's objective political identity.[89] Bigger's conscious motives may be keyed to self-interest and self-preservation, and often motivated by a non-Marxist loathing of whites in general, but the objective import of his actions, which fundamentally challenge a racial and economic system designed to objectify African Americans, positions him on the left.

The concluding courtroom sequence is a contest to define Bigger's actions. The press paints Bigger as "a jungle beast . . . out of place in a white man's civilization." He is also characterized in racist terms similar to orthodox Marxism's moral derision of the lumpenproletariat. A white newspaper editor in Jackson, Mississippi, Bigger's hometown, reports: "Thomas comes of a poor darky family of a shiftless and immoral variety. He was raised here and is known to local residents as an irreformable sneak thief and liar." State's Attorney Buckley uses similar rhetoric in his courtroom debate with Boris Max, vilifying Bigger for refusing to enter the working class: "He said that he did not want to work! He wanted to loaf about the streets, steal from newsstands, rob stores, meddle with women, frequent dives, attend cheap movies, and chase prostitutes!" Bigger, Buckley charged, was perversely "outraged . . . that he had to earn his bread by the sweat of his brow."[90] This rhetoric can be found in bourgeois as well as Marxist normalizations of labor: the opprobrium both level at the lumpenproletariat is largely interchangeable. Wright suggests that labor, rather than reflecting any intrinsic human desire, is mandated and only retroactively validated by both capitalism and orthodox Marxism. Thus, what's revolutionary about Bigger's desire to do something other than work is that it refuses self-obliteration. The Communists, Boris Max and Jan Erlone, recognize this desire, and Max works to define it against Buckley's—and, indeed, Marx's—scorn.

In the final section, Jan and Boris model the functions of Arendt's revolutionary councils. The Communist Party in *Native Son* can be understood as what Michael Warner terms a "counterpublic," a space in which identities suppressed or invisible in hegemonic public spheres are recognized, constructed, and articulated through "active participation." Drawing on Arendt's concept of the polis, Warner thinks of the counterpublic as a site for the production of citizenship, one that does not merely "represent the interests of gendered or sexualized persons in a public sphere," but which constructs "new worlds of culture and social relations in which gender and sexuality can be lived" through "collective world making." It is thus a public in Arendt's sense, a forum for self-revelation and self-construction, rather than that of the "bourgeois public sphere," in which "rational-critical debate around matters common to all" proceeds from the "bracketing" of individual identity.[91] Warner's concept explicates Wright's sense of the Communist Party as a public deriving its revolutionary anticapitalist and antiracist nature not from the collective negation of individuality but from its extension of recognition to African American subjects. Hence, for Wright, the party's revolutionary character lies not in any specific agenda or purpose but in the opportunity for self-expression it grants African American subjects by incorporating them in its organization. In the novel's final book, Jan and Max provide a counterpublic in which Bigger can speak and be heard as the subject speaking, can reveal himself as the agent behind his actions.

The correlation of Communism with individual recognition is established early in the novel, when Bigger first meets Mary Dalton. Mary is a genuine Communist sympathizer and, as Sondra Guttman notes, a transgressive figure herself who actively resists the hegemonic symbolic functions of her race, class, and gender.[92] Bigger is unsettled when Mary, unlike her parents, sees him as more than another hired servant: she looks at him directly, stands "close to him," and asks whether he belongs to a union. The violence threatening black men who interact with white women as equals animates Bigger's fear of Mary, but later, as he drives Mary to meet Jan, he "felt something in her over and above the fear she inspired in him. She responded to him as if he were human, as if he lived in the same world as she." This moment of recognition is fleeting and unable to negate its prohibition: "The guarded feeling of freedom he had while listening to her was tangled with the hard fact that she was white and rich, a part of the world of people who told him what he could and could not do."[93] Bigger's inculcation in the ideology of racial difference, previously demonstrated in his "correct" performance of that difference in the "playing white" game, makes him mistrust Mary. Yet the scene remains instructive. For a moment, Bigger's cinematic fantasy of working for the Daltons—colluding, as a partner in active deception, with a beautiful and clever white woman—is realized, and Mary's politics, rather than simple adolescent rebellion or infatuation, actually instruct the reader as to the essential content of Communism in *Native Son:* its recognition of subjectivity in those individuals objectified by racial and class power.

In this opening section, however, the recognition isn't sustained, as Jan and Mary end up treating Bigger as an object of Communist exhortation rather than a subject. This treatment manifests itself in their insensitivity toward Bigger's racial and class position. Jan and Mary are blind to the ways in which, for Bigger, dominant codes of cross-racial social interaction are lived not as mere restrictions to be defied, but as constitutive components of his sense of safety and self-preservation. They see Bigger as only an oppressed victim without seeing his complicated interior negotiation with that oppression. However, their leftist rhetoric also reveals blindness toward Bigger, as it touts collective sameness rather than the individual recognition Bigger desires. Mary, for instance, expresses her wish to see the South Side: "Never in my life have I been inside of a Negro home. Yet they *must* live like we live. They're *human*. . . . There are twelve million of them."[94] Her egalitarian intent leads her to invoke humanity as an anonymizing category, de-individuating Bigger as merely one of twelve million black humans who are themselves interchangeable with white humans. And indeed, the distinction between egalitarianism and objectification in Mary and Jan's treatment of Bigger is often blurred, as when they feel no compunction in making love while Bigger drives them around Washington Park. Bigger's desire for subjectivity not only makes him unreceptive to narratives of the absorption of the self in the collective, but it prompts him and the reader to appreciate the uncertain distinction between a radical proclamation of cross-racial equality and a refusal to individuate the black subject. Consequentially, in this first section, subjective recognition fails to trump racial difference: Jan and Mary misperceive Bigger as another black victim, he misperceives them as more rich whites.

After Bigger's capture, Jan visits him in jail. He tells Bigger how he was able to transcend his personal grief over Mary's death by considering how African American men have long had to suffer the loss of loved ones: "I thought of all the black men . . . who had to grieve when their people were snatched from them in slavery and since slavery. I thought that if they could stand it, then I ought to." He offers friendship and legal assistance, a move that leads Bigger, for the first time, to see him as a distinct individual rather than a racial type. Wright's images of vision and recognition encode the scene's political logic:

> Jan had spoken a declaration of friendship that would make other white men hate him. . . . For the first time in his life a white man became a human being to him; and the reality of Jan's humanity came in a stab of remorse: he had killed what this man loved and had hurt him. He saw Jan as though someone had performed an operation upon his eyes, or as though someone had snatched a deforming mask from Jan's face.

Jan recognizes the self disclosed in Bigger's actions. "Don't you believe in yourself?" he asks Bigger. "You believed enough to kill. You thought you were settling something, or you wouldn't've killed." Bigger is amazed that Jan could "believe in him *that* much." Jan's new vision corrects his previous misperception of Bigger as only the type of the black victim, while Jan's friendship corrects Bigger's misperception of him as a race enemy. In his first meeting with Bigger, Boris Max similarly acknowledges Bigger's subjectivity by inviting him to explain his motives and experiences to a sympathetic listener. Afterwards, Bigger feels that "his talking had eased from his shoulders a heavy burden. . . . [H]e had talked of his own accord, prodded by excitement, by a curiosity about his own feelings." Max had conveyed "a recognition of his life, of his feelings, of his person that he had never encountered before" and "he had spoken to Max as a man who *had* something."[95] Subjective recognition and political empowerment are fostered within this Communist counterpublic.

Max's courtroom speech further explicates Wright's understanding of political desire. Max historicizes Bigger's desire and actions by relating them to the circumstances of America's founding. He draws on American history to frame Bigger's lumpenproletarian activities as political acts closer to those of the country's founders than to the self-interested depravities of a criminal. His analysis of the American Revolution and the origins of the United States parallels Hannah Arendt's in *On Revolution*. Arendt argues that the American revolutionaries were troubled by slavery primarily because it enjoined absolute anonymity on those who suffered it, "an obscurity even blacker than the obscurity of poverty" that permanently barred the slave from public action, visibility, and democratic participation. The nation's founders knew that slavery was "the primordial crime upon which the fabric of American society rested," and recognized "the incompatibility of the institution of slavery with the foundation of freedom."[96] Max compares Bigger, and African Americans more generally, to America's "forefathers" who "came here with a stifled dream in their hearts, from lands where their personalities had been denied." Like Arendt, Max argues that the founding of the United States was motivated by a desire for personal recognition, but that this was accomplished by enslaving African Americans, by "shut[ting] their eyes to the humanity of other men." Thus, in Bigger "and men like him is what was in our forefathers when they first came to these strange shores.... They are yet looking for a land whose tasks can call forth their deepest and best." Bigger's desire is not for personal gain or financial and material necessities: it stems not from "a lack of bread" but a "lack of self-realization." He discovered that self-realization, in stunted form, by killing Mary. "He accepted it because it made him free, gave him the possibility of choice, of action, the opportunity to act and to feel that his actions carried weight."[97]

In their final meeting before Bigger's execution, Bigger and Max come to disagreement over the meaning of Bigger's actions. Max's speech emphasized how Bigger was driven to crime as the only outlet for self-realization, but Bigger ultimately resists this unfree characterization of his action. Instead, he echoes Jan's recognition that he "believed enough to kill" in telling Max: "But what I killed for, I *am!* It must've been pretty deep in me to make me kill!" Bigger's assertion of I-kill-therefore-I-am insists on the practical nature of subjectivity as inherent in action, and he thus refuses to abandon his (mis)recognition of Mary's death as the

[87]

act that revealed his selfhood. At the same time, however, his choice of words suggests the tentativeness of his equation of murder and subjectivity, as he can only insist that the latter "must've been" represented by the former. His syntax indicates his awareness that only through the fiction of misrecognition can murder be a demonstration of self, but he clings to the import of that demonstration regardless. His closing request to Max, that he "tell Jan hello," indicates that the sense of self he accessed through lumpenproletarian crime anticipates the truer mode of self-revelatory freedom accessible in the counterpublic of the Communist Party.[98]

Bigger's closing sentiment, when coupled with Max's speech, limns the lumpenproletariat's simultaneous orientation toward freedom and unfreedom, possibility and delimitation. The concept's very fluidity in situating its referents as either free agents or products of oppression enables Bigger's paradoxical discovery of freedom in a compelled action. It's the concept from Marxism's repertoire that allows Wright to shape the paradox of the novel's protest, which insists *simultaneously* on the structural, socioeconomic determination of the marginalized and their capacity for action against that determination. To return to Jameson's distinction of Marxism's two "formulae" for parsing sociopolitical transformation, subjectively willed-class struggle and objectively determined historical shifts, *Native Son* derives much of its theoretical power and continued relevance from its complex play, within the contexts of African American modern experience, of these two narratives of revolution.

CODA: WRIGHT, ARENDT, AND THE GENDERING OF POLITICS

The gender dynamics of the jail-cell reconciliation between Jan and Bigger illustrate how the polis provided by the Communist Party is particularly and exclusively defined by fraternity. It forms literally over Mary's dead body, the corpse that enables Jan to recognize Bigger as its creator and, in turn, Bigger to recognize Jan as an individual. As Jan explains, racial difference is transcended through a cross-racial male experience of the loss of female loved ones, a logic that reminds us of how Jan and Bigger must first lose Mary and Bessie—their ties to their respective private, domestic concerns—in order to constitute a counterpublic where subjective recognition is extended across the color line. The gendering implicit in this moment aligns women's bodies with the private or domestic realm, in which one's subjectivity is not revealed in one's actions, in which, as Arendt holds, one is tied to the tasks of bodily necessity. Thus, Mary and Bessie can only be bodies whose destruction illustrates the alternative selfhood of public action. Wright's reliance on this figurative equation of masculinity/public and femininity/private distinguishes the freedom of politics from the passivity of labor, but undermines his depiction of Mary's own rebellion against class and gender norms, as well as his critique of Bigger's internalization of racist and sexist ideologies in his rape and murder of Bessie. This gendering of the novel's political distinctions is indissociable from the devaluation of female bodies enacted by patriarchal and racist logics.

My analysis thus underscores the conclusions of Maria Mootry's reading of Wright's representation of women. "Food, Sex and Religion are the anodynes with which these women [Bessie and Bigger's mother] are associated—everything to narcoticize an intelligent, questioning spirit." As a result, in Wright's fiction, "only to the extent that men define themselves in opposition to women are they validated as recreated, autonomous beings." Because of Wright's gendering of labor and the private realm, women are complicit with the anonymizing functions of racial rule. Mootry reads black women in Wright as "co-conspirator[s] of the oppressor" and as "serious obstacles" to the male characters' "pursuit of Manhood."[99] Trudier Harris also notes the disassociation of black women from public subjectivity in *Native Son*, describing "religion, alcohol, and sex" as "crutches" that "allow none of the women the creative urges associated with a desire to fly planes or to escape from the ghetto." The black women characters also "[preach] subservience" and thus reinforce black passivity.[100]

Other critics have challenged the broad strokes of this interpretation of women in Wright's work. Anthony Dawahare and Cheryl Higashida, for example, argue for Wright's awareness of black women's political agency and his diagnosis of the self-defeating complicity of masculine assertiveness with the patriarchal tendencies of racial nationalism.[101] However, my reading of Wright tends toward confirmation of the interpretation put forth by Mootry and Harris. In *Lawd, Today!* and *Native Son*, he develops a theory of revolutionary passion and action that, on the one hand, thinks the passivity of labor and private life through tropes of feminization, and on the other, figures public political action in terms of masculinity and fraternity. The possible consequences of this figurative distinction are multiple, but what's irreducible in Wright's thought is a fundamental misalignment between his progressive political ambitions and the gendering of the rhetoric in which they're developed.

Arendt's approach to politics also relies on a distinction of private and public that is figuratively established by reference to registers of particularity, principally gender and, as we'll see, race. Adrienne Rich observed that *The Human Condition* uncritically reproduces "the withholding of women from participation in the *vita activa*, the 'common world'; and the connection of this with reproductivity, is something from which she does not so much turn her eyes as stare straight through unseeing."[102] Bonnie Honig concedes that "Arendt does often speak as if her private realm and its activities of labor and work were to be identified with particular classes of people, or bodies, or women in particular."[103] In *The Human Condition*, Arendt observes that the terms for economic labor and for the pains of childbirth are etymologically related in many languages, underscoring her argument that the pain of labor lies in its biological necessity. Arendt describes the household sphere as organized by "natural functions," such as "the labor of man to provide nourishment and the labor of the woman in giving birth."[104] If labor's necessity incorporates and is in part defined by the biological reproduction of life, Arendt's classical conceptualization of labor seems to exert a proprietary claim over female subjects. If childbirth and economic labor are defined in common, then femininity necessarily becomes the figure for the unfree worker and for the anonymity of private or domestic life.

This gender division is racially inflected in Arendt's notorious 1959 essay "Reflections on Little Rock," which dismisses school integration as proper political struggle. The school, for Arendt, is an extension of the household and thus a site specifically for the private, feminized task of child-rearing. Hence, she sees school integration as a violation of the private sphere, where parents' "private right over their children" should remain inviolate. Her refusal to recognize the political dynamics of integration stems in part from an apparent inability to correlate spaces associated with women and children with political action: "Have we now come to the point where it is the children who are being asked to change or improve the world? And do we intend to have our political battles fought out in the school yards?"[105] Ralph Ellison famously disputed Arendt's interpretation, arguing that the children who integrated Little

Rock Central High were offered as a kind of sacrifice: their parents were "sacrificing" them to the racial oppressions of Southern public life, introducing them to the sociopolitical dynamics they'd be forced to understand, master, and protest as adults.[106] As Danielle Allen explains, "Ellison invokes the term 'sacrifice' to explain the actions of the parents of the Little Rock nine but also and more importantly to make the case for the political status of their actions."[107] "You know," Ellison stated in 1961, "the skins of those thin-legged little girls who faced the mob in Little Rock marked them as Negro, but the spirit which directed their feet is old universal urge toward freedom."[108]

Anne Norton attributes the blindness of "Reflections on Little Rock" to the fact that, in Arendt's work, racial blackness often, like femininity, marks a political incapacity stemming from an inability to transcend necessity. Through a close reading of Arendt's writings on African Americans, Norton argues that the founding exclusion of African Americans from the American polis, while critiqued by Arendt, nonetheless leads Arendt to describe African Americans as not capable of entering the public sphere. As a result, Arendt understood African American political movements as only addressing private concerns of black material interests, and incapable of enabling free political action. "The body, for Arendt, was the site of nature's constitutional authority, beyond the reach of politics," Norton writes. So for Arendt, if "African Americans are present in America only in the body . . . [t]hey remain in the realm of nature, outside politics."[109] Wright demonstrates how an Arendtian logic of the political can offer a strident correction to the racial blindnesses of Arendt's work. By focusing on the production of black invisibility as the cause not of political incapacity but of political desire, Wright identifies the African American individual as the political subject *par excellence.*

Cognate analyses of Arendt's conceptualization of gender have read for the ways in which Arendt's own theory deconstructs her tendency to ontologize femininity as, like blackness, the sign of an inability to transcend bodily need. For example, Honig argues that "a gentle subversion of Arendt's treatment of the body as a master signifier of irresistibility" can be effected by excavating Arendt's treatment of labor as a particular mode of self-making whose procedural assumptions, rather than agents, are contrasted with politics. If Arendt's thought suggests that labor and politics are "sensibilities" of activity that all persons potentially perform, then "each would be understood as itself a performative production, not the expression of the authentic essence of a class, or a gender." Arendt's own philosophy thus indicates how "there is no determinate class of persons that is excluded from political action."[110]

To return to Wright in light of these generative readings of the fault lines of race and gender in Arendt, we might conclude by noting that Wright himself performed similar deconstructions of his own political thought. Unlike Arendt, Wright *could* envision the private realm becoming a political space, labor becoming action, and the figure of the African American woman becoming an acting subject. After *Native Son,* Wright's next intended project was a novel examining what Barbara Foley calls "the condition of women as an issue in its own right as well as in its broader social and political connections with racism, capitalism, and fascism."[111] Wright began the novel he would call *Black Hope* soon after finishing *Native Son,* and it constitutes a development in his understandings of politics, labor, and gender. One of the plots in this long text concerns the politicization of Ollie Knight, a young black female domestic worker. Ollie has come from the South to New York to work for an exploitative employment agency run by Mr. Downy, who arranges with white employers to have his domestic workers labor for substandard wages, most of which he pockets directly. Ollie is hired by Maud Hampton, an African American woman who is passing for white and running the large household of a dying, wealthy white man. Maud eventually marries the man, murders him, and inherits his property. Wright's portrait of Maud's psychology rivals his characterization of Bigger in terms of its complexity and nuanced characterization. By focusing on the interior motives and desires of African American women, and exploring the public sociopolitical significances of their actions, *Black Hope* moves past the delimiting gender binaries of Wright's previous fiction.

Ollie Knight is, like Bigger Thomas, a complex character who acts in a manner that encodes objective political possibility. Downy withholds wages from Ollie and eventually forces her to be sexually violated by his dog. In the wake of this horrific assault, Ollie bravely reports both Maud and Downy to the Domestic Workers Union. The union intends to take action against Maud for her part in Ollie's exploitation, but Maud commits suicide, leaving the house to the union and her money to Ollie. At the end of the novel, the union leaders come to convert the house into their headquarters, and Ollie starts directing them in their inventory of its contents:

"I know every speck of dirt in this house by heart. I done cleaned this place it seems like a thousand times." The novel ends with Ollie acting politically, speaking for herself in a polis: "Ollie talked on; she had the floor."[112]

The Domestic Workers Union does not deindividuate Ollie by entrenching her in the anonymity of a laboring identity. Rather, like the Communist Party in *Native Son,* it provides a forum where she can speak and be recognized; where she can, for the first time, receive public recognition. Ollie's characterization is thus a far cry from Bessie's, and Julieann Ulin argues that Wright's research into the experiences of Harlem domestic workers, and his interviews of women involved in the "slave market" of domestic hiring, allowed him "to create a novel in which Bessie's counterpart, Ollie Knight, experiences an alternative fate."[113] Bessie never escapes the routine of labor or the anonymity of domestic space. In *Black Hope,* the domestic space in which Ollie toils is transformed by her own actions, actions which disclose her subjectivity through her refusal to be an object of sexual and economic abuse, into a public polis.

The outlet for self-expression Bigger found in crime is found, by Ollie, in working-class activism. That point of distinction between the two texts deconstructs *Native Son*'s gendering of public and private pursuits: in *Black Hope,* proletarian status positions the black female subject closer to the constructive mode of public action that Bigger only locates at the end of the novel. *Black Hope* suggests, then, that the feminized realm of labor might not just preclude political action, but enable it. However, the political desire animating Bigger and Ollie's actions in both texts remains the same, and the ideal value of a radical institution, political party or labor union, remains its ability to harness that desire to participate in public life and be recognized as the subject of one's participation. *Black Hope* departs from Wright's earlier tendency to figure revolution as lumpenproletarian practice. Nonetheless, Wright's consideration of lumpenproletarian experience and practice, and his recognition that what Bigger Thomas wants is what the revolutionary wants, led him to discover the kernel of revolutionary action that *Black Hope* elaborates.

3

FROM OKLAHOMA CITY TO TUSKEGEE, FROM HARLEM TO DAYTON

The Sites, Levels, and Travels of Ralph Ellison's Marxism

In 1942, Ralph Ellison wrote the critic Stanley Edgar Hyman to encourage him to submit an essay to *Negro Quarterly*, the journal Ellison edited at the time. In response to Ellison's suggestion, Hyman outlined a possible essay on blues music:

> My theory . . . is that the attitudes behind a substantial section of the blues . . . are not actually the values and attitudes of the Negro people, but a small section of it, the lumpenproletariat: whores and pimps and gamblers and saloon people and the musicians and entertainers who work around them. I am referring to such stuff as the constant preoccupation with drink, the emphasis on a woman's primary function as keeping her man, the cracks about dice and razors, etc.

Hyman continued to speculate that the blues, articulating the "primarily sexual miseries" of lumpenproletarian African Americans, the "really declassed," have functioned to symbolize the "social and economic miseries" of the larger black community.[1] Ellison encouraged this project, but with reservations:

> I suggest . . . that you be very careful when applying Marxist concepts to American Negro experience—especially such a term as "lumpenproletariat." I would define the term carefully, remembering the fluidity of Negro class lines. For my own work I find an approach when [sic] defines the American Negro in terms of his consciousness much more exact. Most of us are still of the folk, poised between an American Negro working class outlook, and that of the Negro middle class. And again, the blues are disapproved by respectible [sic] Negro families of the middle class, and by *religious* folk Negroes.[2]

While brief, this exchange illuminates Ellison's understanding of the lumpenproletariat. Hyman offers, in rhetoric that directly alludes to Marx's famous cataloguing of the lumpenproletariat in *The Eighteenth Brumaire* discussed in chapter 1, a definition of the lumpenproletariat as criminal and nonpolitical. For Hyman, the underclass experience expressed in the blues can be a metaphor for the socioeconomic plight of African Americans precisely because that experience seems qualitatively removed from politics and concerned only with sex, drinking, gambling, and the like. And while Hyman defines the lumpen as "de-classed," he associates that status with recreation and vice rather than material want. In seeing underclass life as only metaphorically related to real political concerns, Hyman echoes Marx and Engels's estimation of the lumpenproletariat's moral degradation and sociopolitical irrelevance.

It's easy to read Ellison's response as rejecting any application of Marxism to African American concerns at all, but he actually specifies the care a thinker must take when doing so. It's not that Hyman cannot use Marxism to think black experience, but that one cannot apply Marxist concepts to African American experience without, in turn, modifying those concepts. Ellison thus questions Hyman's (and orthodox Marxism's) assumption that the lumpenproletariat would specify a segment of the black community defined by illicit activity. Rather, the concept signals the "fluidity" of black class distinctions, a definition that preserves the orthodox emphasis on the lumpenproletariat as declassed, but which revises the import of that classlessness. When applied to black life, Ellison implies, the lumpenproletariat references the vicissitudes, complications, and possibilities for "consciousness" that emerge from individuals' mobility across and out of class lines. He augments this redefinition of the lumpenproletariat with one of the folk, which is not an agricultural precursor to the capitalist mode of production but a liminal location between bourgeois and proletarian social and cultural positions. Ellison's investment here in the intersection between the concept of the lumpenproletariat and the on-the-ground realities of black life hearkens back to his earlier 1930s writings. Ellison's Depression fiction enacted an original and sophisticated mode of Marxist theoretical practice by associating the lumpenproletariat and the folk with the political potential afforded by socioeconomic instability.

To link Ralph Ellison to Marxism is, of course, a counterintuitive move given that his political reputation, as established both by scholars and his own postwar comments, has often been framed as an absolute rejection of any leftist radicalism. While he started his career on the Communist left in the Depression, authoring numerous radical fictional works and publishing prolifically in Communist periodicals, Ellison later claimed that he was only briefly drawn to "Marxist political theory" as a youthful "attraction." While admitting that he had written for Communist-backed journals and had produced "propaganda having to do with the Negro struggle," he insisted he "never wrote the official type of fiction."[3] Critics have distanced Ellison from Marxism on the assumption that the latter is a reductive, mechanistic doctrine at odds with Ellison's intellectual and aesthetic sophistication and largely unsuited to the complexities of US contexts and African American experience. As Larry Neal put it: "Ellison had never really internalized Marxism in the first place. . . . [L]ucky for us, his work never took on the simplistic assertions of the literary Marxist" (60).[4]

Barbara Foley has argued that this characterization of Ellison, Marxism, the Communist Party, and the Depression-era proletarian literary movement was a politically motivated discursive project of postwar reaction. The period's anticommunism, Foley argues, "invisibly entered the groundwater of U.S. cultural history" and has shaped the assumptions many critics and readers bring to Ellison. By historicizing Ellison's political reputation as a Cold War–era construction, and by offering the first sustained discussion of his 1930s writings, many of which were never published, Foley opens up new possibilities for reevaluating Ellison's relation to Marxism and the institutions of the Communist left.[5]

To that end, this chapter recovers the theoretical problematic of Ellison's Marxism, the undergirding and enabling conceptual structure of his work, the scaffolding of his epistemological priorities. The influence of Ellison's own lumpenproletarian experience on his Marxism are visible and enacted in his 1933 journey from his home in Oklahoma City to

Tuskegee Institute in Alabama, where he intended to study music. Lacking financial resources, Ellison hopped a freight train to get to Tuskegee. He was accompanied on the first leg of his trip by Charlie Miller, a friend of Ellison's mother and veteran transient who taught Ellison how to ride the rails. Before arriving at Tuskegee, he had a racially charged encounter with railroad bulls in Decatur, Alabama.[6] His trip lasted only a few days but was formative of his intellectual priorities, and Ellison would still recall it decades later. His distinct brand of Marxism animates his 1930s stories, essays, and correspondence, as well as two longer works of fiction that Ellison began in the 1930s but never finished: *Tillman and Tackhead* and *Slick*. Long neglected by scholarship, these narratives of African American characters who enter the social underworld of the lumpenproletariat and there discover political opportunity demonstrate the ingenuity with which Ellison used fiction to advance the protocols of his Marxism.

As he encouraged Hyman to do in 1942, Ellison's Depression work refashions the concept of the lumpenproletariat. As we've seen, Marx considered the lumpenproletariat to be a dead end for revolutionary politics: because it has no role in capitalist production as a class, it is self-interested, resistant to organization, and prone to reactionary co-option. Ellison's 1930s work preserves Marx's understanding of the lumpenproletariat as figures inhabiting the margins of class struggle and the interstices of social structures, but reimagines Marx's political estimation of them. For Ellison, the economic conflicts of American capitalism create politically generative encounters, accidents, and events within the social superstructure. In his Depression writings, transient figures navigate the margins and gaps of the social and metaphorically figure this social manifestation of revolutionary possibility. To further describe that possibility, Ellison employs another repurposed concept, a departicularized definition of the folk drawn from Communist discussions of black folk identity in the period. What I term lumpen-folk figures trope, for Ellison, the origin and operation of revolutionary politics.

OKLAHOMA CITY AND THE FORM OF THE SOCIAL

Jesse Wolfe voices a critical consensus when he writes that Ellison's love of "the fluidity and unpredictability of American democracy" is a "patriotic American, and anti-totalitarian, impulse [that] was a constant throughout Ellison's career."[7] That impulse characterizes Ellison's 1930s work, where, however, it is Marxist in orientation. This paradox is illuminated when Ellison is read alongside Louis Althusser and Antonio Gramsci, who despite considerable differences between their political careers and national contexts, explore materialist conceptions of social "fluidity and unpredictability." Both define a given social order as determined by economic relations of production but complex and internally variant in its own right. For Althusser, that definition is essential to the materialism of Marxism itself, which "establishes in principle the recognition of the givenness of the complex structure of any concrete 'object'. . . . There is no longer any original essence, only an ever-pre-givenness. . . . There is no longer any simple unity, only a structured, complex unity." Reducing the social to a simple reflection of an underlying economic "essence," and flattening its multivalent ontology, is an idealist error.[8] For Althusser and Gramsci, the economic determination of the social or superstructural is realized *as* the irreducible complexity of the social. They thus help us see the materialism of Ellison's 1930s work, which approaches the superstructure as the terrain of revolutionary possibility, where the fluid and shifting conditions of American society are simultaneously shaped by, facilitate, and complicate racial domination and class exploitation.

In his well-known post-Depression essays, Ellison would use the quasi-existentialist term "chaos" in connection with a sense of American social life as unpredictable, fluid, and resistant to static categorization. Sometimes the term names an epistemological and moral danger that the novelist must recognize and contain: Arnold Rampersad calls it "a threat to social order" while Foley situates it as "the existential void threatening to engulf those courageous enough to explore complexity and fluidity."[9] But it can also invoke a political potential in American experience. In his speech accepting the National Book Award for *Invisible Man*, Ellison urges novelists to "challenge the apparent forms of reality," those deceptively "fixed manners and values of the few" that underwrite social hierarchies, in order to reveal the true "mad, vari-implicated chaos" those hierarchies conceal.[10] John F. Callahan points out that chaos is linked to agency as "the front man for possibility. It is, Ellison believes, man's fate to defy the formlessness of chaos and the abyss, and at the same time to recognize that possibility flows from chaos."[11] Given Ellison's postwar turn away from the left, one can interpret this celebration of chaotic possibility as a denial of the reality of any structural oppression in American life. But the political as opposed to quietist ramifications of this concept of America are foregrounded when we see in it traces of Ellison's 1930s Marxism, which foregrounded the "chaos" of a social ontology determined by capitalist exploitation and organized around racial domination, but at the same time enabling resistance to both.

Ellison began his 1933 trip to Tuskegee by leaving Oklahoma City, which he would long recall as representative of the form of American society itself. The city, Ellison wrote in the introduction to *Shadow and Act* (1964), though officially dominated by white supremacy, was a "chaotic community" that allowed Ellison and his friends to "[explore] an idea of human versatility and possibility which went against the barbs or over the palings of almost every fence which those who controlled social and political power had erected to restrict our roles in the life of the country."[12] In the essay "Hidden Name and Complex Fate" (1964), Ellison attributes the richness of black life in segregated Oklahoma City to an interplay of historical and social contradictions that complicates the workings of Jim Crow. The same city in which Ellison found "card[s] warning Negroes away from the polls" is also the city in which he was able to read Shaw and Maupassant "in the home of a friend whose parents were products of that stream of New England education which had been brought to Negroes by the young and enthusiastic white teachers who staffed the schools set up for the freedmen after the Civil War." While the composition of Oklahoma City is defined by Jim Crow, it nonetheless challenges racial rule by being temporally and culturally uneven: the legacy of Reconstruction, supplanted by Jim Crow in the late nineteenth century, is residually present in this family that introduced Ellison to modernist literature.

Ellison lists other elements of Oklahoma City that imprinted themselves on his consciousness:

> I was claimed by weather, by speech rhythms, by Negro voices and their different idioms, . . . by music, by tight spaces and by wide spaces in which the eyes could wander, by death, by newly born babies, by manners of various kinds, company manners and street manners, the manners of white society and those of our own high society, and by interracial manners . . . .
>
> I was impressed by expert players of the "dozens" and certain notorious bootleggers of corn whiskey. By jazz musicians and fortunetellers and by men who did anything well. . . . I was fascinated by old ladies, those who

had seen slavery and those who were defiant of white folk and black alike, by the enticing walks of prostitutes and by the limping walks affected by Negro hustlers....

And there was the Indian-Negro confusion. There were Negroes who were part Indian and who lived on reservations, and Indians who had children who lived in towns as Negroes.... There were certain Jews, Mexicans, Chinese cooks, a German orchestra conductor and an English grocer who owned a Franklin touring car. And certain Negro mechanics—"Cadillac Slim," "Sticks" Walker, Buddy Bunn and Oscar Pitman—who had so assimilated the automobile that they seemed to be behind a steering wheel even as they walked the streets or danced with girls. And there were the whites who despised us and the others who shared our hardships and our joys.[13]

Multicultural interactions, residual energies and cultural forms, interracial "confusion," lumpenproletarian prostitutes and hustlers, and access to modern technology make black life more than a reflection of Jim Crow and capitalism. For instance, black auto mechanics certainly experience racial marginalization and economic exploitation, but they also dwell among premodern preachers and fortunetellers and bear heroic, folkloric personas. Ellison's love of the fluidity of the American scene stems from a materialist recognition of its actual contradictions and their productive capacities.

Recognizing the possibilities of social complexity is Louis Althusser's intention in describing the social as an overdetermined structure in dominance. Althusser theorizes a given social formation as a unified set of relatively autonomous sites of practical activity, related to each other, yet related—like the social components shaping black life in Oklahoma City—unevenly, through difference rather than equivalence. The economic determines the social by aggregating the uneven relations between all sites into a totality or "structure in dominance" unified by its overall dedication to reproducing capitalism's relations of production. However, the structure is characterized not by a uniformly consistent reflection and implementation of economic exploitation, but by the heterogeneous determinative relations shaping its component social sites and levels. Althusser thus describes the social as overdetermined: internally inconsistent and variant, or to quote Althusser, "complexly-structurally-unevenly-determined." Since that complexity does not uniformly reflect or effect ruling-class dominance, but combines both domination and disruption as elements of social form, overdetermination makes revolutionary change possible:

> Only overdetermination enables us to understand the concrete variations and mutations of a structured complexity such as a social formation... as so many concrete restructurations inscribed in the essence, the 'play' of each category, in the essence, the 'play' of each contradiction, in the essence, the 'play' of the articulations of the complex structure in dominance which is reflected in them.... [U]nless we... think this very peculiar type of determination once we have identified it, we will never be able to think the possibility of political action.[14]

Since overdetermination theorizes play or fluidity as a structural quality of the social, it enables one to identify chances for structural disruption and change. To quote Alain Badiou, "overdetermination puts the possible on the agenda... [and] is in truth the political place."[15] Ellison describes black life in Oklahoma City in a similar manner, as determined by capitalism and white rule, but also by figures, traditions, and practices that work in tension with or against that determination, making opportunity and resistance possible.

Recalling his youth in Oklahoma City, Ellison describes his childhood friendship with a white boy nicknamed Hoolie. Ellison's family was living in a white neighborhood (another sign of the unevenness of segregation) and Ellison, fascinated with radios, spent his time searching through the trash for items that could be of use to a radio amateur. One day he met Hoolie, who was engaged in the same search, and they struck up a brief friendship. "Knowing this white boy was a very meaningful experience," he recalled. "It had little to do with the race question as such, but with our mutual loneliness... and a great curiosity about the growing science of radio."[16] This experience of a technologically enabled encounter across racial lines recurs in his 1930s fiction, where technological products of modern capitalism (cars, radios, and airplanes) figure the social as porous to opportunity because it is internally uneven. In Ellison's fiction, technology moves characters and situations from across the social landscape into new relations, and these encounters allegorize the formation of interracial political alliances and action. That Ellison uses modern technology to figure this process indicates that he understands such opportunities to be enabled *by* the modernity of capitalist production.

John S. Wright has paid the most attention to the role of technology in Ellison's work, arguing that Ellison does not share high modernism's suspicions of modern technology. Rather, "revolutionary technological modernity" is for Ellison a crucial component of African American identity in the modern era. Wright indicates how technology, for Ellison, exists in a synecdochic relationship with social relations, "as an extension of human lives, as something *someone* makes, *someone* owns, something *some* people oppose, most people *must* use, and *everyone* tries to make sense of."[17] Similarly, I see Ellison's Marxism as enacting the practice Rayvon Fouché argues African Americans have long performed with the technological products of modernity: "produc[ing] meanings for technological artifacts, practices, and knowledge that regularly subvert the constructed meanings of these technological products."[18]

"A Party Down at the Square," one of Ellison's earliest literary efforts, uses technological symbolism to demonstrate how the form of the social itself gives rise to opportunities for political resistance. This story of a lynching in a small Southern town is narrated by a racist white youth. The lynching is interrupted by an airplane whose pilot, seeing the light of the blaze on the town square through the pouring rain, mistakes it for the runway lights of the nearby airport and starts to make a landing. The pilot corrects his mistake in time, but the plane's landing gear knocks over power lines, electrocuting a white woman. The lynching is resumed and carried off, but it gives rise to some unusual aftereffects. Afterwards, the town's blacks "look mean as hell when you pass them down at the store." Additionally, white sharecroppers are grasping materialist critiques of white supremacy: "it didn't do no good to kill the niggers 'cause things don't get no better" says one who, according to the narrator, "looked hungry as hell." Finally, the airline has launched an official investigation into the event "to find who set the fire that almost wrecked their plane."[19]

The plane disrupts the practice of Jim Crow by revealing its contradictory relations with the capitalist social totality. Antagonistic scrutiny from modern, corporate eyes outside the rural South, the airline and its investigators, may complicate future rituals of racial violence. Yet at the same time the incident has revealed white supremacy's hidden complicity with capitalism as an ideological compensation, thematized around white female sanctity, for exploited white workers. Jim Crow is rendered vulnerable due to its overdetermined nature: it is regionally peculiar yet contiguous with the larger social structure, temporally residual as well as an apparatus of modern capitalism. The plane's *descent* reveals that overdetermination as enabling the *dissent* of empowered African Americans and white sharecroppers.

THE PRACTICE OF POLITICS: DECATUR AND THE LUMPEN-FOLK FIGURE

Ellison's theory of revolutionary political action revises two concepts and figures: the lumpenproletariat and the folk. His memory of black Oklahoma City auto mechanics bearing folk legend status suggests an alignment, in Ellison's thought, of the ability to manipulate technology, to work the overdetermined complexity of social form, with an organic mode of individual agency. In his Depression work, he associates that agency with lumpenproletarian outsiders who craft possibility from the gaps and margins of the social. As we've seen, Althusser's theory of social form is designed to enable revolutionary action, and Gramsci's work further theorizes such action and thus furnishes an additional theoretical vocabulary for the specification of Ellison's Marxism.

Gramsci approaches the traditional Marxist framing of base and superstructure through his attention to what he terms "organic" (economic) and "conjunctural" (superstructural) components of social structures. Economic conditions are epistemologically grasped, however, when they are manifested on the "terrain of the 'conjunctural,' " where the objective dynamics of production are subjectively apprehended in various social and ideological forms. Class struggle, in other words, is actually waged in terms that orthodox Marxism might dismiss as merely superstructural: cultural, political, and so forth. Gramsci thus interprets Marx's famous preface to *A Contribution to the Critique of Political Economy* as arguing that "men acquire consciousness of structural conflicts [i.e., economic class conflicts] on the level of ideologies," but that this is "an affirmation of epistemological and not simply psychological and moral value." The economic ultimately determines this acquisition: the presence of anticapitalism in an ideological or social form indicates, Gramsci argues, that the economic "premisses exist . . . for this revolutionising."[20]

Catharsis, then, describes how economic conditions can be manipulated by subjective action at the level of the superstructure. For Gramsci, catharsis is "the passage from the purely economic . . . to the ethico-political moment, that is the superior elaboration of the [organic] structure into [conjunctural] superstructure in the minds of men." When this occurs, the capitalist totality is no longer approached as "an external force which crushes man, assimilates him to itself and makes him passive" but is "transformed into a means of freedom, an instrument to create a new ethico-political form and a source of new initiatives." Catharsis redefines the objective conditions of capitalism as routes of subjective anticapitalist action: it is "the passage from 'objective to subjective,'" from structural exploitation to active resistance, and inculcating the "'cathartic' moment" is Marxism's top priority. As Norberto Bobbio explains, "the very moment in which the material conditions are recognized, they become degraded to an instrument for whatever end is desired."[21]

Ellison's experience in Decatur, Alabama, in 1933 would guide his thinking about politics in similar channels. In Decatur, railroad bulls seized him and other hobos, "forty or fifty of us, black and white alike," from their train. "Not only was I guilty of stealing passage on a freight train," Ellison recalled, "but I realized that I had been caught in the act in the very town where, at that moment, the *Scottsboro* case was being tried."[22] The Scottsboro case had begun two years prior, when police took nine black male hobos off a train and accused them of raping two white female transients. Their trial would become a rallying point for the Communist Party, which provided them with legal representation and turned their defense into a national antiracist struggle. Ellison had been following the trial, and in the Decatur freight yard, when he realized that some of his fellow hobos were white women dressed as men, he feared the worst.[23] He was saved, however, by an act of spontaneous resistance: "when a group of white boys broke and ran, I plunged into their midst." He escaped and hopped another train, but "the fear, horror and sense of helplessness before legal injustice" he felt in Decatur "was most vivid in my mind," he recalled more than four decades later, "and it has so remained."[24]

Analyzing the significance of this moment requires specifying Ellison's 1930s understanding of Jim Crow. As the ending of "A Party Down at the Square" indicated, Ellison understood Jim Crow as a practice of dominance complexly connected to capitalist economic exploitation. In a note to himself when working on his aborted 1930s novel *Slick*, Ellison wrote: "The presence of Southerners in the North coupled with the fascist minded of that region make life for the Negro as miserable as in the south." Just as in the South, "Northern capitalists exploit" blacks "and attempt to keep them at the same level. Use police force to intimidate them."²⁵ Ellison generalizes Jim Crow as a national social order that ultimately reflects and achieves ruling-class economic dominance. If racially driven repression is the distinctly American sociopolitical articulation of capitalism, to battle Jim Crow is to wage anticapitalist struggle in sociopolitical terms. Ellison's approach thus resembles Stuart Hall's famous Gramscian claim that "race is . . . the modality in which class is 'lived,' the medium through which class relations are experienced, the form in which it is appropriated and 'fought through.'"²⁶ Fleeing Jim Crow, and thereby defying and demystifying the naturalness of its repressive routine, is an act with anticapitalist as well as antiracist significance, as it articulates the resistance of the economically marginalized to both racial dominance and economic exploitation.

Ellison's escape from Decatur proceeds cathartically, as it involves reapprehending structural dominance as political resistance. At first, the presence of white women among the hobos occasions fear and passivity in the face of impending violence. But Ellison is then drawn into action by those same individuals whose presence he initially feared. After all, how does Ellison know that some of those "white boys" he recalled breaking and running weren't *also* white women dressed as men? In a cathartic instance, the racial and gender significance of white women and black men together shifts from a catalyst of objective structural repression to a means of subjective action.

The incident in Decatur resituates a defining feature of the lumpenproletariat's social and economic marginality, its transience and mobility, as resistance. The incident thus resonates through Ellison's Depression fiction, in which the experiences of the lumpenproletariat connect the complexity of the American social scene to revolutionary action. Extricating the lumpenproletariat from Marx's dismissal of it as a politically unconscious or reactionary social segment guided only by vice and self-interest, Ellison reimagines lumpenproletarian agency in terms of a political subjectivity normally reserved, in classical Marxism, for the collective proletariat. As the socially and economically displaced, Depression lumpenproletarians navigate the interstices, underworlds, and margins of the social, those illicit routes and spaces capable of troubling the functioning of race and class rule. Ellison, fully as much as Wright or the later theorists of the Black Panther Party, situates the experiences of the lumpenproletariat at the center of his Marxism.

In Ellison's unpublished memoirs, Charlie Miller, the transient who accompanied Ellison on the first part of his 1933 journey, demonstrates the possibilities accessed from navigating the complexities of social form. Miller was a light-skinned African American who crossed racial, social, and class boundaries, and Ellison's description of him echoes Marx's of the heterogeneous social locations of the lumpenproletariat: "Sometimes footloose wanderer, sometimes taxi driver, butcher, man of all work, circus roustabout and gambler, he knew America like the palm of his hand." Refusing to define himself through fixed identities of either class or race, he was "as irreverent toward the Protestant work-ethic as he was toward the mystique of race and color." Miller is a "proven master" of transience not only in his capacity to read freight manifests and avoid the multiple perils of life on the bum, but in a figuratively political manner as well, in that he grasps how the fluid complications of American society can be manipulated against racial and economic power.[27]

Ellison explores this political potential figured within and by lumpenproletarian experience in his 1930s story "I Did Not Learn Their Names." The unnamed main character, based on Ellison himself, is African American and has gone on the road to earn money to pay his college tuition as a music student. Unable to find any work during the Depression, he rides freight trains across the country. He travels with Morrie, a white drifter he met in a hobo jungle in Oklahoma. Morrie has once saved his life, and helps him fight the racist white transients they often encounter. The train is figured as a vehicle of interracial, antiracist allegiance with larger, revolutionary implications: its rapid movement gives off sparks "dancing red in the whirling darkness," and on the morning of the story's main action, the protagonist "woke to see the line in the east turning red with the dawn." These allusions to Communism and the Soviet Union, the utopian "red" promise rising in the east, cast the mobile world of the lumpenproletariat as the origin of revolutionary practice.

The story explicates that origin through the protagonist's accidental encounter, in a boxcar, with an elderly white couple traveling to Missouri to meet their son, who is being released from prison. At first he assumes the white couple will be offended to discover him in the same car as dawn breaks: "In the dark, I was like all the rest who were on the freight and it didn't make a difference. Now it did." But the two welcome him, invite him to join them for a meal, ask after his own life, and relate the story of their son's troubles. The red light of dawn brings not the imposition of Jim Crow, as the protagonist initially feared, but its suspension, a suspension secured by the social marginality of the space itself. Still suspicious of the couple at first, he nonetheless refuses to address the man as "sir" because "Saying 'sir' was too much a part of knowing your place. I had learned that on the road you really had no place; you were all the same though some of them did not understand that."[28] Out of place and moving freely in the margins of the social, lumpenproletarian experience accesses human communion free from sociopolitical hierarchies.

The couple encourages the protagonist to continue his studies, and tells him that even though "the money is gone . . . our boy will be back with us. We are very happy." Lumpenproletarian crime and transience circumscribe the possibility of a collectivity and fulfillment that forecast the means and ends of revolutionary practice. After his encounter with the couple, the protagonist "thought of them a few days later" after he is arrested by railroad police in Decatur, who suspect him of traveling in the company of white women. In jail he learns of the Scottsboro case, and is relieved when Morrie is able to secure his release. While Ellison doesn't explicitly identify why the arrest puts him in mind of the couple, the implication is clear: his encounter with the couple stands in contrast to Jim Crow, and the racial violence of the latter is contiguous with the state violence suffered by the couple's son, who is approximately the same age as the protagonist. "I thought of the old couple often during those days I lay in jail, and I was sorry that I had not learned their names."[29] This closing regret is less a lament than a subtle foreshadowing. Among the lumpenproletariat, he has found white allies whose friendship allegorizes revolution by, in a reworking of Ellison's own escape from Decatur, defying Jim Crow. That friendship is colored red by the allusion to Scottsboro, and forecasts a new world in which the true names and true identities of human beings will, because outside of social and economic stratification, be known. The story thus combines romantic and realistic framings of the lumpenproletariat. Ellison depicts the violence and racism of the freights, echoing the brutal and unredemptive representations of lumpenproletarian life found in the Depression bottom dogs fiction described in chapter 1. Yet Ellison also sees a forecasting of postclass society in the marginal lives and encounters of the lumpenproletariat.

Alongside the lumpenproletariat, Ellison theorizes political action by drawing on an unusual concept of the folk, one inspired by the particular place of the African American folk in Communist discourse. As the instinctual humanity of the couple in "I Did Not Learn Their Names" suggests, Ellison reconceives the folk as a principle of positivity, an undeconstructible kernel of human will and the impulse to act that, while often associated with African Americans, nonetheless transcends racial identity. As a conceptualizing of transracial human impulses, it describes *ante*capitalist and prediscursive energies that can invigorate anticapitalist discourses and projects. The folk in Ellison's Marxism is thus a conceptual abstraction from the familiar definition of the black folk as a premodern Southern peasant class preserving the authentic cultural roots of the black community. Raymond Williams, however, points out how such purportedly empirical definitions of the folk are actually discursive responses to industrial society that position historically residual cultural practices as modes of oppositional authenticity.[30] J. Martin Favor and David G. Nicholls have identified the primarily discursive and instrumental presence of the folk in African American writing, where it often tropes problems of modernity and authenticity. Ellison's Marxism similarly repurposes the folk, situating it not as an empirical demographic but as an instrumental trope, one that associates human authenticity with the origins of political action.[31]

Ellison's recasting of the concept of the folk is informed by the Communist Party's approach to black folk culture in the Depression, when the party's "Black Belt" thesis described African Americans in the South as an oppressed nation and prioritized their struggle for self-determination. Party discourse defined the authenticity of Southern blacks, their folk identity, as working-class in nature, making their objective allies not the black middle class, but the interracial proletariat. The party sloganized black cultural identity as "national in form, but proletarian in content." The Communists thus developed nonessentialist and politically empowering concepts of black folk identity and black nationalism, understanding nations as historical formations and approaching national struggles as articulated modes of resistance to capitalism and imperialism.[32]

As historical materialists, both Ellison and Wright were interested in the meaning of Southern agricultural black folk identity in the capitalist North in the wake of the Great Migration. In a reading of Wright and Ellison's writings on the folk during World War II, Robin Lucy argues that Wright saw the folk as having been negated by modernization. Accordingly, for Wright, black folk culture had become "an element of an unusable past that cannot be translated into modernity."³³ Ellison, however, understood black folk identity and culture as having been transformed, in the North, into a mode of collective working-class consciousness and resistance. For Ellison, this modernized folk consciousness and cultural practice "defines a strategic, self-conscious, and radically transformative black national politics."³⁴ I argue that Ellison's 1930s fiction similarly developed a political, nonethnographic definition of the folk, one associated not with the proletariat, as Lucy holds, but with individual lumpenproletarian figures.

While affirming the historical eclipse of the agricultural folk, black Communist writers in the period tended to retain and reassign the senses of racial authenticity and communal and individual strength associated with the folk. Folk culture was considered the authentic expression of the black masses and the expressive kernel or motor of black revolutionary consciousness, and thus needed to be creatively updated for the current historical moment. In "Blueprint for Negro Writing," Wright describes black folk culture as a vital raw material for the black writer who must synthesize it with Marxist theory.³⁵ Marian Minus, a friend of Wright and Ellison, advanced a similar argument a few months prior to the publication of Wright's more well-known essay. In "Present Trends of Negro Literature" she insisted that black writers must reject the middle-class values of the Harlem Renaissance and return to the "earthy, burning, vital forces" of the folk culture of the masses. The writer must modernize this culture from a Marxist perspective, mastering its "social implications" in order to totalize it, to link its rich particular content to "the total configuration of world-wide human emotions, ideals and struggles."³⁶

Such arguments contextualize Wright's portrayal of boxer Joe Louis as a folk hero capable of uniting the masses in revolutionary struggle. Despite seeing the empirical Southern black folk as historically outmoded, Wright, like Ellison, deploys a folk-derived rhetoric of organic or essential capacity in order to think the origins of political action. Wright's *New Masses* report "Joe Louis Uncovers Dynamite" describes the mass celebrations of African Americans in Chicago following Louis's 1935 victory over Max Baer. Wright gives voice to the celebrants' nascent revolutionary consciousness as they storm a streetcar and take the money that spills in the chaos: "They stole it from us, anyhow." Louis's prowess makes him a folk avatar of the revolutionary capabilities of African Americans: "We ain't scared either. We'll fight too when the time comes. We'll win, too." Gramsci might note that this instance of unleashed, inherent folk militancy represents the acquisition of anticapitalist revolutionary agency on sociocultural terrain and in ideological terms. Concluding his narrative, Wright exclaims to his Communist reader: "Say, Comrade, here's the wild river that's got to be harnessed and directed. Here's that *something*, that pent-up folk consciousness. Here's a fleeting glimpse of the heart of the Negro, the heart that beats and suffers and hopes—for freedom. Here's that fluid something that's like iron. Here's the real dynamite that Joe Louis uncovered!"[37]

In a similar manner, Ellison's Marxism synthesizes the irrepressible strength and human agency associated with the folk with the socially displaced mobility of the lumpenproletariat in the archetypal figure I call the lumpen-folk, a figure for and elaboration of the "fluid something that's like iron" of politics.[38] Morrie and the elderly couple in "I Did Not Learn Their Names" reference this figure, and Ellison develops it further in his 1937 story "Hymie's Bull." Here, the protagonist is again a black drifter riding freights in the Depression. The narrative opens within a lumpen-proletarian social fluidity determined by economic crisis: "We were just drifting; going no place in particular, having long ago given up hopes of finding jobs." The narrator recounts the spontaneous emergence of a lumpen-folk hero, "an ofay bum named Hymie from Brooklyn." Hymie is legendary because he killed a railroad bull in a knife fight, an individual act of self-defense but one that will enable, like Joe Louis's heroic victory over Max Baer, collective political action. The day after Hymie kills the bull, the train the hobos are riding is stopped and the transients taken off. "We knew Hymie's bull had been found and some black boy had to go." But just then, "the storm broke and the freight started to pull out of the yards." The hobos make a run for the train, hop it, and escape.[39]

As a Jew from Brooklyn who saves black transients from Jim Crow, Hymie invokes the Communist left and its leading role in the Scottsboro defense and other antiracist causes. His act sets in motion a cathartic response to racial oppression. When they are pulled off the train, the narrator and his fellow drifters expect racial violence as the outcome of an apparently inevitable law. But in a fortuitous moment the conditions of the social totality, as figured by the technological symbol of the train, are cathartically transformed into an instrument of escape and freedom. Both the train and Hymie, the modern conditions of capitalism and an irrepressible human agency, make resistance to racial and class rule possible.

Rampersad points out that nowhere in his recollections of the 1933 journey does Ellison mention anyone like Hymie.[40] Ellison is instead extracting and departicularizing the themes of a black folk legend he heard on that journey. "I remember that when I was riding freight trains through Alabama to get to Tuskegee Institute there was a well-known figure of Birmingham, called Ice Cream Charlie, whose story was also told over and over again whenever we evoked the unwritten history of the group," Ellison later explained. Charlie was an ice cream maker. His success in this trade led his white competitors to send the police after him, "and it ended with his killing twelve policemen before they burned him out and killed him."[41] Ellison takes Ice Cream Charlie, a figure of both lumpenproletarian criminality and the agency of the black folk, and reimagines him as Hymie, thereby combining the potential of the lumpen-folk with the efficacy of organized interracial action Ellison experienced in Decatur.

Recalling his childhood in Oklahoma City, Ellison described how he and his friends worshipped a wide range of African American figures who appeared to freely defy racial subordination, including lumpenproletarian "gamblers" or "some local bootlegger." Ellison characterizes this practice as "projecting archetypes, re-creating folk figures, legendary heroes, monsters even, most of which violated all ideas of social hierarchy and order and all accepted conceptions of the hero handed down by cultural, religious and racist tradition."[42] In "Hymie's Bull," he translated this practice into explicitly political terms, crafting a new kind of transracial revolutionary folk hero. Ellison's story thus follows Marian Minus's injunction to black writers to comb the "legends, myths and ballads . . . in which Negroes have immortalized their culture heroes for those elements of universality" and to identify black folkloric figures "touched with the super-human, who reflect the aspirations and failures of all humanity."[43]

CRITERIA FOR INSTITUTIONS: TUSKEGEE AND HARLEM

A theory of institutional revolutionary leadership forms the final level of Ellison's 1930s Marxist problematic. When Ellison arrived at Tuskegee in 1933, he entered an institution dedicated to Booker T. Washington's accommodationist political paradigm. He would soon discard that paradigm by leaving Tuskegee for New York in 1936, where he would affiliate with another institution, the Communist Party. As a result of these two encounters, institutional critique is a priority of his work. When Wright turned to his Communist reader and, pointing at the Louis-inspired crowds, exclaims "*here's* the wild river that's got to be harnessed and directed," or when Wright offered Bigger Thomas as a lumpenproletarian figure possessed with the capacity for revolutionary action, he indicated the need of the party to recognize and administer such potential. This criterion also drives Ellison's analysis of ostensibly radical institutions.

The ability to link leaders and intellectuals with the masses is, for Gramsci, a distinguishing feature of Marxist institutions, which must "construct an intellectual-moral bloc which can make politically possible the intellectual progress of the mass and not only of small intellectual groups."[44] Revolutionary parties and organizations foster reciprocity between the spontaneous feelings and thoughts of the masses and the theoretical knowledge of informed leaders. Marxist intellectuals must theorize the "elementary passions of the people" by relating them to the terms of "the particular historical situation" and to a general Marxist worldview. The masses in turn contribute "passion" to the intellectuals and leaders, enabling the institution to move from theory to praxis. "In the absence of such a nexus" Gramsci warns, "the relations between the intellectual and the people-nation are, or are reduced to, relationships of a purely bureaucratic and formal order."[45] In the context of a Marxist critique of the African American leadership of the Communist Party, Ellison questions how revolutionary institutions can avoid becoming bureaucratic and provide the intellectual cohesion and strategic leadership capable of harnessing and exploiting the fluid possibilities of the social and the "passion," or agency, troped by the lumpen-folk.

In the spring of 1940, Ellison attended the Communist-backed National Negro Congress (NNC) in Washington, DC, where he was impressed by the passion of the black sharecroppers and workers in attendance. As he reports in *New Masses,* the delegates came to see if and how the institutional Communist left could advance their interests. Ellison describes the delegates as having already fashioned folk culture into a kind of anticapitalist agency: "They were people sure of their strength. . . . In many of the speeches I had heard the names Gabriel, Denmark Vesey, Harriet Tubman, Frederick Douglass. And in these mouths the names had a new meaning. And I suddenly realized that the age of the Negro hero had returned to American life." In the speech of one delegate, Ellison hears a moment of Gramscian catharsis: "all the violence that America has made our Negro heritage was flowing from him transformed into a will to change a civilization."[46]

Yet at the same time, he was skeptical that the party—particularly the Harlem Branch, whose leaders he and Wright knew—could recognize this source of potential. He wrote to Wright that the NNC was "the first real basis for *faith* in our revolutionary potentialities I have found," a faith that the black masses can correct the "stupidities of black CP leaders. Some morning they [the Communist leaders] will be awakened from their 'Marxist' fog by the people who think they are carrying out God's wishes when they fight for freedom, telling them 'Comrades, us dont want to disturb youall, but us thought youall would like to know that us got the revolution going like youall been talking about.'" Reminding Wright of his own conclusion to the 1935 Joe Louis article, Ellison writes of his report on the congress: "I guess what I am trying to say in the article ... is that the 'river' is harnessing *itself!*"[47] Ellison's comments suggest a general theory of the measure of any revolutionary party. That the masses grasp revolutionary consciousness in ideological terms of "God's wishes" doesn't make that consciousness false, since this subjective articulation expresses objective economic contradictions cathartically, in politically empowering terms. The danger Ellison describes is the blindness of institutional leaders to political opportunity when it emerges in new and unusual forms beyond their prescription— forms which, for a Marxist, might well be cultural or ideological, and articulated in idioms of the black folk rather than the international proletariat.

A few weeks prior to his letter about the NNC, Ellison describes to Wright a suggestion he's heard, in Communist circles, that writers should submit their manuscripts to the party for prepublication inspection. Ellison is open to the idea, but only "if the inspectors are people the writers can respect. However, I understand the suggestion originated in Harlem!"[48] Ellison doesn't renounce institutional supervision per se: committed writing could benefit from an active exchange between writer and party, but the Harlem CP, he suggests, would be unsuited to that exchange. His complaint suggests that his criticism of the Harlem leadership's political acuity stemmed from his experience as a party writer, and in 1940 Ellison was especially frustrated by what he saw as the failure of party leaders to properly read *Native Son*. Wright's novel was published on March 1, Ellison's twenty-seventh birthday. Ellison's remarks in May about the "stupidities of black CP leaders" derive from his ardent defense of Wright's novel against criticisms from within the Harlem Communist Party: he saw the literary inadequacy of these leaders as a symptom of a more general political inadequacy. Of all his intellectual efforts in the Depression period, his defense of *Native Son* most clearly develops his criteria for institutional effectiveness.

In a 1941 *New Masses* article, Ellison praised *Native Son* as "the first philosophical novel by an American Negro," a text that utilized modernist techniques in order to access "unlimited intellectual and imaginative possibilities." The novel's theoretical understanding of black life in modern America set it apart from previous black writing, which was "apologetic in tone and narrowly confined to the expression of Negro middle-class ideals."[49] For Ellison, *Native Son* was literature as philosophy and socially engaged theory rather than sentimental or didactic propaganda.

As I discussed in the previous chapter, *Native Son* explores the lumpenproletariat's unique capacity for revolutionary politics through Bigger Thomas's gradual self-recognition of his ability to act, to transcend racist and economic marginalization and distinguish himself as an individual capable of altering his environment. Through Bigger, Wright theorizes the subjective processes through which African Americans might attain revolutionary agency, and Ellison saw *Native Son* as compensating for Marxism's lack of a psychoanalytic or existential component, its "almost total failure . . . to treat human personality."[50] The capacity to transform one's situation is for Wright both the defining capacity of human subjectivity and the existential germ of the revolutionary impulse. In gradually discovering that capacity, Bigger simultaneously reclaims his humanity from its structural devaluation and reminds the reader that such devaluation can be actively challenged. Communist leaders, Wright's novel holds, must recognize and educate the impulsive mode of agency Bigger discovers. That the specific actions through which Bigger makes this discovery are ethically repugnant is Wright's challenge to both liberal *and* radical readers seeking to consume heroic political narratives with self-affirming pleasure—with the "consolation of tears," as Wright put it in "How 'Bigger' Was Born"[51]—rather than with the epistemological consideration appropriate for a "philosophical novel."

As I discuss below, Ellison's own fiction of the 1930s explores similar thematic and conceptual territory. He thus dedicated himself in 1940 to defending Wright's project to Harlem Communists who felt Wright distorted African Americans and the party. Ben Davis Jr. wrote a lengthy review in the *Sunday Worker* that especially irked Wright and Ellison. While mostly positive, Davis critiqued Wright for politically consequential representational inaccuracies: misrepresenting black people as "beaten and desperate," ignoring "the progressive developments among the Negro people," and failing to accurately document the cultural and political strength of the black masses and the antiracist efforts of the party.[52]

Wright was living in Mexico in the spring of 1940, and Ellison kept him updated on his efforts to defend the novel within Communist circles. "I have talked about the book, trying to answer attacks against it until I am weary."[53] They discussed criticism like Davis's as a sign of the party's inability to learn from revolutionary writing. Worried about the mimetic accuracy of Wright's representations, Communist leaders overlooked the novel's unorthodox insights. For example, Davis objected that the legal strategy Max uses in Bigger's trial is one no Communist lawyer would implement: "Max should have argued for Bigger's acquittal in the case, and should have helped stir the political pressure of the Negro and white masses to get that acquittal."[54] Davis, in his concern over how accurately Wright represented Communist legal activism, misses the connection of Bigger's guilt to his discovery of agency and corresponding refusal to cede responsibility for his actions.

Ellison sent Wright a copy of the *Baltimore Afro-American*'s review of *Native Son*, which found that the novel reinforced racist stereotypes, was gratuitously graphic in its representation of sex and violence, and needlessly inflammatory in its inclusion of racial slurs and other "curse words."[55] Ellison complained to Wright that "practically every garbled opinion expressed in the piece has been expressed by" Harlem party leaders Abner Berry and Theodore Basset, "both of whom should know better." Ellison ultimately doubted whether "cp leaders" really were "emancipated from bourgeois taboos."[56] In a later letter, Ellison asserted that they "refuse to see the revolutionary significance of Bigger and while professing to be revolutionaries they have yet to rid themselves of their wornout [sic] Christian ethics." These so-called revolutionaries are concerned with moral palatability: "They worry about whether you *justify* Bigger," and "fail to see that whats [sic] *bad* in Bigger from the point of view of bourgeois society is *good* from our point of view." In other words, they read the novel through a lens of moral and ethical judgment rather than Marxist analysis. And ironically, as Ellison writes, Bigger's actions and Max's speech lay bare the function of "the whole ethic of moral justification" as an ideological cover for an exploitative social system.[57] Bigger's agency invokes the contours of revolution as the rejection of that system in its entirety, but Communist objections show symptoms of a decidedly nonrevolutionary attachment to ideological elements of that system. Ellison declares that "Native Son [sic] shook the Harlem section to its foundation and some of the rot it has brought up is painful to smell."[58] That rot is the party's unconscious influence by the ideology of the present that it is supposed to be negating.

The insight of James Baldwin's later critique of *Native Son*—that its political agenda entails a dehumanizing distortion of black life that undercuts its ambition to portray Bigger's humanity—indicates that Ellison is too quick to discount the party's concerns, many of which anticipate Baldwin's, as bourgeois hang-ups.[59] But the logic of his defense of *Native Son* reveals a theory of institutional leadership, one that stresses the need to evaluate the revolutionary will of a given institution. A radical institution should be able to incorporate, without ideological blinders imposed by its own doctrine or by the dominant social order in which it's located, insights and practices gleaned from the fluidity—and in the case of *Native Son*, the illicit lumpenproletarian undercurrents—of American society.

Ellison's brief time among the rail-riding transients of the Depression helped shape his development of a theoretical project that uses lumpenproletarian life to triangulate the form of modern US society, principles and origins of revolutionary action, and criteria for institutional leadership. In *Tillman and Tackhead* and *Slick*, Ellison mines this problematic at length in order to explore the radical stakes of black lumpenproletarian experience. Both works try to figure out chances for revolutionary practice obtaining not in proletarian subjectivity or class position, but in the socially marginal position of African Americans during the Depression.

ELLISON'S DAYTON PERIOD: *TILLMAN AND TACKHEAD* AND *SLICK*

Ellison began writing *Tillman and Tackhead* and *Slick* in the winter of 1937–38 in Dayton, Ohio. Ellison had travelled to Dayton for his mother's funeral in October, and was forced to remain there until March, waiting for one of her life insurance policies to be paid. He and his brother Herbert struggled to make ends meet, hunting rabbits and quail to both eat and sell to local grocers.⁶⁰ They moved between temporary lodgings, at times sleeping in garages and shops, battling, in Rampersad's words, "hunger, cold, and homelessness."⁶¹ Yet Ellison was also able to use this period to, as he put it, focus his "full attention to the task of learning to write fiction."⁶² In Dayton, Ellison was relatively isolated from the Communist milieu of New York. He complained to Wright that he was unable to locate copies of the *New Masses* or *Daily Worker,* and that there was no radical political activity to be found anywhere.⁶³ He managed to write by borrowing office space, a typewriter, and paper from a local lawyer and Republican Party figure known to Marian Minus, and from an architect named Frank Sutton.⁶⁴ The two longer fictional works he began in Dayton, *Tillman and Tackhead* and *Slick,* reflect the circumstances of what Ellison called his "exile."⁶⁵ Both deal with protagonists who fall outside of established socioeconomic positions, and who must, like Ellison, shift on the illicit margins of social structures in order to survive. As Ellison took advantage of his poverty and limited resources in Dayton in order to write politically innovative fiction, his lumpenized characters access politically constructive knowledge and agency.

Tillman and Tackhead and *Slick* resemble Wright's Depression fiction in their themes and characterizations. According to Ellison, Wright found his Dayton work too similar to his own, and his anger at Ellison formed an early rift in their relationship: "I never showed him another piece of fiction," Ellison claimed.⁶⁶ Yet this similarity in both writers' 1930s work is inadequately understood if framed as a foreshadowing of their later break and the critical positioning of the two, by Cold War and Black Power-era critics, as polar alternatives for black fiction. Ellison and Wright were close during the 1930s in their understanding of Marxism's conceptual applicability to US and African American circumstances, and while Ellison was certainly influenced by Wright, he was never merely derivative. *Slick* resembles *Native Son* in its treatment of the education of a politically unconscious black male protagonist, yet Ellison was writing *Slick* at roughly the same time Wright worked on *Native Son:* Wright began drafting his novel in earnest in the summer of 1938.⁶⁷ Rather than seeing the Depression-era Ellison as laboring under the shadow of Wright

Winslow Homer, *The Gulf Stream*. 1899.
Oil on canvas, 28 1/8 x 49 1/8 in.
Catharine Lorillard Wolfe Collection, Wolfe Fund, 1906.
The Metropolitan Museum of Art,
http://www.metmuseum.org.

or struggling to find an authentic authorial identity, we should see him and Wright as coarticulators of a lumpenproletarian black Marxism.

Tillman and Tackhead is set in a club in Oklahoma City. The protagonist Tillman is one of the African American waiters who work at the club and who, as the story starts, are moving tables in preparation for dinner service. As they pass the open door of one of the club members' private rooms, another waiter, Tackhead, notices a painting of a black man hanging on the wall: "somebody done made a picture of a mose!" he exclaims in surprise.[68] Another waiter tries to get them to return to their labor, but Tillman leads them into the room to investigate the painting. From their comments, it's evident that the artwork in question is Winslow Homer's 1899 painting *The Gulf Stream*, which depicts a black seaman adrift and alone in a shipwrecked vessel, surrounded by threatening sharks and an oncoming storm. The water runs red with blood, suggesting the sharks have already devoured the man's crewmates. A ship appears in the far distance, but it's unclear whether it will come to the rescue. The man himself seems passive in the face of these dangers: one art critic describes his "stoic resignation to his fate."[69] Or as one of the waiters puts it, "That mose is tryin t play like he dont see them sharks."[70]

The waiters read the painting as a representation of black experience in America. One suggests that the central figure represents all black men, "The more Ah look at that mose the more he looks like a boy Ah usta know," while another notes the origins of the man's plight in racial oppression: "Wouldnt nobody but a white man put a mose in that fix." Tillman, who used to harbor ambitions of being an artist himself, reads the painting as an instance of art's complicity with racial rule. Since whites are "the only ones who paint," when a white man appears in a nautical-themed painting, he has "pretty gals sittin all ova im" or he's triumphantly wrangling a fish with "a fightin look on his face." However, "when white folks went t paint a colored man they put him out in a piece a boat with a bunch of sharks around him. And instead of havin im fight t git out, hes jus laying back on his behin n lookin out cross tha water like hes waitin fo somethin t happen." Tackhead defuses Tillman's comments with a joke about how the man is safe from the sharks, who "dont care fo no dark meat," and the rest of the men return to work.[71] Tillman, however, stays behind to study *The Gulf Stream* further.

According to Peter H. Wood, interpretations of *The Gulf Stream* that move beyond a purely formalist approach have often seen it as either a universal allegory of the human condition, or as a narrative illustration of the drama of shipwreck. Taking into account Homer's sympathy for African Americans and progressive racial views, and situating the painting within the racial struggles and discourses of the 1890s, Wood himself argues that *The Gulf Stream* encodes an allegorical protest against Jim Crow and the period's racial violence.[72] Tillman offers an illicit counter-reading, one that assigns a repressive sociopolitical function to the painting. As Tillman's comments indicate, the painting serves Jim Crow by fabricating essential natural differences between whites and blacks: the former are defined by mastery over their environment, and the latter as passive and powerless. The painting's place in the club room indicates its function. Like other paintings on the wall, it is set in a "rich [frame]" and

Tillman notices how "light from the chandelier played upon blue and red pigments" of the canvas: class rule both frames and animates the racial violence of the painting. *The Gulf Stream* aestheticizes and naturalizes the subservience of black working-class men like Tillman. "They said you didn't fight. That was what the picture was saying." If the painting reproduces the subservience of black viewers, achieved here when the other waiters laugh off the image and return to work, it also reproduces the power of white elites, who "probably laugh like hell" when they view it.[73] In this setting, the painting reifies the power arrangements of Jim Crow and capitalism.

Through a cathartic sequence of reflection, Tillman reapprehends those objective arrangements as an occasion of subjective action. He begins by recognizing the falsity of the representation: it's not that, as a black subject, "you didnt fight," but that "you fought yourself into not fighting them. They dont know that. . . . Theyll never know that. When they know that itll be the last thing they'll ever know." When the elevator door in the outer hall opens, Tillman ducks deeper into the room to conceal himself. No one emerges from the elevator, but his physical response dramatizes both the illicit nature of his study and his commitment to it. And that instinctual movement of simultaneous self-preservation and resistance shifts his understanding of *The Gulf Stream*: "From where he stood the colors seemed brighter. He studied the Negroes face and the muscles of his arms." The apparent passivity of the figure's expression conceals the actual power lying dormant in his arms. The painting now subtly reveals the agency of black men that is contained but not cancelled by the enforced subservience black men must perform to survive under Jim Crow. This recognition makes Tillman reconnect with that agency inside himself, and the painting shifts from a pronouncement of white class rule to a catalyst for action: "The painting stirred something deep within him and a feeling of bitterness grew. As he watched the painting something vague stirred within him, which for a long time had tried to die away. Something he had tried to help die."[74]

Ellison's theoretical understanding of the folk here frames a sophisticated rendering of Tillman's conflicted consciousness. Tillman's irrepressible "something" echoes Wright's description of "that fluid something that's like iron" contained in "the heart of the Negro," and expresses Ellison's use of the folk as naming an irrepressible quality of human perseverance, desire, and action. Tillman describes the "something" as "that clear, sharp, penetrating feeling, this thing" that responds to the aesthetic beauty of the world about him. In his youth, the discovery of this "something" had led him to want to be an artist, an ambition thwarted by Jim Crow. Barred from art by racial rule, he can find no outlet for his aesthetic desires in the blues or African American Christianity, since both form the culture of an insular "black world" that is also defined by Jim Crow. "Whenever this thing rose up he became lost between two worlds, one too narrow and the other refusing him his needs." The double consciousness imposed on him by racial hierarchy gives rise to a potent revolutionary "desire to create a new world, a world which he had not the strength to imagine."[75]

If living under Jim Crow requires Tillman to routinely suppress that desire, the painting now brings it out as a motive force of agency, one that Ellison describes in terms of criminal violence, liberatory creation, and revolutionary action:

> Standing before the canvas he experienced a longing to paint such a picture. But with the Negro fighting some enemy more human and more defeatable than the sea. He became gripped with a high sense of exhilaration, as when . . . he . . . fought, watching the face of his opponent change shape under the blows of his fists. Then his whole being seemed caught up and thrown into a region where he stood tall and free.

With a knife, Tillman slashes the painting into "colored shreds."[76] Symbolically, his act has both negative and positive political valences. It represents a liberation of the human agency visually suppressed in the resigned black victim and destroys the order of Jim Crow naturalized by the painting. It's also an act of creation, giving an outward, if negative, representation of a new world defined by the shredding of race and class oppression.

Through this criminal act of vandalism, Tillman feels he has entered a new existence on the margins of Jim Crow's familiar structures of racial and class power: "he had destroyed the picture of a Negro as white folks wanted him; even if in doing so he had suddenly found himself in a strange region where nothing was secure or familiar." Tillman has deproletarianized himself and entered the ranks of the lumpenproletariat, those who no longer belong to any defined socioeconomic strata. He recognizes that he has redrawn the significance of the lone black figure in *The Gulf Stream*: "Now he was adrift in a current which swept in a direction he feared, yet a

[121]

vague feeling of power pulsed deep beneath his dread of the journey."[77] He has painted his own image of black subjectivity, has undergone a cathartic transformation from the object of exploitation to the empowered subject of resistance. As discussed in chapter 1, the trope of the rag here suggests the liberatory, open-ended potential figured in lumpenproletarian experience. By turning the canvas to rags, Tillman opens exploitable gaps in the composed, framed articulation of Jim Crow rule.

His sense of power is quickly replaced by fear. Leaving the private room, he returns to the work of preparing for dinner service, hoping his act isn't discovered before he can get away at the end of his shift. Returned to his proper socioeconomic location in the black working class, Tillman once again resembles the passive figure in the picture he's just shredded. As he drapes a white cloth over one of the tables, it "billowed up and fluttered, settling down as he gave it a jerk and pulled the crease skillfully to the center."[78] The image of the tablecloth is here aligned with that of both the canvas and a sail: the routinized labor Tillman performs contrasts sharply with the rebellion enacted against the canvas, while his setting of the cloth invokes the labor of a seaman raising a sail. In the wake of his symbolic rebellion, Tillman has returned to the subservient position of the black sailor in *The Gulf Stream*.

Tillman's cathartic response to the painting is later replayed in a direct confrontation with Jim Crow. At one point during dinner, Tackhead again draws Tillman's attention to an unusual sight, this time directing him to the window of a hotel across the alley from the club. He spies the hotel's black bellboy and a white woman having sex, "framed in the window" like Homer's canvas. Tillman, who has witnessed the devastation of the 1921 Tulsa race riot, is angered by this illicit coupling, afraid that it will incite a similar mass lynching if discovered. Tackhead reassures him: the white women of the hotel are "high-class whores" who are "crazy" about the bellboy, and their servicing of wealthy white men grants them and the bellboy a degree of freedom from the racial and sexual prohibitions of Jim Crow. "Ain no cops gonna bother em," Tackhead explains.[79] Tillman discovers a lumpenproletarian underworld existing in the interstices of, and defying the normative operations of, white supremacy. He glimpses a measure of freedom and desire afforded by the overdetermined complexity of Jim Crow society.

Tillman then waits on a white couple who provoke him with racist remarks. When the couple return to their table from dancing, the woman "[brushes]" against Tillman, prompting him to recall his earlier fears about the scene in the window: "this crackerd raise hell if he could see" the white prostitute and black bellboy. Well aware of the violent prohibition of physical contact between black men and white women, Tillman's unnoticed contact with the white woman reminds him of his social status, which recalls that of the sailor in *The Gulf Stream*. "The painting and window were becoming mixed in his mind." If the window depicts resistance to Jim Crow through a defiance of its codes, the content of the painting reminds him that white racist narratives of such illicit activity form the alibi and occasion for the subservience-inducing violence of Jim Crow. Tillman next hears that the vandalism of the painting has been discovered and "had the sensation of falling. The painting came back to him vividly, giving him a sense of water and isolation."[80] Like his sense of the interracial coupling in the window, his destruction of the painting passes, in his consciousness, between being an emboldening act of resistance and a frightening infraction.

Agency and powerlessness, resistance and repression, are thus "mixed" in Tillman's consciousness when the man he's serving accuses him of stealing his companion's purse. The man tries to attack Tillman, who protests his innocence, knowing that the charge could incite lynching and riot. He notices the window again, and he "became sharply conscious of his blackness. You were all of one miserable piece. If the Negro in the window was caught, other Negroes would suffer; just as he was suffering because someone had stolen." As the man continues to hit Tillman, the "shipwrecked Negro flashed through his mind" but now, rather than signifying a passive "sense of water and isolation," the painting strengthens his resolve to resist victimization. The "thing inside him," that desire for a better world he has to suppress in order to survive, finally escapes as action, and he slashes the man with his knife. "He felt a strong sense of power, he was slashing the painting again." His earlier fears about the bellboy's irresponsibility are supplanted by the recognition that, under Jim Crow, black masculinity itself is criminalized: black men are "of one miserable piece," their existence a crime regardless of whether they violate racist sexual taboos, destroy white-owned artworks, or commit theft. This recognition changes the nature of criminal resistance for Tillman from reckless behavior (sleeping with white women, destroying the private property of the club) to the necessary

[123]

means of reclaiming black humanity. As he later reflects, "the knife had cut through a mold into which he had been forced and he had stood free and experienced for the first time a sharp sense of his manhood."⁸¹ The story has built to this cathartic redefinition of objective structural powerlessness as subjective agency: in a social system in which blackness is criminalized, criminal action ceases to be merely for private or personal advantage, and instead becomes collective and political.

After this act, Tillman is able to escape the club through two strategies. First, he finds the switchbox and cuts off electricity to the building. Second, he encounters Breck, the club's bellboy, who gives Tillman his uniform. Tillman "heard the rustle of cloth" as Breck takes off his jacket to give him: the sail-like tablecloth that earlier, like *The Gulf Stream*, signified his racial and economic subjugation, is now cathartically resignified as a means of escape from that subjugation.⁸² Taking advantage of the dark to elude the white owner's searchers and obscure his own identity, he uses his disguise to convince Pop, an elderly employee of the club, that he's a bellboy the club's owner has sent to the hotel across the alley for tools to restore the electricity. The owner has ordered that no one can leave the building until Tillman has been found, but Pop lets him go anyway. The escape sequence allegorizes the revolutionary stakes of Tillman's act. In defending himself against the white man, he has momentarily cut off and interrupted the operating "power" of Jim Crow. In the darkness and freedom that follow in the wake of that interruption, Breck and Pop are also moved to violate the rules of the Jim Crow club. Tillman's individual act thus inspires collective black agency. By escaping in the garb of a bellboy, Tillman performs a symbolic re-creation of himself: he is no longer the passive, working-class black seaman in *The Gulf Stream* resigned to his circumstances, but the bellboy in the window who refuses to accept and who illicitly challenges the orders of white supremacy. His act provides him with an escape from his place in a repressive socioeconomic system into the possible freedom of lumpenproletarian social margins.

Tillman returns to the home he shares with his mother. He knows that she too will be wounded when she hears of his act, dismayed that he has not been able to accommodate himself to Jim Crow: "He had to drive the knife home again, even into mom." His act violently rejects Jim Crow in its entirety, including the limited hopes it provides the black community. Tillman tells her he had no choice but to fight back if he was to reclaim his humanity: "Ah had t fight t live," he explains, "n now Ah got to go on fighting and running." He hops a freight train away from Oklahoma City, entering the socially unfixed fluidity of lumpenproletarian life. "He belonged to a different world now, a world he had created with his knife."[83] This ending is ironic: alone on a freight train, Tillman has come again to resemble the sailor adrift in *The Gulf Stream*. Yet unlike that sailor, Tillman has created his own circumstances, endowing them with the possibility for freedom and self-definition he saw in his glimpse of the lumpenproletarian underworld framed in the hotel window. Tillman's act isn't literally revolutionary, yet by destroying the "mold" of black subjectivity depicted in *The Gulf Stream*, a mold which Jim Crow enforces and on which it depends, Tillman's vandalism allegorizes the stakes of revolution. Furthermore, the narrative enables Ellison to depict the turns of consciousness through which political agency can be realized by the subject caught within a social system dedicated to suppressing that subject's humanity. *Tillman and Tackhead* is a tale of the political possibilities inhering in lumpenproletarianization, a story of how freedom, dignity, and action are accessed by the subject who drops out of his stable socioeconomic and ideologically codified position into the margins and interstices of the social.

Ellison also wrote *Slick* in Dayton, and while he excerpted an episode from the text for his first published work of fiction, "Slick Gonna Learn" (1939),[84] he never finished the novel. *Slick* details the experiences of Slick Williams, a recently laid-off African American worker in an unspecified Northern city. Needing to support his pregnant wife Callie and his two children, and owing money to his white landlord Snodgrass, Slick is strained financially. And while Slick is at first oblivious to this development, the workers at his former factory have gone on strike and the city is embroiled in class struggle. When Callie falls ill from a pregnancy complication, Slick must resort to gambling in a dice game with the black pimp Bostic to win money to pay for a doctor. He loses, and pleads with Bostic to lend him the money. Bostic replies by suggesting Slick pimp Callie to raise the funds. Slick attacks Bostic, cutting his face with a bottle in the ensuing melee. When a white cop intervenes to break up the fight, Slick impulsively punches him in the face, an action he knows should seal his fate in a racist social system.

Here Ellison juxtaposes an orthodox Marxist critique of the lumpenproletariat with his own revisionary appropriation, contrasting the realistic and romantic valences of the concept described in chapter 1. Bostic, complicit with capitalism in denying Slick the material resources he needs, references the orthodox account of the lumpenproletariat as co-opted by, structurally aligned with, and emulating capitalist exploitation. Before Slick punches the cop, he confuses his "white face" with that of Bostic's, as well as with that of the white foreman who laid him off at the factory in order to "make jobs for white folks." Bostic is a black underworld operator, yet he participates in the socioeconomic oppression of white supremacy.[85] Slick's criminal actions, attacking Bostic and the cop as equivalent "faces" of that oppression, will thus induct him into a socially marginal mode of lumpenproletarian existence infused with politically productive possibilities of agency and knowledge.

Slick is arrested, and in jail he has a dream about fighting in World War I. In his dream, however, Slick and his fellow black troops are led by Joe Louis to fight not the Germans but a giant white figure wielding a noose and leading white troops. Referencing Wright's 1935 essay on Louis, the scene figures the agency of African Americans through reference to Louis's folk status as an avatar of black action. Just like the South Side celebrants who were encouraged by Louis's victory over Max Baer, Slick dreams he takes on Louis's power himself: "He was Joe himself! He had a machine gun."[86] Ellison adopts Wright's reading of Louis's fight and draws on the experience of blacks in World War I to underscore their collective agency, but at this point, Slick's dream of violent resistance remains only a dream that indexes his real-world helplessness. Furthermore, it is not politically informed: like Jake Jackson in Wright's *Lawd, Today!*, he simply dreams that all whites are his enemies and all blacks his allies. He longs not for transformative struggle but for race war. Slick's dream thus resembles the fantasies of fascist and nationalist power that initially captivate Bigger Thomas. Like *Native Son*, *Slick* will explore how a passionate yet politically unconscious propensity toward action can be translated into revolutionary politics.

As Slick is brought to court, Ellison describes how, somewhere below the jail/courthouse, a building dedicated to white supremacy, "a motor was humming . . . causing the building to shake at regular intervals." This technological symbol indicates the infrastructural determination of Jim Crow: capitalism is the "motor" of racial oppression. Yet it also hints at the irregularity of that determination. The social may shake at *regular* intervals due to its determination by the economic as a structure in dominance, but the possibility of *irregular* shaking, the disruption of dominance in the social occasioned by the unpredictability of economic overdetermination, is foreshadowed. That irregularity occurs when Slick enters the courtroom. Slick knows the rules of Jim Crow and expects to suffer, but economic class conflict disrupts those rules. The judge, not wishing to draw extra attention to the town's legal apparatus in the midst of the factory strike, lets Slick go. "He had knocked the hell out of a white man and gotten away with it! The law had let him go. With this thought, something seemed to surge in his mind." In an act that recalls the inherent, folk-inflected prowess he accessed in his dream, Slick challenges the cop who arrested him: "Someday . . . Yuh gonna learn to leave colored folks erlone."[87] In retaliation, a group of cops later kidnap Slick and drive him out to the country to lynch him. However, en route they receive a radio call summoning them to disperse strikers at the factory. After dealing him several blows, the cops let Slick escape, and he is picked up by a white truck driver. Noting the poor weather and Slick's injuries, the driver is genuinely concerned for him, and the episode implies that Slick must learn to overcome his suspicion of all whites and see white workers like the driver as his objective allies against Jim Crow capitalism.

Ellison deploys technology in this episode to once again figure the emergence of political resistance from the ontology of social form. The "motor" beneath the jail/courthouse first references a straightforward Marxist analysis of Jim Crow law as not a premodern or regionally specific social order, but one determined by technologically advanced modern capitalism. Extended by Ellison as the motor of the police car, the motor also figures the extralegal violence of Jim Crow. Yet because the police car also contains a radio, the device that here ties Jim Crow to the overdetermination that *interrupts* its repression, the car can be cathartically refigured as an instrument of revolutionary action, the driver's truck. "A man sure needs a car," the driver tells Slick, hinting at the necessity of politics to overcome his current abused condition.[88] Technology passes from an objective and oppressive force to a subjective and empowering vehicle. With this cathartic sequence of technological symbols, Ellison indicates how the complexity of social form gives rise to political opportunity.

Slick returns home but still needs money for Callie's worsening condition. The next day, he goes downtown and sees a car full of white men returning from a hunting trip. He is reminded that he has hunted before when out of work, and had made money selling quail (which the law prohibits hunting) to rich whites under the table. Slick also recalls that last year, he had hunted with Dr. Baldridge, a white doctor who had offered to help Slick if he ever needed it. Slick visits Baldridge, who arranges for Callie to be taken to a Catholic hospital without charge. This is an act of off-market exchange, as Baldridge expects Slick to bring him a pheasant in payment.[89] Hunting for this black market is the novel's form of lumpenproletarian practice or hustling, the illegal measures to which those who fall out of economic production are forced to resort.

The Catholic hospital is a symbolic rendering of the complexity of American society. The novel suggests that it's the Catholic specificity of the hospital that makes it willing to accept Callie: "they says theys good to colored," Slick notes.[90] When he later visits Callie in the hospital, he notices multiple statues of the Virgin Mary in the halls. For one, the statue signals the temporal heterogeneity of the hospital to the reader: this is a modern institution, but one containing residual cultural overtones, and the contradiction between the modern and the residual seems to partially account for why Catholic hospitals are "good to colored." The differential element in this singular hospital, Catholicism, distances it from the organizing power relations of modernity, as Slick notes that one statue of the Virgin has "so many flowers it dont even smell like a hospital." One statue resembles Callie: "Mary had a sweet expression on her face too. Callie had had that funny sweet look when she had the first baby."[91] The statues speak to a shared experience that transcends racial, cultural, and temporal boundaries. Manifesting that unelaborated human universalism implies a challenge to systems like Jim Crow and capitalism that define, divide, and hierarchize subjects, and the hospital figures the possibility of sociopolitical transcendence. Slick's ability to hunt while unemployed, Baldridge's willingness to help in spite of racial difference, and the willingness of a Catholic hospital to work outside the rules of Jim Crow, all combine to offer Callie a chance at survival.

Yet the Catholic hospital, like the social, is by no means free from racial and class rule. Initially, Slick is optimistic about the hospital because it is modern and will offer superior care. "He hoped Callie would not be afraid to go to the hospital. Last year Tom Slade wouldnt go when the doctor told him to and two days later his appendix had burst and killed him. Folks oughta git outa that kind stuff. This heahs a 'enlightened age,' he thought, remembering a phrase from a newspaper." But even though he decries this apparent antimodern prejudice among blacks, he then intuitively grasps its legitimacy. "Hope that ambulance don come [for Callie] too soon," he worries, because he recalls one night when he came upon an ambulance parked in the street. Its motor had broken down, and the attendants were trying to repair it. "As he came along side he saw a woman lying inside with her throat cut. It had been strange. The street silent, the attendants working silently and the big black woman framed in the glass like a picture, bleeding on the white sheets."[92]

The scene recalls the framed image of the black sailor in *The Gulf Stream,* and offers a similar revelation. When the operations of modern society are interrupted, when the ambulance motor breaks down, Slick gets a glimpse of their ulterior purpose. This "strange" memory of his suggests how, as institutions of modern America, hospitals are implicated in the social death of black subjects. Callie initially fears the hospital, citing the real possibility of being subjected to forced sterilization: "Aw lawd, they gonna cut me up. Ah know it. That's whut they [do] to colored folks. They gon let them student doctahs practist on me!"[93] And while the hospital at first treats Callie, Ellison's notes seem to suggest that he considered having Callie die because the Catholic hospital refuses to perform an abortion to save her life.[94] The hospital is thus contradictory in multiple ways: as an institution, it offers modern medical care to all but also participates in a social system that routinely threatens black life. Catholicism, as its organizing ideology, both enables and delimits its ability to protect black life. The statues of the Virgin Mary symbolize a shared humanity that transcends racial stratification, but they are also white. The hospital thus represents American society itself as an overdetermined structure in dominance operating to maintain class and racial rule while still containing internal inconsistencies that make it possible to conceive of and enact resistance.

After Callie enters the hospital, Slick is visited by his white landlord, Snodgrass. Slick threatens Snodgrass with a fire poker when he asks Slick for rent: "I oughta take this poker and whip yo fucking head. You was trying to come in my house, thats what you was trying to do. You caint do that to me. Long as I'm renting this lousy shack dont you never let me even hear tell of you tryin that agin." As with Bostic and the white cop, Slick again spontaneously defies racial and class authority. Slick defends "my house" as if he owned rather than rented it. By claiming it as *his* house, he expropriates the security and sustainability that capitalism and white supremacy have expropriated from him. Slick acts impulsively, but his acts have revolutionary significance.

Slick is terrified, afterwards, by his response to Snodgrass. He rightly fears retaliation, but he also cannot understand why he did it:

> Any other time he would have hidden his anger and made an excuse about the rent money. He would have acted safe, as his life had taught him Negroes had to act. . . . It would have been like going to the grocery and asking the man for a dimes worth of sausage and the man giving you the sausage and you laying the dime on the counter and walking out of the grocery and forgetting it. But since he had been taken for a ride by the policemen he could no longer trust himself.

Slick's personal safety and the operation of Jim Crow both depend on his passive acceptance of standardized codes of cross-racial and cross-class interaction. But since he escaped legal and extralegal victimization due to the overdetermination of Jim Crow repression, he feels he has "washed away his self-control. . . . And now he had to *think* to protect himself." Slick acted out of ignorance—he doesn't know why he punched one cop and challenged another, or why he threatened Snodgrass—because, like Bigger's in *Native Son,* his actions are the precondition for knowledge. Slick can and must now think critically because he has "stepped outside the iron ring of action placed upon Negroes" by impulsively defying a social system designed to stifle any cognition by making him "act safe."[95]

Ellison read psychology in an attempt to give Slick's impulses a scientific grounding. He was especially influenced by William H. Sheldon's 1936 study *Psychology and the Promethean Will,* from which he copied multiple passages.[96] Sheldon identified the "Promethean conflict" as a conflict between two instincts of the human character: "The Promethean element of consciousness is the forward straining dream of a better world. When dominant, this element gives rise to radical idealism. The Epimethean or backward straining element is the wish for safety and for the security of righteousness. Epimetheanism is conservative idealism."[97] Sheldon primarily applies this distinction to the mind's engagement with religion; Ellison adapts it as a model for the revolutionary stakes of human action. When Slick challenges Snodgrass, he renounces the Epimethean prioritizing of safety and security and makes a Promethean gesture for a "better world." Sheldon's vocabulary allows Ellison to ascribe a political dimension to untutored instinct. As Barbara Foley writes, Ellison gleaned from Sheldon how "the universals of myth provide access to a dialectical psychology that maps the conflicts within individuals along the axes of contradiction in society at large."[98]

Two characters, the proletarian activist Liles Jackson and the Communist organizer Booker Smalls, seek to equip Slick with the sociopolitical cognition his Promethean impulse has enabled him to access. At the local pool hall, Liles commends Slick for his assault on Bostic: "I'm just naturally polite to prizefighters and guys like that," he jokes. Liles's comment transforms the novel's earlier invocation of a prizefighter. In Slick's dream, Joe Louis was the avatar of black strength in a race war. Liles suggests that such strength was more appropriately directed toward Bostic, the black pimp who, by refusing Slick a loan and suggesting that Slick pimp Callie, enacted the racial and class violence of Jim Crow. The struggle through which Slick's problems can be solved is not waged against the white race, but against Jim Crow and capitalism, and Liles urges Slick to join the interracial striking workers. He speaks to the need for blacks to translate empowering black cultural practices into revolutionary struggle: "Nigguhs *been* knowing how to out smart white folks in little things. Now its time to learn to out smart em in the big things."[99] In this scene, lumpenproletarian experience—Slick's exteriorization from production, his delving into the underworld, and his acts of criminal defiance—is not presented in orthodox Marxist terms as a mode of false consciousness that must be transcended. Rather, Liles indicates that it can furnish the very kernel of revolutionary consciousness and proletarian solidarity.

The final episode of *Slick* is Slick's encounter with Booker Smalls, a black Communist intellectual. As Slick walks the streets one night, he finds himself pursued by police for violating a curfew imposed due to the strike. In his flight, he breaks into the Abraham Lincoln Republican Club, a room above a drugstore.[100] In this socially marginal and politically suggestive social site—accessed through lumpenproletarian ingenuity manifested as the criminal defiance of social rules (the curfew, private property)—he encounters Booker. While Booker aims to bring theoretical clarification to Slick's experiences in their long conversation, he also learns from Slick. Together, they form a Gramscian "intellectual-moral bloc," synthesizing Booker's theories with Slick's experience. Their relationship models the ideal form of the revolutionary party as an institutional cohesion of agential passion and theoretical insight.

Booker explains the connection between Slick's experiences with the police and the strike, so that for the first time, Slick realizes that "his life had been saved by the radio call, by the pickets." He performs an act of cognitive analysis, connecting, through the technological mechanism of the radio, the immediacy of his experience to its larger structural causation. So it seems at first that Booker will be a political mentor who brings theoretical light to Slick's experiences. But then they start discussing hospitals. Slick, based on his experiences with the Catholic hospital, thinks a hospital is "bout the best place to be in the whole damn town." With no work available, and with the kinship structures of the Southern folk negated by Northern industrialization, Slick sees the hospital as the only place blacks can receive aid. Booker objects and tells the story of how Bessie Smith died after suffering a car accident and being refused treatment at a whites-only hospital in Memphis. Booker condemns hospitals as mere apparatuses of Jim Crow rule, and he denounces blacks' reliance on them as an unconscious accession to their own social death: "we'll have to keep dying like Bessie until we learn that they dont want us in the hospitals." Slick concurs, but then tells him about Callie being cared for in the Catholic hospital. Booker is taken aback and apologizes. "Thass allright," Slick responds, "Yuh didnt know nothin bout it."[101] On one level, this is merely a failure of etiquette and consideration on Booker's part. But on another, Slick's comment that Booker "didnt know nothin bout it" indicates how Callie's admission to the hospital complicates Booker's understanding of the form of American society, bringing to light the heterogeneity and inconsistency that complicate its functional domination. Slick provides an experiential corrective to Booker's theory, offering the lesson foregrounded by Ellison's Marxism: change and opportunity can happen *because* of disjunctures between racial and economic dominance and social complexity.

Eventually, their conversation turns to the lumpenproletariat. Slick tells Booker his plans to make a living hunting illegal game and selling it on the black market, which leads Booker to recall hunting in his youth. "We were poorer that winter than any I can remember and that was the winter I had the most fun." Slick understands: "That was because of the hunting. . . . You caint beat hunting for sport. If I was well off that's all

I'd ever do." Here, lumpenproletarian subsistence is symbolically transformed from desperation to potential. Slick's illicit survival method, romantically amplified by Booker's memories, foreshadows the pleasure and possibility of activity liberated from material need. The freedom of the lumpenproletariat from the economic mandate to labor, a freedom that enables creative practical activity like hunting for a black market, prefigures the freedom of all in postcapitalist society, when labor will no longer be a matter of necessity. Booker agrees to Slick's proposal that they hunt together to make a living. "This will be like history repeating itself for me," he exclaims, referencing his childhood. But the words immediately remind him of the famous opening of *The Eighteenth Brumaire:* "Hegel remarks somewhere that all facts and personages of great importance in world history occur, as it were, twice. He forgot to add: the first time as tragedy, the second as farce." Marx, he tells Slick, "meant that the first time an incident occurred in history it was tragic, like death. But the next time it happened it was foolish and something to laugh at, like Mussolini who tries to play Julius Caesar." Slick asks him what that has to do with him and hunting. Booker responds, "I dont know yet."[102]

In his subsequent effort to puzzle out that connection, he recasts the place of the lumpenproletariat within Marxist thought. He begins by telling Slick about Marx. Slick's false consciousness makes him resistant. He is suspicious of Marx because "them Reds" like him, and because "he was a Jew wasnt he?" Booker educates Slick not by dictating over his ideological confusions, but by comparing Marx to Frederick Douglass. Both were brilliant and eager to fight oppression on the international level. Booker speculates that Douglass "might have met Marx in Europe when he met many of the other well known revolutionists." Booker connects Douglass and Marx to Slick through a shared impulse toward action. Douglass, he explains, "was . . . a guy like you: mad and wanting to fight." Douglass convinced Lincoln to arm blacks in the Civil War, and Booker describes the fight of blacks against the Confederates in Marx's terms for the revolutionary struggles of the proletariat. Slick is impressed, both newly receptive to Marx and newly aware of his own agency: "It makes you feel proud. You can respect a guy like old Frederick Douglass." Booker underscores the comparison by stating that Douglass and Marx resembled each other: "They both looked like lions. If you go down to the library and ask for pictures of them you'll see that they both have big heads, thick manes

[133]

of hair, with large beards and bushy eyebrows. And in the pictures I've seen of Marx he was almost as dark as a Negro." Booker's account causes Slick, much like Tillman after viewing *The Gulf Stream*, to "feel that he was remembering some long forgotten, necessary thing."[103] By imagining Marx and Douglass as both racially black, Booker seeks to empower Slick with a Marxism and a black political tradition both characterized by the lion-like strength of individuals who, like Slick himself, are "mad and wanting to fight." Booker here performs the work of creative leadership that Ellison requires of revolutionary institutions.

Booker explains that his own knowledge of Marx and Douglass comes from an inherent political impulse, from seeking out others who felt the need to combat racist dehumanization as strongly as he did. Those others, he explains, were not traditional African American bourgeois leaders, who are radically unlike Marx and Douglass: "they dont have guts and they dont have hate and they have no yearning deep down in them for change, or for real freedom." Those with Marx and Douglass's guts, hate, and the desire for change are the black lumpenproletariat—"those who sing the blues, shoot crap, drink corn, and fight with razors and tell white folks to keep their distance"—and the Communists.[104] This is a dramatic revision of Marx's understanding of the lumpenproletariat's political tendencies. For Booker, black lumpenproletarian figures with no place in and thus no investment in the extant social order are not self-interested and open to bribery by the ruling class, but, because of their total exteriorization, possess a powerful desire for social change, a desire productively harnessed by Communist activism.

Booker then realizes what his spontaneous citation of *The Eighteenth Brumaire* had to do with hunting. When he hunted for survival as a child, it was "tragic" because he didn't understand the sociopolitical causation of poverty behind that necessity. But now it's a farce, since he sees how he has been forced again, by racial and economic oppression, to this measure. He understands it not as fate, but as the consequence of a socioeconomic system. "When you see it as something that people could stop if only they would and they dont then its a farce," he tells Slick. Slick objects that "a man cain do nothing bout being out of work." To which Booker responds: "You could if you had enough people who wanted to stop it badly enough."[105] Here, the lumpenproletarian necessity of hustling, of hunting for survival, incites not, as classical Marxism would hold, false consciousness or reaction, but revolutionary consciousness. Booker here exemplifies the ideal analytical work of a revolutionary institution in his ability to recast fate as agency, objective conditions as subjective political resources. Booker connects Ellison's theory of political possibility with his theory of the structure of American society, rendering the latter not as a set of given oppressive conditions, but as a farce in which the big joke is that Jim Crow capitalism, for all its oppressive power, is also fissured, inconsistent, irregular, and disruptable.

Ellison did not continue the narrative past this point, but this scene serves as a logical climax, since Booker and Slick's conversation synthesizes the novel's conceptual and political themes. Though incomplete, *Slick* offers the fullest theoretical explication of Ellison's 1930s Marxism, which conceptualized revolutionary action in relation to both the possibilities inherent in the ontology of American society and the proper functioning of revolutionary institutions.

4

PROSTITUTES, DELINQUENTS, AND FOLK HEROES

Margaret Walker's Lumpenproletariat

Although her career on the Depression-era left is less well known than that of Richard Wright or even Ralph Ellison, Margaret Walker was committed both to Communist activism and Marxist thought in the 1930s, and she was an active member of the Chicago literary left. However, in later years she was circumspect about this involvement. In a 1991 interview, Walker expressed her surprise to be included in *Writing Red*, a 1987 anthology of Depression-era women writers on the left.

> I said to someone, once, "I didn't know I was that radical. I never published in any left-wing magazines. They wouldn't have me. I published in *Crisis.*" They said, "Yes, and that was black, wasn't it? But it was considered red, too." I didn't realize that, but I did know that was the decade of socially conscious writers. And that is where I belong.[1]

Here, Walker's reluctance to admit her inclusion in the canon of 1930s leftism is in part inaccurate: for instance, her claim that she only published in the NAACP journal *Crisis* is belied by the fact that she did indeed publish a short story—"The Red Satin Dress," discussed below—in *The New Anvil*, a "red" proletarian magazine. She also published poetry in the single 1937 issue of *New Challenge*, a black left journal aligned, in no small part by Richard Wright's editorial work, with the Communist movement. In part because of Walker's reluctance, and in part because much of her poetry and fiction of the period was never published, scholarship has generally neglected her 1930s leftism: Carolyn J. Brown's recent biography, for example, does not cover Walker's involvement with the Communist left.[2]

Walker's admission above that she nonetheless "belong[s]" in the ranks of Depression-era committed writers enables a new approach to Walker scholarship, one that recovers her role as one of the decade's innovators of Marxist thought from feminist and African American cultural perspectives. First, we should note that her institutional involvement with the Communist left was sincere and multifaceted. She was close with Wright in this period, and his influence and encouragement deepened her interest in Marxism and Communist politics. Walker joined the Young Communist League and then the Communist Party in Chicago in 1937, where she was a member of the Writers Unit and attended the party's Workers' School.[3] As an employee of the WPA Federal Writers Project, Walker was acquainted with left writers like Nelson Algren and Jack Conroy, and she participated in a planning meeting for Conroy and Algren's *The New Anvil*.[4] She attended Communist rallies, spoke to a meeting of African American members of the Young Communist League about proletarian literature, and chaired a "practice course in Creative Writing" at the Workers' School.[5]

Beyond such institutional involvements, Walker was also committed to Marxist theory. Her letters to Wright testify to her effort to study Marxism and incorporate it in her work. In September of 1937, she announced her interest in attending lectures on "Dialectical Materialism" and "Marxist-Leninism" [sic] offered at the Worker's School.[6] She later asserted her progress in her study of "Communism and Marxism" and "the relation between the two and my work," telling Wright that "I have begun to see all life around me with a clarity that almost stumps me."[7]

Yet in a November 1937 letter, she admitted a certain frustration with her study of classical Marxism: "I haven't done well with the Dialectical Materialism at all. I get a fair understanding of the fundamental laws but I don't think, nor act, nor reason dialectically."[8] I propose to read this admission not as evidence that her interest in Marxism was superficial, or merely performed to impress Wright, but as an indication that her engagement with Marxism was of a revisionary nature. In an unpublished poem from the 1930s, "Radical Revolutionary," Walker defines the essence of revolutionary activity as epistemological revision. The poem's speaker describes "My way of breaking brackets from accepted facts / My way of willingness to learn another way."[9] Her comment about dialectical materialism is typed in the margin of her letter to Wright, a fitting indication of how Walker's engagement with Marxism during the 1930s would expand and reshape Marxist protocols from their margins, from the perspective of the lumpenproletarian figures and practices excluded from Marxism's consideration. Like Wright and Ellison, Walker was familiar with the tenets of Marxist thought but nonetheless used her written work to craft an African American innovation of Marxism that, like Wright's and Ellison's, turned around the concept and figure of the lumpenproletariat.

In a 1938 letter to Wright, Walker discusses her in-progress novel *Goose Island*, which examines "the problem of Juvenile delinquency" in the titular North Side Chicago slum. The key moment in realizing how to approach the problem, she claims, was realizing its structural economic determination: "the system breeds slums," she notes, and "the whole economic system makes for juvenile delinquency and criminals are an indictment of class society."[10] This is a major recasting, based on Walker's own familiarity with the denizens of Goose Island, of Marxism's understanding of the lumpenproletariat. As we've seen, Marx and Engels saw criminality and social marginalization as the result of willed self-interest rather than structural exclusion: the lumpenproletariat is not a product of capitalism, but exists beyond production and thus beyond the considerations of Marxist epistemology. It is, for both capitalism and Marxism, that which doesn't count, which bears no determinative or dialectical relation to production or historical transformation. Walker, however, uses her Depression-era work to reevaluate the concept of the lumpenproletariat within revolutionary theory. By designating the lumpenproletariat as a symptomatic *indictment* of capitalism, Walker resituates it within Marxist social and political analysis. Her poems about urban prostitutes, her unfinished novel *Goose Island*, and her folk ballads about African American heroic outlaws reorient both procedures.

Walker approaches the lumpenproletariat by artfully combining the concept's realistic and romantic valences—its allusions, by turns, to both the immiseration of social exclusion and the freedom of the margins. For instance, she depicts the poverty and exploitation of the urban lumpenproletariat of Chicago as an indictment of capitalist depredation, a symptom of capital's socioeconomic operations. She depicts her outlaw figures as the victims of intersectional economic, racial, and gender oppression. But in doing so, she relocates the lumpenproletariat from the margin to the center of Marxist epistemology: underworld and transient figures displace the proletariat as the target and embodiment of capitalist exploitation. The lumpenproletariat thus also catalyzes Walker's sociopolitical critique of that exploitation, replacing the proletariat as the vantage point for knowledge of capitalist processes. In other words, by arguing, *contra* Marx, that the lumpenproletariat rank *among* capitalism's oppressed and exploited, Walker accesses, in her literary treatments of the lumpenproletariat, forms of revolutionary insight typically associated with proletarian class consciousness. Accordingly, she takes the measure of the urban lumpenproletariat's political viability, following Wright and Ellison in departing from Marxism's alignment of the lumpenproletariat's political leanings with mere opportunism or reaction. For Walker, the slums of *Goose Island* generate revolutionary activity, and black outlaws recoup their marginalization as empowerment.

Her commitment to writing about the lumpenproletariat departs from that of Wright and Ellison in some key ways, however. For one, her work examines the sociopolitical implications of the actions of a wider range of lumpenproletarian types: prostitutes, juvenile delinquents, underworld criminals, and black folk heroes all function, in her poetry and prose, to map the sociological and experiential diversity of lumpenproletarian life. Because of her attention to that diversity, Walker is able to imagine the lumpenproletarian individual as both an outside agent of resistance as well as a symptom of the damages of being socially excluded, whereas for Wright and Ellison, the tendency is to focus on, and perhaps glamorize, the lumpenproletariat's potential for agency. Furthermore, Walker attends to the figure of the lumpenproletarian woman, supplementing the exclusively masculinist framings of the figure in Wright and Ellison. In her folk ballads, for instance, African American lumpenproletarian women access antipatriarchal agency and selfhood through criminal practices and, in doing so, disrupt racial, gender, and capitalist modes of repression.

Walker's approach to the lumpenproletariat is, to quote "Radical Revolutionary," "another way" for Marxism, but it is also a black Marxism firmly located within her mobilization of African American culture. The second section of *For My People* (1942) features ballads of various black folk heroes, and mines these tales for their radical political insights. Reframing the black outlaw hero Stagolee as an agent of antiracist resistance, Walker uses the modern criminal heroes of black culture to reimagine the political agency of the lumpenproletariat. Rather than self-interested individuals irrelevant to class struggle or prone to reactionary recruitment, Walker's outlaw figures become revolutionary actors against capitalist, racial, and patriarchal domination. Indeed, as Southern African American criminals navigating a world shaped by Jim Crow, their exteriority to the law is by definition an act of political defiance.

Walker's folk ballads politicize and radicalize what Cecil Brown describes as the "bad nigger" trope. "As one of the earliest examples of the antihero," Brown writes, "Stagolee is a figure who embodies and perpetuates a counterculture." He is a black cultural antithesis to a figure like John Henry, who did not resist "the white system" but who "sacrificed his life for that system." In *For My People*, Walker constructs a similar opposition between the lumpenproletarian Stagolee and the working-class John Henry. Political potential lies with the socially marginal status and criminal agency of the former, whereas the latter represents the proletariat's co-option by structures and rhythms of labor. Reading "Bad-Man Stagolee," Walker's poem in *For My People*, Brown notes how Walker strips this archetypal figure of his lumpenproletarian attributes and makes him a political agent: "there is no reference to the traditional Stagolee as pimp, gambler, or cold-blooded murderer. But the fact that Walker's Stagolee kills a policeman with a pocket knife ties it in . . . with the theme of police brutality."[11] What Brown identifies is Walker's lumpenproletarian reworking of Marxism, her relocation of revolutionary potential from labor and proletarian collectivity to the heroic acts of resistance encoded in African American vernacular culture. Walker's Depression-era Marxism is one in which the archetype of the revolutionary agent is not the superhuman producer of surplus value John Henry, but various "bad" lumpenproletarian individuals like Stagolee, individuals marginalized by racial and economic exclusion who because they, as Eldridge Cleaver would put it, lack a place or "plug" in the system, offer a radical critique of and resistance to that system.

WORKERS, PROSTITUTES, AND REVOLUTIONARY DESIRE

One of Marx's more idiosyncratic references to the lumpenproletariat occurs in the *Economic and Philosophical Manuscripts* (1844), in which he describes prostitution as "only a *particular* expression of the *universal* prostitution of the *worker*, and since prostitution is a relationship which includes not only the prostituted but also the prostitutor—whose infamy is even greater—the capitalist is also included in this category."[12] Roderick Ferguson argues that this passage positions the prostitute as the "symbol of that dehumanization" of the worker by processes of commodification. The symbol tropes "man's feminization under capitalist relations of production": the prostitute is a symptom of the ways in which capitalism unsettles heteropatriarchal norms and roles. The passage thus elaborates Marx and Engels's moral scorn of the lumpenproletariat, adding sexual deviance and the scrambling of gender roles to their dismissal of these types from Marxism's purview. Ferguson writes, "We may imagine Marx asking, 'How could she—the prostitute—be entrusted with the revolutionary transformation of society?'"[13] Ferguson's purpose is to cite the need for a queer disidentification from Marxism, a repurposing of historical materialism conscious of its limitations by heteropatriarchy. Walker's poems about prostitutes, as we'll see, enact a similar revision of Marxism's dismissal of the lumpenproletariat, and a similar reclaiming of sexual practice and desire as not perversions produced by capital, but as vehicles of anticapitalist political and theoretical sensibilities. Walker, in other words, *does* imagine ways of entrusting the prostitute with the revolutionary transformation of society.

Walker thus "lumpenizes" a basic tenet of classical Marxism: that the socioeconomic location and laboring conditions of the proletariat position it as the class historically destined to negate the capitalist mode of production and bring a new world into being, a world defined in part as a dialectical redefinition of the socialized production practices already experienced by workers under capitalism. As Engels explains, the proletarian revolution "transforms the socialized means of production, slipping from the hands of the bourgeoisie, into public property. By this act, the proletariat frees the means of production from the character of capital they have thus far borne, and gives their socialized character complete freedom to work itself out."[14] This dialectic is at work in Walker's poems about prostitution, though she relocates it to the experiences and conditions of these lumpenproletarian types. In her poems, this lumpenproletarian figure's various desires—for sexual fulfillment, consumer pleasures, money, and personal empowerment—represent the desire for capitalism's historical negation. Her prostitutes' desires are "queer" in that their allegorical object lies outside the bounds of the present and cannot be conceptualized except as a revolutionary alternative to that present.[15]

Walker's work, however, recognizes a further contradiction in Marx's passage about prostitution. By using a particular lumpenproletarian practice as a figure for working-class exploitation, Marx effaces, if only rhetorically, the distinction between lumpenproletariat and proletariat that he establishes in other writings, where the former is politically opposed to the latter. In his economic writings, Marx also draws a distinction between the two groups. As we saw in chapter 1, *Capital* delineates "vagabonds, criminals, prostitutes, in short the actual lumpenproletariat" from the relative surplus population of unemployed workers: the former are not merely out of work, but by their own volition and self-interest remain fundamentally beyond productive relations.[16] Yet his remark about prostitution troubles this distinction. Apart from its gender and sexual connotations, Marx's metaphor positions the lumpenproletariat as the *product* of capitalist exploitation: the actual prostitute becomes a symptom for the universal "prostitution" arising from capitalist relations.

Thus the line between what Marx otherwise understands as the self-interested, disreputable practices of the lumpenproletariat, and the historically progressive tendencies of proletarian labor, is blurred. One theoretical advantage of such a blurring is to enable the transfer of revolutionary capacity from the proletariat to the lumpenproletariat. If, for Marx, labor conditions prepare the proletariat to overthrow capitalism—the point of his famous remark about capital producing the proletariat class as "its own grave-diggers"[17]—and anticipate the full socialization of production after capitalism, the rhetorical instability of this comment about prostitution suggests that lumpenproletarian methods of surviving on the margins, *outside* of productive labor relations, could be used to enact similarly revolutionary diagnoses. Walker's work motivates that possibility and thus anticipates the form of Eldridge Cleaver's 1972 argument, discussed in chapter 1, that the experience of the lumpenproletariat, because it occurs outside the constraints of labor and class identity organized by labor, better presages the classlessness of socialism. For Cleaver, the lumpenproletariat's desire for *"equality in distribution and consumption"* is a more radical desire than the protective, working-class demand for work or jobs.[18] In Walker's treatment of prostitution, the prostitute's desire for pleasure and opportunity similarly figures radical alternatives to extant political orders. Walker's repositioning of the lumpenproletariat is thus less a departure from Marxism then a deconstructive, recuperative reading of Marxism. Or rather, it stands as a revision licensed by orthodox Marxism's own dialectical logics and textual instabilities.

Walker's poems about prostitutes were authored at the same time as multiple poems about the working class that are unusually pessimistic, for a Marxist, about the possibility of revolutionary consciousness or change emerging from proletarian experience. While the laboring conditions of workers in her poems make them unable to grasp the possibility of structural change or socioeconomic critique, the life conditions of prostitutes often lead these figures to such forms of consciousness. In a radical reclassifying and regendering of classical Marxism's revolutionary agent, the prostitute often functions in Walker's Depression poetry as the heroic proletariat functions in Marx's political texts.

Walker's interest in Marxism is conventionally assumed to have followed from her close friendship with Wright, whom she met for the first time in 1936, in Chicago, at a planning session for the Communist-backed National Negro Congress.[19] However, in an unpublished 1934 poem, Walker had already begun to question the revolutionary capacity of the proletariat. "Factory-hand" depicts the working-class woman as a mere reflection of capitalism's exploitative relations of production. The only potential exit from those relations is neither collectivism nor class consciousness, but death. The titular subject is "a fragile little thing / All bent with toil and quivering." The manuscript contains multiple revisions to the poem's final lines, but in one ending the speaker concludes: "And when I saw her pale and worn / Humble in death I could have sworn / Such sweet release was God's kind hand."[20] Death is the only escape from labor because the figure of the worker here accesses no dialectical opposition to her exploitation. Her body bears the traces of that labor to the extent that it is nothing more than its gradual destruction by labor. In a highly sympathetic anticipation of the claims of Black Panther thinkers like Cleaver, Walker's vision of working-class status here entails not revolutionary agency but total co-option—to be a worker is to be wholly the product of one's oppression.

Walker explores this problem in terms of political consciousness in the 1936 dialect poem "Rich Fokes Worl." The speaker, a black worker who, like the archetypal John Henry, "aint nevah been scairt of hard work," describes his struggles to retain consistent employment, both in the Jim Crow South and the industrial North. He accurately attributes his struggles to racism, the mechanization of the labor process, being barred from union membership, and ultimately, a work-related illness that forces him off his WPA relief job. While he grasps that his racial and class status determine his misfortunes, he never sees how capitalism and racism work together to *produce* class and racial difference in the name of maintaining exploitative relations of production. Instead, he chalks his lot up to fate: "po' cullud fokes jes natchelly has a hard time in a rich fokes worl." Walker's manuscript revisions suggest that this line originally referenced a "white fokes worl" before she changed it to "rich fokes worl" (she also made the same change in the title)—a revision that reflects her recognition of the complicity of racism and capitalism.[21] It's clear to Walker's reader that racial difference functions to keep oppressive working relations intact: the speaker, for instance, recollects working as a strike-breaker, a common tactic for pitting black and white workers against each other. But nothing in his experience on and off the job has provided him with an awareness of the socially fabricated nature and attendant political vulnerability of race and class lines. It's simply nature, or fate, that he is black and working-class in a white, rich folks' world. Like the woman in "Factory-hand," this worker's experience reflects a Marxist indictment of capitalist labor that he is not himself able to access or act upon. Like Jake Jackson in *Lawd, Today!*, or the black worker who wants to turn Bigger over to the police in order to protect his job in *Native Son,* the worker in these poems never reaches the heroic, world-changing capacity of Marxism's proletarian.

Walker's replacement of the proletariat with the lumpenproletariat as Marxism's world-historical agent is suggested in the 1936 poem "Men At Work." The title prepares the reader for a typical proletarian ode, but the first four stanzas characterize the titular subject in lumpenproletarian terms of transience and social dislocation: "We were the breadlines," the "Flop house fellows; proud park bench sleepers." They are also described as "the destitute" and "The unprepared unfortunates. / The miserables." Peter Stallybrass notes that Victor Hugo used the title of his novel *Les Misérables,* to which Walker certainly refers, as a designation for the classless individuals Marx would include in the lumpenproletariat.²² But alongside these depictions of material destitution, Walker associates the declassed with political activism: "We were the stump speakers," "fighters," "riot radicals." This political potential is directly correlated with their unemployment: because they are not working, because they are exterior to capitalist relations, they are able to be at once "the idlers, the slackers, the schemers" *and* "the dreamers."

In the final two stanzas, Walker shifts to the present tense and to more familiar proletarian rhetoric: "We are the marching men / Bearing a pick and shovel over our shoulders," the poem declares. "We are the men at work."²³ The proletarian imagery of these stanzas, which emphasizes labor and collectivity, might seem a contrast to the lumpenproletarian tone of the first part of the poem. However, it indicates that Walker is situating the lumpenproletariat, because of its dislocation from labor and capitalist exploitation, in the role classical Marxism assigns to the proletariat by reassigning the decor of proletarian militancy to those who, because idle, can dream of alternatives to alienated labor. The proletariat, in other words, is invoked here as a structural component of revolutionary process rather than an actual set of laborers. André Gorz argues that Marxism's proletariat is less an empirical category than a theoretical abstraction, that "the historical role of the proletariat" in the world-historical negation of capitalism is a "transcendental guarantee" rather than a factual description of actual workers.²⁴ Within classical Marxism, the term is perhaps best understood as a future and inherently revolutionary collective identity to which the empirical working-class is structurally suited and toward which it is developing. But the gap between the concept and its potential empirical referents allows for a certain revisionary fluidity, and the play of proletarian and lumpenproletarian associations in "Men at Work" registers Walker's revision of Marxism. The group best positioned to initiate the historical eclipse of capitalism is in fact the one on its margins rather than at its center.

"Gun Moll," a poem from 1936, suggests the opportunities of lumpenproletarian life as an alternative to the dead ends of labor. The speaker opens with a different invocation of socioeconomic fate than that which closes "Rich Fokes Worl": "I was born to be a harlot/From my birth/I trod the streets/Of scarlet women." Her childhood, lived in proximity to prostitutes, was shaped by antiheteronormative family arrangements. She indicates that the sexual licentiousness of her mother, who "could not remember/The names of all her lovers," meant that "I never knew my father" and that "my half-brothers and sisters/Were none whole bloodied." "Bloodied" might be an error, but its use in place of the expected "blooded" suggests that this nonpatriarchal family unit is not a sociological deviation, but an *escape* from the structural violence of patriarchal concerns with lineage and property, as well as racist concerns with bloodlines and purity. Because the family is not "whole blooded" it is not "bloodied" by patriarchy and racism. Walker thus situates lumpenproletarian experience on the margins not only of labor, but of racial lines, patriarchal kinship structures, and heteronormative sexual arrangements. Without occluding the poverty of her origins, and the destitution of social exclusion suffered by the lumpenproletariat more generally, Walker's speaker finds a generative value in her childhood: "We were nurtured on the crumbs of the rich" while "the slime of the slums/Was our first playground." This dialectical play of deprivation and sustenance suggests the restorative potential of lumpenproletarian alternatives to economic, social, and gender norms.

The speaker then enters the workforce and loses some of the freedom of lumpenproletarian life. The sites of labor here include not only "factories" and "kitchens," but "Bawdyhouses." Unlike the "scarlet women" whose place on the streets, outside of labor relations, inspired possibilities of freedom, the bawdyhouse is a site of labor. Walker demonstrates an awareness of prostitution as both an alternative to and a mode of labor, both a marginal practice located in the streets and an exploitative confinement located in a brothel. What seems like a contradiction, therefore, between framing prostitution as freedom and as labor, is in fact Walker's careful attempt to refigure lumpenproletarian life as freedom without losing sight of its real limitations. Prostitution only works as a figure for freedom, in other words, when it is exterior to capitalist productive relations, an exteriority that is fragile and which the poet must then preserve.

Accordingly, after the speaker becomes a worker, she and her contemporary working-class women find pleasure only outside of work. As with the working-class poems, work itself offers nothing in terms of personal or political fulfillment, only a "sorrow" that the women "learned to drown . . . / In a glass of sparkling blood." Again, the unexpected resituating of blood not as a sign of patriarchal lineage or the human cost of hard labor, but as a playful, "sparkling" euphemism for alcohol and its pleasures, indicates the freedom of the places and practices that thrive outside of the workplace. Like the scarlet women and unlike those who work in the bawdyhouse, "We were happy in the forgotten streets."

The speaker soon commits to her desire for this freedom by joining the lumpenproletariat: she begins dating a gangster. This section of the manuscript is marked by various changes and deletions of unclear priority, but one version indicates how this lover provides the speaker with the pleasures and the freedoms lacking in labor:

> I was pretty and young
> And he was adventure,
> Romance and danger that I craved.
> Life with him was never a dull moment.
> He bought me beautiful clothes
> And jewels and a car.
> He taught me to gamble
> And confidence the foolish
> And the wealthy of their gold.

Lumpenproletarian life provides collectivity, activity, adventure, material goods, and, beyond these pleasures, a criminal form of class-based struggle.

The pleasures of consumption, for the speaker, extend to her sex life with her lover, who was "a warm, passionate lover / He fed me rapture / And glory from a spoon." The desire that characterizes this part of the poem—a desire whose object shifts between her lover's body, her material goods, and the thrill of activity itself—is nowhere found in the two poems of working-class life discussed above. In finding working-class life devoid of fulfillment, "Gun Moll" anticipates the findings of sociologists Horace Cayton and St. Clair Drake in their landmark study *Black Metropolis* (1945). Cayton and Drake describe how the "inability to secure satisfying employment" is a significant catalyst of African American women in Chicago turning to prostitution:

Thus, one young woman in a buffet flat exclaimed: "When I see the word *maid*—why, girl, let me tell you, it just runs through me! I think I'd sooner starve." Another, who lost her white-collar job during the Depression, first took work as a maid and then became a prostitute: "I didn't want to do housework. Here I had been in some kind of office since I was fourteen years old. Now why should I start scrubbing floors at this late date in life?"[25]

Working-class life in "Factory-hand" and "Rich Fokes Worl" is a kind of death-in-life, a life devoid of desire and governed entirely by the necessity of laboring to survive. Desire, represented in "Gun Moll" as the motive force to transcend necessity, the impulse that carries the speaker away from labor, thus carries a distinctly Marxist political charge in itself, allegorizing *revolution* as another escape from capitalist relations of production. As a gangster's girlfriend, a status on the margins of both class and sexual normativity, the speaker realizes, materially and personally, what Cleaver would later call "the ultimate revolutionary demand": to access the fulfillment of consumption without the exploitations and compulsions of production.[26]

The speaker goes on to claim of her lover that "I was his slave," but in this context the term suggests less gender or racial subordination than the kind of loss of self in a larger, postindividualized collective Marxism associates with the formation of the proletariat. For Marx, lumpenproletarian individuals, lacking a collective class status, were self-interested and thus ruthlessly individualistic. For Walker, individual alienation is negated not at the point of production but in the hustling, practical, and collaborative activity of lumpenproletarian life.

Eventually, her lover leaves her for another woman who ends up murdering him. So she uses a gun he had given her to kill her in revenge. The last lines reveal that she is delivering this monologue to the police: "Yes. Sure I did it. / I told you that already a half a dozen times!"[27] The speaker ends up in the same position as Bigger Thomas, using lumpenproletarian crime to access self distinction—"*I* did it." She also upsets normative gender roles by claiming the phallic agency provided by her romance with the gangster. Her liberation and empowerment is only temporary and somewhat figurative in nature: she arrives, like Bigger and like the working-class speakers, at a dead end; crime fails, as it does in *Native Son*, to actually substitute for activism. Furthermore, Walker's awareness of the potential for exploitation alongside freedom in the experiences of her prostitutes, her juxtaposition of mobile "scarlet women" and confined brothel workers, indicates her awareness that the positive freedom of lumpenproletarian life is shaped in part by the imaginative license of a poet's perspective. That means, however, that in the hands of a poet and on the blank pages of Walker's drafts, the speaker's experience can be temporarily refigured to allegorize revolutionary alternatives to the intersectional workings of racial difference, patriarchy, heteronormativity, and capitalism.

Walker acknowledges that a politically empowering depiction of lumpenproletarian life is in no small part a capacity of literary imagination and form. In the 1934 poem "Prostitute," the titular speaker wonders if prostitutes "were ... meant for this alone? / Only this: slaves to the flesh and spirit of men? / Nothing but chattel? Nothing but so much property? / Nothing but so much meat and bone—fat and skin?"[28] Walker here acknowledges the exploitations of prostitution, guarding against uncomplicated romanticization. The dehumanization of the prostitute here echoes Marx's comment in the *Economic and Philosophical Manuscripts*, where "prostitution" names the alienation, under capitalism, of all individuals from their human essence. In the poem "Whores," published in *For My People*, Walker refuses any distinction between the prostitute and the worker and refuses to read prostitution as socially exterior. Prostitutes are described by the speaker as "fascinating sights" but ultimately "old women working by an age-old plan / to make their bread in ways as best they can" who "[learn] too late in unaccustomed dread / that easy ways" cannot "leave them satisfied."[29] Rather than living an alternative to social norms, these prostitutes are workers who, in the era of global warfare, might "be surprised by bombs in each wide bed" just like anyone else. Nancy Berke observes how the poem contrasts with other pieces in *For My People* that romanticize black female resistance; "Whores" not only carries a tone of moral judgment but also "suggests black women's powerlessness as it depicts real, not mythical, female transgressors."[30]

These takes on prostitution perform an important corrective to Marx (one he realized rhetorically, at least, in his *Economic and Philosophical Manuscripts* comment), reminding us that, despite Marx's assumptions to the contrary, lumpenproletarian individuals do not necessarily perversely elect to live outside of productive relations: they may not work on the factory floor, but prostitutes here are just as much exploited modern workers as those who do. Realistically, Walker knows the human costs of prostitution and recognizes the presence of economic, racial, and gender exploitation in the oldest profession. This more sober analysis of lumpenproletarian life might seem to contradict the tone of "Gun Moll." But both poems also suggest a certain imaginative opportunity, for the poet, in prostitution. In describing the prostitutes in "Whores," the speaker notes how "from their hands keys hung suggestively." Literally a tool of their debilitating trade, the key also is a figure of possibility that is recognized by the poet and, to a certain extent, enacted in the poem. The speaker describes them as "whores on special beats," a phrase which, as Berke notes, "alludes to police involvement in the city's underworld activities" and implies a critique of the structural complicity of prostitution and the law.[31] As discussed above, the hardship of their sexual labor is also tied to the destruction of World War II. In this way Walker can reimagine the despised and discounted whore as not, here, an agent of political desire and change, but as still bearing the key to a suggestively extensive critique of modern capitalism, the state, and modern warfare.

In "Prostitute," the speaker attributes her entrance into prostitution to a basic libidinal desire: "I only wanted love and men" and "Nobody wanted Purity/Nobody wanted Innocence./Nobody wanted—God—the only things I had to give./I was too plain—I was too poor."[32] Prostitution indexes the sexual commodification of the "pure" self, but it also functions as a symptom of the contradiction between libido and material circumstances. Similar to "Gun Moll," the speaker's desire for "love and men," the fulfillment poverty denies her, allegorizes the revolutionary desire for the transcendence of economic limitations. Walker thus challenges sex-negative bourgeois moralism without romanticizing away the sufferings entailed by the prostitute. Jane Addams evinces such moralism, for example, in her 1912 book *A New Conscience and an Ancient Evil*, when she blames the desire of individual women for their entrance into prostitution: "a girl always prefers to think that economic pressure is the reason for her downfall, even when the immediate causes have been her love of pleasure, her desire for finery, or the influence of evil companions."[33] Walker redefines and destigmatizes the moral and sociopolitical valences of desire as manifested in prostitution. The poem thus simultaneously explores prostitution as both, realistically, a mode of economic victimization and, figuratively, an escape from such victimization.

Walker stages this dialectic of lumpenproletarian suffering and freedom later in the poem, when the speaker wonders if all prostitutes are merely "meant to be manikins only? / Human Rags? Discarded Hagars?"³⁴ These three images chart Walker's understanding of the rags and paper trope. Lumpenproletarian life is the dehumanizing condition of being society's discards and outcasts, but through the literary technique of Biblical allusion, that condition is recast as potential. In Genesis, Hagar is the slave of Abraham's wife Sarah, and gives birth to Abraham's son Ishmael. When Abraham later casts Hagar and her son into the wilderness, God reaches out to them and promises her that her son will be the originator of a nation. Hagar's status as a slave reflects the speaker's exploitation, and her banishment by Abraham reflects the struggles of the lumpenproletarian social outcast. Yet in Hagar's story, from exteriorization comes the possibility for futurity and utopian transcendence: the "human rag" is a symbol of human detritus, but the "discarded Hagar" tropes the constructive and progressive political potential of the discarded.

In these poems Walker furnishes a more sensitive understanding of the gender, racial, and economic complexities of lumpenproletarian experience than we find in the works of Wright and Ellison. If the exploits of a Bigger, Tillman, and Slick are in danger of conforming to what Madhu Dubey calls the "romance of the residual," the tendency to read exteriorization and marginalization exclusively as conditions of empowered resistance, Walker's representations of prostitutes preserve an awareness of the continuity of capitalism's exploitation beyond normative economic and social relations.³⁵ While similarly redefining lumpenproletarian experience as providing radical political potential, Walker doesn't lose the opportunity to simultaneously represent such experience, in a different yet equally critical register, as a manifestation of intersectional oppression. By motivating both poles of the rags and paper trope, Walker can offer positive and negative revolutionary framings of lumpenproletarian experience: it is by turns a damning condemnation of social and economic injustice and the alternative to such injustice.

In an early short story, Walker uses the trope of the rag to correlate working-class identity and lumpenproletarian practice with allegorical possibilities of personal and collective empowerment. "The Red Satin Dress" appeared in 1939 in *The New Anvil*. The father of a working-class family brings home, for his wife, a red satin dress that he claims to have found under his seat on the train. The dress is new and expensive, and it occasions some conflict between the narrator's parents. The mother feels they should return it to the store in hope of finding its purchaser, and her husband suspects she thinks that he "stole it." Their dispute then turns into a sociopolitical one about the advisability of resorting to lumpenproletarian tactics in the face of economic deprivation: "Daddy said poor folks can't afford to be so honest, being honest like that is too expensive. Mama said she thinks it's just the other way around, poor folks have to be extra careful because folks are so quick to say we steal." Eventually, she wears the dress to a party and slowly is reconciled to keeping it, and the dress becomes a catalyst for the strengthening of the narrator's parents' erotic relationship: "every time she put it on Daddy had another fit of beaming and kissing her." When the dress starts to wear, her mother transforms it "into a ruffled cape to wear evenings over other party dresses that were cheap but were always set off by the cape." At the end of the story, the narrator reports that her grandmother plans to make a quilt from "this red satin rag," so that "we can look at it a long time" and "maybe one of us can even have the quilt some day in our hope-chest."[36]

The dress is acquired on the margins of capitalist socioeconomic relations rather than purchased with wages that represent the exploitation of the father's labor power. It thus symbolizes a kind of fulfillment, here figured in erotic and familial terms, that working-class life, and thus capitalist productive relations, cannot yield. It suggests the potential lying on the margins of those relations, a potential always in danger of being derided as theft and moral degradation. The satin dress, by the end of the story, is the "rag" that is repurposed as a point of departure for the future happiness of the family, and its color suggests the political tendency Walker associates with that future. If her poems about prostitutes and other outcasts often reimagine, on paper, the suffering of being discarded "human rags" as in fact a condition of future-oriented revolutionary possibility, the grandmother's quilting in "The Red Satin Dress" allegorizes Walker's own committed literary practice.

GOOSE ISLAND: REVOLUTION FROM THE SLUMS

Walker graduated from Northwestern University in 1935, and in her final year as a student she worked for what she later characterized as a "re-creation project sponsored by the WPA" and focused on juvenile delinquency. The project she describes seems to be sociologist Clifford Shaw's Chicago Area Project, a program to combat juvenile delinquency through neighborhood-based community-building activism and recreation.[37] Shaw's research into delinquency, in studies like *The Jack-roller* (1930), had suggested that, to quote Solomon Kobrin, "delinquency may often represent the efforts of the person to find and vindicate his status as a human being, rather than an abdication of his humanity or an intrinsic incapacity to experience human sentiment." As a result, for Kobrin, the "spirit" of the project realized Shaw's "sense of the naturalness or inevitability of violative activity in the youngster who, whether singly or in groups, is neglected, despised, or ignored as a person."[38] This recognition of the positive desire of the delinquent figure, a desire produced by socioeconomic marginalization, suggests how the project's approach led a writer like Walker, fascinated by both Marxism and Chicago's urban underclass, to reimagine delinquency as not a social problem but as the kernel of revolutionary political volition.

Walker's work on the project introduced her to various lumpenproletarian types in the North Side "Italian-black neighborhood" of Goose Island:

> They gave me a group of so-called delinquent girls to spend time with, to see what kind of influence a person with my background and training would have on them. Primarily, they were shoplifters and prostitutes.... I learned that prostitution and gambling were vices tied up with city politics. One of the straw bosses on the project was a pimp whose brother was a smuggler and a narcotics dealer.[39]

Walker incorporated her experiences into *Goose Island*, a novel she began in the 1930s but never finished. In her preface, she describes Goose Island as a place of discards: "This area is called the Low End by Negroes who live in that section. It is characterized by dirty streets and filthy alleys full of refuse garbage and swept only at election time." Besides indicting civic government for its structural role in maintaining urban poverty, Walker also suggests the political exploitability of this "Marginal or Interstitial District."[40] The garbage of Goose Island—including the persons who, cast off from society, inhabit it as refuse themselves—is "swept" only when it serves political interests. This passage echoes Marx's suspicion of the lumpenproletariat's susceptibility to political bribery and suggests that

Chicago's lumpenproletarians are bribed tools of city political interests. Like the literal and human trash of Goose Island, Marx's lumpenproletariat "may . . . be swept into the movement by a proletarian revolution" but is much more likely to be recruited by the forces of reaction.[41] But unlike Marx, and like Wright or Ellison, Walker doesn't see the political malleability of the lumpenproletariat as necessarily aligned with conservative or reactionary forces. *Goose Island* considers the progressive political insights and opportunities emerging from the socially marginal, interstitial spaces of urban lumpenproletarian life.

The protagonist is Henrietta, an African American woman who, after her marriage fails, gets a job working for the Experiment, a sociological project studying juvenile delinquency in Goose Island. Before working with the project, her first encounter with the lumpenproletarian "Low End" catalyzes the dissolution of her marriage. After her aunt tells her she saw Henrietta's husband, Arthur, with a prostitute in the Low End, Henrietta investigates the neighborhood. The Low End is, for her, "a place that stood for the worst things in life. All the gambling and vice holes, the prostitution houses, the headquarters of gangs and gangsters, were clustered in the Low End." Her apprehensions about the Low End echo the proliferative rhetoric of Marx's catalogue of the Parisian lumpenproletariat in *The Eighteenth Brumaire*, a reminder that Henrietta's moral repulsion is readable as, simultaneously, bourgeois and classically Marxist.

Yet when she enters this "Marginal or Interstitial District" she gains a degree of authority over her husband, whom she encounters on the street. He challenges her presence there: "You've got no business down here in the Low End." She challenges him in turn: "What *business* have you got down here?" In response to his "Well, but I'M a man!" she asserts that "Yes, and dont you forget one day that I'm every inch a woman and I'll stand every foot of my ground, you understand."[42] The gender prerogative Arthur claims, framed as his freedom to be in the Low End, is reclaimed by Henrietta as a protective and defiant resistance to the prescribed gender roles Arthur's comment invokes. Henrietta initially perceives the Low End as a place of "vice holes," a sexually connotative phrase that indicates how the area's nonconformity to normative gender roles is what occasions her moral scorn. Yet her entrance into this space where gender prescriptions are less stable, her removal to the margin of those prescriptions, enables her to challenge the patriarchal authority of her husband. The criminal world of the lumpenproletariat is thus introduced as a space of freedom, and its perceived deviance redefined as potential resistance, a resistance that is lost in bourgeois as well as Marxist dismissals of the lumpenproletariat as beyond the bounds of proper consideration.

Henrietta and Arthur eventually separate, and Henrietta searches for a job in the midst of the Great Depression. The experience is again one of moving out of a stable social position and into the margin, and is here described with careful use of free indirect discourse, as Goose Island is characterized from Henrietta's shifting perspective: "Always here in Goose Island life had moved for her easily enough without being luxurious. . . . Now she walked out into the world of hopelessness. The streets were filled with tramping people like her searching for work. She was part of the giant army of unemployed. Drunks littered the corner pavements; beggars were everywhere, and the peddlers were innumerable." Her gaze still includes the scorn found in Marx: the rhetoric of this catalogue of the Depression dislocated references moral repulsion (drunks "littering" the streets as human trash) and Marx's hostility to self-interested lumpenproletarian hustling (the "innumerable" peddlers). But it also includes "beggars," a signifier invoking stark material need without clear tones of repugnance. Thus she notes how "the parks were full of men who were not yet tramps but steadily becoming demoralized. Through this maze she walked out of her dream, into a realization of the depression." Lumpenproletarian life now appears as economic victimization, its immiseration the product of a structural crisis in capitalism—"it looked as though the whole economic system in America and the world too, for that matter had been wrecked"[43]—rather than the result of individual moral failings. Furthermore, the social margins of Goose Island become a "maze" that, for all its bewildering connotations, stands in contrast to the "dream" that was Henrietta's prior, relatively stable social situation. The margin, in other words, is an interstitial space where epistemological gains can be sought and found.

The Depression makes lumpenproletarian transience visible as a consequence of structural flaws with capitalism, and that enables Henrietta to begin to work her way through the "maze" of lumpenproletarian life toward a critical awareness of capitalism: "People dared not walk the streets at night, especially women. There seemed to be a wave of purse-snatching and hold ups and murders and rapes." In her previous visit to the Low End in search of Arthur, she had reflected how "she had always thought it would be dangerous walking these streets," but then the perception of danger was clearly bound up, in her mind, with her moralizing aversion to the "worst things in life" contained in the Low End. Now, she reframes lumpenproletarian danger as the product of economic deprivation: "People were tense with desperation; a man might do anything for a few dollars."[44] The Depression allows Henrietta to move from the obfuscatory "dream" of seeing Goose Island as Addams saw prostitutes, as defined by willed decadence, to the more complex, "maze"-like reality of lumpenproletarian misery as a symptom of economic inadequacy—a move Marx never quite made himself. Henrietta's experiential education is how Walker's novel recasts the rags of lumpenproletarian misery as the blank page troping new epistemological departures.

Henrietta is eventually hired as a secretary on the Experiment, a sociological project studying juvenile delinquency in Goose Island and seeking to cure it through community organization and recreation. Henrietta begins associating with Bud Haynes, an African American underworld operator from the neighborhood who works with the Experiment. Bud is a "legend" in the neighborhood, and Henrietta had long heard of him from her aunt: "Some of the things she told her he later corroborated unconsciously. Some of the things were obviously gossip, hearsay, and near legend." Bud had migrated from the South "upon the death of his father"; had organized gambling for Tranchina, an Italian gangster; had his wife—"one of those extremely interesting women who had made her living not only by her wits but by peddling love"—to whom he may not have been legally married, confined in an asylum; and had worked as a pimp and eventually established his own underworld enterprise comprising "Bookies, Prostitution, Gambling Dens," which allowed him to don "good pin striped suits and [smoke] ten cent cigars." Bud paid for police protection, and although his money filled city coffers, "there was really never any improvement in the neighborhood. The alleys were always full of refuse and filthy; the streets were swept only at election time; no garbage man removed garbage regularly and in general the whole neighborhood of Goose Island was like a dump upon which the whole city discarded everything undesirable."[45]

Bud is both a lumpenproletarian operator and a sort of folkloric hero of the community, someone who uses crime, in the face of social oppression, to become economically successful and larger than life in reputation. His coming from the South after the death of his father raises the likely possibility of his having left to flee racial persecution. He foreshadows the black outlaw figures of Walker's poetry collection *For My People*, who use illicit measures to resist structures of power. His legend romanticizes the underworld and glosses over his exploitation of his prostitutes, but it also encodes the possibility of criminal measures being empowering for African Americans. Walker captures this instance of the rags and paper trope through her alignment of the steady accumulation of "hearsay" about Bud with the steady accumulation of "refuse" in the Goose Island streets. The material immiseration of the slum is suggestively linked to the freedom and ingenuity of the lumpenproletarian hustler: refuse is recycled as possibility.

This dynamic is disrupted by the Depression, when Bud "went ragged," lost connections and illicit trade and, figuratively, lost the romantic potential associated with his pre-Depression legendary status. It's at this point that he begins working for the Experiment with Henrietta, and he provides her with insight into "all the undercurrent movements in the neighborhood": what crimes had been committed, which gangs had been involved, etc. "At first Henrietta was horrified at the stories he told, then she gradually withdrew from her reserve and fascinated by the language he used, the jokes he cracked, and the almost unbelievable tales he told she began listening with more than professional interest." Bud uses his storytelling arts to deconstruct Henrietta's bourgeois, moralizing horror of lumpenproletarian life. But as he does so, he also teaches Henrietta about the complicity of capitalism in producing crime and juvenile delinquency. Critiquing the "foolish gushing women interested in charity work" whom the Experiment courts, he exclaims: "What do they care how these kids live, and how they die? . . . These kids ain't bad because they're born bad; they're bad because they're where they are."[46] While he destigmatizes the lumpenproletariat, he also doesn't romanticize outcasts and delinquents but identifies them as symptoms of capitalism's neglect of the slums. Rather than those who simply don't count for Marx's anticapitalist critique, lumpenproletarian figures are at the center of Haynes's anticapitalist epistemology. As a result, Henrietta begins to grasp the political limitations of the Experiment's sociological and philanthropic approach: before Colman, the Experiment's head administrator, Henrietta and Bud "did not voice any such sentiments about the Gold Coast

[157]

being the breeder of the slums, in turn devouring and regurgitating the people living in the back ways."

As she did in some of her 1930s poems, Walker situates the lumpenproletariat of Goose Island in a manner that aligns it with the structural role played, in classical Marxism, by the industrial proletariat. "The Gold Coast depended upon these people for labor," Henrietta and Bud know, "and they in turn depended on them for 'a crust of bread and a corner to sleep in.'"[47] For Walker, the lumpenproletarian types of the "back ways" are not, as in classical Marxism, irrelevant to capitalism's functioning, excluded from its consideration of the factory or the market and relegated, out of sight, to back alleys. Nor, she indicates, does the lumpenproletariat categorically renounce legitimate labor. Bud and Henrietta recognize that lumpenproletarian deviance is not the result of a willed refusal of work and legitimate social status but is produced by the inadequate returns of the labor available to the denizens of Goose Island. Thus what capital offers the slums is not material sustenance but a mere allusion to it: the "crust of bread and a corner to sleep in" is a phrase from a Paul Laurence Dunbar poem.[48] Discussing one youth involved with the project, Bud exclaims: "What chance has she got? Look at the house they're living in. Look at the days they got to go hungry? And her old man finished college! A college graduate! Yes and he did post graduate work in the Penitentiary for making counterfeit money."[49] Counterfeiting works as a general figure for lumpenproletarian recourses in the face of the inadequacy of socioeconomic relations that maintain the poverty of the slum: money must be made through criminal means since it isn't reliably provided by labor. In this way, Walker theorizes the tenuous criminal resourcefulness of the lumpenproletarian individual in the same way Marx theorized proletarian militancy: as an organic consequence and symptomatic indictment of capitalism.

Doing so, of course, allows her to position the lumpenproletariat as potentially negating capitalism. The denial of livable conditions to these persons, symbolized by the accumulation of trash in the streets of Goose Island, has the potential to dialectically empower them against capital, a process figured by the accumulation of legends about Bud as a romantic social outlaw. The Experiment cannot recognize this transformative potential, and when revolution is voiced in Goose Island, it falls outside of the project's bounds. At neighborhood meetings held by the project, for instance, two brothers, one of whom "[gives] his name as Black" and who "were both known as crazy Reds who styled themselves as Radicals or Communists" often disrupt the discussion. Black articulates a Marxist critique of the Experiment: "As long as things go on like this where a man can't get a piece of bread thout he begs for it and can't get work and got to live in these no good building [sic] the Project can keepa going till doomsday they ain't gonna cut out no devilment."[50] The brothers reiterate the critique Bud had made earlier, framed now as a "Communist" insight. They also raise the question of whether a "black" Marxism, emerging not from official institutions but from the neighborhood itself, might not be better suited to the needs of the slum than are the philanthropic efforts of the sociologists.

Events come to a head when four African American youths rob a business and, in the process, get into a shoot-out with a police officer. The officer and one of the criminals die, another is captured by the police, and the other two go on the run. Concurrent with this moment of crisis, the Experiment elects to pull out of the neighborhood. Henrietta comes to the office to discover Colman "packing papers together": the possibilities for renewal that the Experiment sought to bring to the discarded human rags of Goose Island are being withdrawn. Henrietta tells him of the incident with the shot police officer. "Well they never seem to learn," Colman explains. "They see what a life like that gets them everyday, yet they do the same thing over and over again."[51] Colman is giving up on the lumpenproletariat because he, like Marx or like any bourgeois moralist, sees their criminal tendencies as an inherent failing beyond organization or repair.

In response to the shooting, a "police terror" descends on Goose Island as cops comb the neighborhood and harass residents, seeking the two fugitives. The scene resembles the manhunt for Bigger in *Native Son*, but with a key difference: rather than neighborhood sentiment turning against Bigger for threatening the tenuous job security of working-class blacks, Goose Island organizes and resists, and with the help of the institutional left. The Communist-backed International Labor Defense gets involved in defending a victim of police brutality, and sponsors a "mass meeting" in collaboration with other radical organizations, a meeting which "half of Goose Island" attends. "After this meeting the terror abated slowly," and the resistance of the neighborhood is the key factor in that abatement: "At the last house searching the housewife, who was an energetic worker in the neighborhood branch of the Workers' Alliance demanded that police or no police they couldn't search her house without a search warrant and if they didn't get out of her house she'd made [*sic*] them tell the reason why. That ended the house-searching."[52] The Workers' Alliance was a Communist-supported organization of unemployed workers: workers who don't work and thus aren't quite proletarians. The International Labor Defense had been instrumental in the legal defense of the Scottsboro Boys, the primary antiracist cause of the Communist left in the Depression. This confluence of organizations suggests that the resistance to the police terror is a black and red instance of lumpenproletarian militancy. After all, it is initiated by a criminal act, and the nature of that criminal act—resistance to the rule of the police—is expanded and organized into a mass movement. If Wright's *Native Son* was skeptical about the ability of criminal activity to effectively disrupt racial and economic oppression, Walker's scenario imagines a process whereby the crime of resisting arrest becomes the positive revolutionary impetus of a community resisting the state.

Even in its fragmentary and unfinished state, *Goose Island* demonstrates Walker's interest in the 1930s left. It also speaks to her close interest in Marxist theory, a facility demonstrated in her attempts to resituate the lumpenproletariat as the dialectical counterpoint of capital, and it serves to put lumpenproletarian criminality in place of labor as the activity catalyzing political action. Her depiction of Bud Haynes anticipates her later efforts, in the poetry of *For My People*, to rethink the lumpenproletarian figure as the outlaw hero of black folklore. Her situating of Goose Island as an alternative to normative gender and sexual roles is also realized in *For My People*, where her outlaw figures challenge racial, patriarchal, and economic systems of oppression at once.

FOR MY PEOPLE: THE LUMPENPROLETARIAN AS THE BLACK FOLK CULTURE HERO

The title poem of Walker's volume narrates black history in a Whitmanesque fashion, but thematizes that history as one of labor and submission: rather than yielding revolutionary consciousness and agency, labor entails subjugation. The culture of black laborers is defined by passivity and powerlessness, by a fetishization of social and material oppression.

The first stanza describes "my people everywhere singing their slave songs repeatedly: their dirges and their ditties and their blues and jubilees, praying their prayers nightly to an unknown god, bending their knees humbly to an unseen power." This sacrifice of agency in black culture derives from the ceaselessness of labor, labor that, contrary to classical Marxist dictates, provides African Americans no class or revolutionary consciousness. Instead, Walker renders it as "washing ironing cooking scrubbing sewing mending hoeing plowing digging planting pruning patching dragging along never gaining never reaping never knowing and never understanding." The rhythmic shift that accompanies "dragging along" registers the simultaneously unending yet directionless, dragging nature of this work: for all of its activity, it leads to nothing, certainly not to "knowing" or "understanding."

The poem continues to hold out the possibility of African American fulfillment under these conditions only to revoke it. After citing "the boys and girls who grew in spite of these things to be man and woman," the poem notes how they then "die of consumption and anemia and lynching." The poem then charts the Great Migration, addressing itself to African Americans in Chicago and New York, but the move out of the Jim Crow South also fails to bring satisfaction, as African Americans become "lost disinherited dispossessed and happy people filling the cabarets and taverns and other people's pockets needing bread and shoes and milk and land and money and something—something all our own." The "something" the community needs isn't fulfilled by the move to the North, and the social institutions governing black urban life hold out the promise of transcendence but only in a duplicitous manner, in order to exploit African Americans.

The penultimate stanza addresses "my people standing staring trying to fashion a better way from confusion, from hypocrisy and misunderstanding, trying to fashion a world that will hold all the people, all the faces." However, nothing in the narrative of black history that the poem has offered suggests how such a "better way" could be created. Oppression has not molded the black working class into the dialectical negation of capitalism and racism, but has only produced obfuscation, false consciousness, and servility. In the final stanza, therefore, the poet must invoke revolution as an abrupt, caesural break from the body of the poem. Each previous stanza consisted of a long line beginning "For my people," but the final stanza declares, in sharp short sentences, "Let a new earth rise. Let another world be born."[53] The vision of revolution it goes on to outline is conventionally didactic, but its apparent simplicity is ironized by its unaccountable origin: if black life, organized around labor and oppression, fails to galvanize resistance, where does the possibility of thinking this revolution come from? The poem leaves this question open in order to frame it as its central political problem: where can revolutionary agency come from if, in African American experience, it doesn't come from where classical Marxism says it should?

Walker elaborates this theme in another poem from the volume's first section. "Lineage" characterizes the speaker's relationship to her grandmothers as a rupture. "My grandmothers were strong. / They followed plows and bent to toil." The human agency of their labor, however, is curiously effaced, as their work is described as an organic process, almost an extension of the natural world: "They moved through fields sowing seed. / They touched earth and grain grew." Hence when the poet repeats "my grandmothers were strong" at the end of the first stanza, the line is ironic: it's a strength that precludes freedom, and is defined entirely by necessity. The second stanza recollects these women with fondness and posits their strength again before ending the poem by asking, "Why am I not as they?" In this reading the poem speaks somewhat conventionally of a modern speaker's felt alienation from her family, roots, and traditions. The speaker might lack the confidence and strength of previous generations of women in her family, who were "full of sturdiness and singing," but this strength is what kept her grandmothers doing nothing but work: a circuitous routine that made their sturdiness indistinguishable from stasis, and their songs the songs of submission and acceptance described in "For My People."[54] The speaker thus distinguishes herself as a woman "unlike" previous generations of workingwomen, and the emergence of African American political agency is here presented as a disruption in lineages of black women's experiences.

Accordingly, the second section of *For My People* features African American men and women who refuse to limit themselves to labor, sturdiness, and repetition, and who break from lineages of racial, economic, and gender submission. As Derek Furr notes, "Walker exploits the ballad tradition's fascination with criminals and shady characters, not in the conventional interest of sensationalism, but as a means of giving a compelling, sympathetic voice to marginalized figures."⁵⁵ Nancy Berke, in language echoing Marx's tendency to name the lumpenproletariat through a heterogeneous catalogue, writes that these poems "describe the exploits of tricksters, conjurers, gamblers, bootleggers, pimps, and laborers, accentuating the nuanced lives of African American folk heroes and heroines."⁵⁶ While this section does include one ballad devoted to John Henry, that legendary black laborer, the section continues the first section's suspicion of work and labor. Here, the figures that find empowerment are nonworking black lumpenproletarians whom Walker presents as legendary outlaws. They opt for occult, illegitimate, or criminal tactics to survive and thrive on the margins of racist, capitalist, and patriarchal social formations. These poems redefine Marx's lumpenproletariat within African American culture, where the socially marginal status of lumpenproletarian figures renders them neither politically irrelevant nor self-interested and reactionary. Rather, these legendary black lumpenproletarians perform resistance to normative structures of oppression; it is in their experiences, and not in the ceaseless labor of socially incorporated black workers, that the revolutionary possibility of "another world" and a "new earth" is figured.

The titular figure of "Molly Means" is "a hag and a witch" whose "heavy hair hung thick in ropes" and whose "blazing eyes was black as pitch." Her physical features, rendered as ropes and pitch, invoke the imagery of lynching. Furthermore, "some say she was born with a veil on her face," alluding to W. E. B. Du Bois's famous symbol, in *The Souls of Black Folk* (1903), for double consciousness, the internal destabilization of self-consciousness caused by white America's discounting of the individuality of black persons. Thus, despite her status as a singular, legendary sorceress, Molly Means embodies collective black experiences of racist violence and social exclusion. Yet she recoups such exclusion as a form of agency: her features signify not victimization but an occult power, and her veil does not disempower her, as does Du Bois's, but allows her to "look through unnatchal space/Through the future and through the past/And charm a body or an evil place." Molly is marginalized from mainstream society, shunned and feared, but her social exteriorization, far from anonymizing or delimiting her, allows her to become legendary for her "evil powers."

The main action of the ballad is initiated when Molly casts a spell on a new bride who recently moves in near her: the bride's husband discovers his wife "barking like a dog/And on all fours like a common hog."

Molly's motive for casting this spell isn't specified, and sexual jealousy over the woman's husband is certainly one possible implied explanation. But the description of the spell's effect suggests a larger, sociopolitical dimension to Molly's act: it hints at a sexual empowerment and license provided by Molly's spell, one that defies the husband's ownership of his wife's sexuality, which Molly's arts have now made "common." The presence of a powerful woman like Molly, who refuses to conform to social norms and whose practices actively disrupt them, challenges the normativity of patriarchal gender roles. The bride's husband avenges himself on Molly, therefore, by finding a "man who said he could move the spell" to Molly herself, causing her "to bark and bleed / Till she died at the hands of her evil deed." A certain ideological operation of patriarchy is allegorized here: the threat or challenge of the woman who refuses to conform to gender and sexual norms is cancelled by the derogation of her nonconformity as animalistic perversity.

The ballad concludes by describing how Molly's ghost still "rides along on a winter breeze" and continues to inspire fear.[57] The threat she posed to the social order survives her repression by that order, and continues to trouble it. "Molly Means" is a clear distillation of Walker's Marxist feminist commitments. It outlines an African American vision of sexual freedom and female empowerment, an empowerment that, because it refuses incorporation in and redefinition by social institutions, always remains beyond their repressive grasp. Her occult arts figure the socially illegitimate recourses and practices adopted by those on the margins. Unlike Marx, Walker sees such practices as politically constructive in their ability to haunt and disrupt the structures of society.

"Bad-Man Stagolee," as discussed above, transforms the archetypal black folk outlaw into a figure of political resistance. Nancy Berke notes that this poem performs a "twist" on the Stagolee tale by having Stagolee kill a police officer and thus "stretches the legend from its celebration of Stagolee as a mean individualist, to a tale with political undertones." Berke finds this maneuver to be in part a "problem": it aggrandizes a figure whose legendary acts are merely criminal rather than constructive for African Americans, and it risks glamorizing crime at the expense of a more realistic portrayal of its dialectical sociopolitical causes and consequences.[58] Yet we've seen Walker do this before, in *Goose Island*, when the delinquents' criminal acts of robbing a store and shooting a police officer catalyze community-wide resistance. Her retelling of the Stagolee story plays with a similar relationship between the criminal individual and the black community. William Scott argues of the ballads in *For My People* that "while they are ostensibly about individuals, they all invoke a community around these individuals in order to convey a sense of the latter's actions and effects."[59] Their status as folk tales, in other words, implies a community that receives them, tells them, and takes instruction from them. In "Bad-Man Stagolee," Stagolee, despite the apparently apolitical nature of his criminal acts, comes to figure the black community's desire for revolutionary transcendence.

Walker's redefinition of Stagolee opens the poem:

That Stagolee was an all-right lad
Till he killed a cop and turned out bad,
Though some do say to this very day
He killed more'n one 'fore he killed that 'fay.

Rather than an underworld gangster, Stagolee is "all-right" *until* he kills the cop, but the poem then suggests that while he was considered "all-right" he had also killed whites before, a simultaneity that suggests a tacit communal approval of Stagolee's actions. Furthermore, the lines indicate that the image of Stagolee as an "all-right" individual brave enough to defy and even kill whites is itself a product of the community's oral traditions. Like Ice Cream Charlie, the black folk hero who killed twelve cops in defiance of Jim Crow and whom Ellison discussed with other black drifters while riding freights in 1933, Stagolee "evoke[s] the unwritten history of the group."[60] His actions as a criminal express the community's desire to resist the statist forms of racial oppression enacted by the police. After he kills the police officer, the poem notes the peculiarity of the story's resolution: "the funniest thing" is that Stagolee escaped punishment and "missed the lynching meant for his hide / 'Cause nobody knows how Stagolee died." In a circumstance as magical and inexplicable, as peculiarly "funny," as Molly Means's occult powers, Stagolee fails to experience the racist violence his act should precipitate. His story thus narrates the fantasy of resisting racial rule and triumphing in that resistance. His death remains a mystery, "But his ghost still walks up and down the shore / Of Old Man River round New Orleans / With her gumbo, rice, and good red beans!"[61]

By rendering his death mysterious and making him become a ghost, the ballad indicates how the fantasy of empowering action his story enacts cannot die: Stagolee's ghost is the spirit of black political desire that transcends any specific historical place and time and lives on in the face of its repression. The apparent non sequitur in the final line, about the food in New Orleans, figures the utopian aim of that desire: the sensory richness of gumbo, rice, and "red" beans (a color doing double duty here as a political signifier) gestures toward the quality of life in a moment when white racial rule has been negated.

"Kissie Lee" regenders the narrative of "Bad-Man Stagolee." Kissie Lee is "the toughest gal God ever made" and like Stagolee, who carried a "blade he wore unnerneaf his shirt," she "drew a dirty, wicked blade."[62] As a phallic symbol, the knife here represents not patriarchal social power, but a mode of individual resistance available to lumpenproletarian men and women: Stagolee and Kissie's knives are in this sense antiphallic symbols, symbols of their refusal of and challenge to the social order's relations of race, gender, and power. Kissie, the poem tells us, "warn't always tough," and her grandmother was regarded as "the town's sin and shame." However, as a child, Kissie was always getting into fights, so her grandmother gave her some formative advice:

> "Whin I was a gal wasn't no soul
> Could do me wrong an' still stay whole.
> Ah got me a razor to talk for me
> An' aftah that they let me be."

Unlike in "Lineage," where the only inheritance from previous generations of socially incorporated African American workingwomen is a passive resilience in the face of constant toil, Kissie's socially outcast grandmother passes down to her a tactic of individual resistance. The female proletarian lineage of "Lineage" is supplanted by a lumpenproletarian and feminist lineage in "Kissie Lee": Kissie's grandmother gives her the ability to "hold her likker and hold her man / And she went thoo life jus' raisin' san."

One day Kissie encounters, in a bar, "a guy what spoke too soon; / He done her dirt long time ago." Kissie shoots him and then, the poem suggests, castrates him with her knife. "Evvy livin' guy got out of her way / Because Kissie Lee was drawin' her pay." Kissie strips this man of the phallic authority granted him by patriarchy with her knife, an instrument that symbolically demonstrates her resistance to the gender relations codified by patriarchy. Not the factory floor, and not the kitchens in which previous generations of women toiled in "Lineage," but the nonlaboring space of the saloon enables Kissie to "draw her pay" in a nonproletarian manner. Marxism's signature understanding of the wage is that it represents not the true value of a worker's labor but a fraction of it designed to keep the worker functional and producing the surplus value that, because it is not remunerated, becomes profit for the capitalist. But in Kissie's case, "drawin' her pay" refers not to the exploitation of labor but to the gains of defying social power through crime. Her criminal prowess offers an escape from patriarchal gender roles, just as Stagolee's provided an escape from white supremacy. Kissie becomes a bootlegger, and the poem concludes by stating how she "died with her boots on switching blades / On Talladega Mountain in the likker raids."[63] She dies in a legendary manner, one that thus preserves, for future folkloric retellings and for future generations of African American women, the socially illegitimate yet empowering agency that her grandmother bequeathed to her. In Stagolee and Kissie Lee's stories, Walker offers a vision of revolutionary agency missing from poems like "For My People." Instead of emerging dialectically at the point of production, revolutionary consciousness and capacity are simultaneously lumpenproletarian and culturally African American, accessed on the margins of society and passed down in the tales and collective wisdom of the black community.

"Big John Henry" furnishes a counterpoint to figures like Molly Means, Stagolee, and Kissie Lee. If Stagolee is the archetypal black lumpenproletarian figure, John Henry is the archetypal black worker, and as such featured in African American proletarian writing. For instance, when the black leftist writer John Oliver Killens wrote the young adult novel *A Man Ain't Nothin' But a Man: The Adventures of John Henry* (1975), he did so in part, Keith Gilyard argues, to clarify his commitment to Marxism by offering a narrative of "cross-ethnic, working-class consciousness." In the novel, John Henry's death while trying to demonstrate the superiority of proletarian labor to automation carries a proletarian critique of capitalism's relations of production. As Gilyard explains, Henry feels that "the enemy is not machines but rather the unwise use of them."[64]

Walker's John Henry, however, for all of his mythical strength, is simply born to labor and never accesses an anticapitalist critique.

> The day he was born in the Mississippi bottom
> He made a meal on buttermilk and sorghum
> A mess o' peas and a bait o' tunnips
> And when he finished he smacked his lips
> And went outside to help pick cotton.[65]

Derek Furr writes that the last line of this passage, about picking cotton, "falls flat—a cold, hard fact" after the mythical richness of his meal. Furr notes that the abrupt entrance of labor into the myth of John Henry's birth foreshadows the "sober ending" of his life while laboring.[66] As in "Bad-Man Stagolee," food signifies the sensory abundance of an order of experience apart from labor, which then cancels any such fulfillment and offers only death. For all of John Henry's heroic strength and exploits, he ends the poem "cold and dead," with no hint of the kind of ghostly immortality accorded to the spirit of resistance embodied by Stagolee or Molly Means.[67] If, as Furr argues, the ending of the poem "calls for . . . heroes who move beyond nostalgia to political action," those heroes do not emerge from the ranks of black workers.[68] Walker's John Henry poem reiterates the problem of "For My People": if black life is defined by labor in a racist, capitalist mode of production, and labor leads nowhere in terms of sociopolitical consciousness, then how is such consciousness discoverable? Molly Means, Stagolee, and Kissie Lee all suggest her answer: it can be found on the margins, among the lumpenproletariat rather than the proletariat.

"Two-Gun Buster and Trigger Slim" delineates this lumpenproletarian alternative to labor by offering a narrative of deproletarianization. Two-Gun Buster is a "railroad han'" whose quick aim with a gun allows him to terrorize his fellow workers, especially at meal times. Since each worker is only allowed one serving, and Two-Gun "had a belly he couldn't fill / With what the cook had on the bill," he bullies other men into giving him their food. The sociopolitical lesson here is obvious: capitalism keeps all workers from sufficient amounts of food, which, as we've seen for Walker, is aligned with the utopian qualities of a fulfilled, rich life. Two-Gun's bullying of his fellow workers alludes to the structural exploitation of labor itself, and Two-Gun is thus aligned with the figure of the capitalist, who deprives workers of the value of their labor. One day, a worker known only as "the Lil Lad" resists Two-Gun's attempt to take his food. Lil Lad is a strong worker like John Henry and thus "sho did earn his plate of food." Lil Lad's labor should entitle him to its remuneration in the form of food, which the capitalist mode of production, in the person of Two-Gun, expropriates.

Lil Lad challenges Two-Gun in a manner that is literally criminal and allegorically revolutionary, shooting him when he tries to take his meal. Lil Lad calmly finishes eating and not only leaves the labor camp, but abandons his proletarian status: "He didn't come back to draw his pay." Instead, he "draws his pay" as Kissie Lee did, becoming an outlaw figure who resists the relations of production in which drawing one's pay signifies one's exploitation and submission. He thus gains individual distinction and popular renown, joining the ranks of famous, socially ostracized and criminal individuals like Molly Means, Kissie Lee, or Stagolee: "So they gave the Lil Lad a name / And they called him Trigger Slim."[69]

In these ballads, Walker brings a black cultural lens to Marxist theory, revaluing the political and intellectual gains of labor and proletarian identity from the perspective of African American historical experience, and rethinking the types Marx dismissed as lumpenproletarian scum as the heroes of a black folk culture of revolution and utopian aspiration. Walker's Depression-era work constantly asks where African American life doesn't align with Marxist theory, not in order to debunk or abandon Marxism, but to appropriate and transform it. The points of nonalignment she finds are often located where they were for her more well-known black leftist contemporaries, Wright and Ellison: in the theoretical and political evaluation of those persons, practices, lives, and resources lying beyond relations of production and on the margins of a society defined by those relations. What Marx called the lumpenproletariat and banished from the theory of revolution and postcapitalist futurity, Walker sees as the heart of an African American culture of resistance, enabling her to craft a black Marxism that is revisionary and, at the same time, a realization of the essential spirit and priorities of Marxism.

[169]

CONCLUSION
AFTERLIVES OF THE DEPRESSION LUMPENPROLETARIAT

Writing about Richard Wright in 1963, Ralph Ellison commented that it was "awful" how Wright had "found the facile answers of Marxism before he learned to use literature as a means for discovering the forms of American Negro humanity."[1] Ellison crystallizes a set of assumptions here that has often guided the ways readers and scholars understand the place of Marxism in African American literary history: an enabling if intellectually and aesthetically limited influence that black writers had to move past in order to achieve both literary excellence and to furnish complex, accurate representations of African American life and culture.

Ellison's comment also indicates how, in the postwar period, writers who had started out on the Depression left often gravitated toward other sociopolitical sensibilities. His career in particular has been cited as demonstrating the necessity for black writers to transcend Marxism's "facile answers," in no small part because he helped construct that narrative of his own trajectory. In a nuanced account of Ellison's shift away from the left, Lawrence Jackson argues that he switched his literary and political allegiances to the liberal establishment after black leftists read *Invisible Man* (1952) as "trying to earn bourgeoisie success by way of abstract symbolism, Freudian psychoanalysis, and anticommunism, the coin of the day." Their attacks on his novel meant that "Ellison had an impossible time convincing fellow black writers of his political credentials." Such criticisms responded to how *Invisible Man* "seemed incapable of admitting the value of principled black resistance" and how "the complex novel that contemplated the symbolic structure of individual will could easily be read as anticommunist." Faced with this situation, Ellison "buried his leftist past" and embarked on a new track defined by Cold War liberalism and apolitical aestheticism.[2] As a result, Barbara Foley writes, "*Invisible Man* is read as testimony to Ellison's maturation; the novel's repudiation of leftist authoritarianism and scientism and its embrace of democratic pluralism and epistemological ambivalence exhibit not just its protagonist's development from ranter to writer, but the increasing sophistication of the text's creator as well."[3]

Margaret Walker would also, in later years, bury her Depression-era investments in the left and Marxism. In 1986 she claimed: "I couldn't have even had a full flirtation with the Communist Party, because they simply rejected me. . . . I realize I was considered *petit bourgeois,* Black Nationalist deviationist." Walker claims this alternative aesthetic and political classification: "I'm very Black Nationalist."[4] Ellison and Walker's retrospective revisions of their time on the left helped legitimate a consensus described by Anthony Dawahare: "most scholars of black literature and culture remain entrenched in anticommunist and pronationalist theoretical paradigms," he writes, and as a result, scholarship often assumes that "if blacks were communists, then they simply must have been duped by left-wing political parties that did not have their best interests in mind."[5] Both Ellison and Walker produced narratives that reinforce a common set of assumptions about Marxism: its protocols are not suited for explaining US and African American contexts, and commitment to Marxism produces stunted, simplified renditions of black life. As a result, the ostensibly more authentic political and aesthetic paradigms of cultural nationalism, or the ostensible moral and artistic sophistication of postwar liberalism, are often characterized as superior alternatives for black expression.

Only recently have scholars like Foley and Jackson begun the process of recovering Ellison's Depression-era leftism from the charge that it was merely facile. I have sought to further that project by delineating the epistemological and literary sophistication of his 1930s Marxism. By exploring Walker's archive of unpublished writings from the Depression period, *Ragged Revolutionaries* also reveals her encounter with Communism, an encounter that not only involved a serious manipulation of

[171]

Marxist concepts, but that synthesized Marxism with modern African American experience and cultural expression. During the Depression, Walker may indeed have been invested in black cultural nationalism, but given her own revolutionary commitments and the ways Communist discourse of the period privileged black culture, it was an investment which, at that time, was shaped by Marxist priorities.

Richard Wright made a more public break with the left than either Ellison or Walker, but this was largely due to his stature as one of the Communist left's most celebrated authors. He announced his disillusion in his 1944 *Atlantic Monthly* essay "I Tried to Be a Communist," citing, among other charges, the party's failure to live up to its revolutionary ideals and its suppressions of writers and members. Hazel Rowley writes that the essay was an early entry in a genre of "disillusioned voices of ex-Communists" that would become "fashionable" in Cold War America.[6] Yet in part because Wright had published successful pro-Communist works in the Depression that continue to be dominant in scholarship on Wright, and in part because writers and critics in later decades attacked or championed Wright as a model of the politically committed black author, the pertinence of Communism and Marxism to Wright's writing has always been visible.

Nonetheless, the complexity of Wright's efforts in the Depression can be lost in the implications of the "protest" label, which implies the sacrifice of complexity to the exigencies of antiracism and anticapitalism. This sense of Wright as an inadequate writer because of his political commitment informed James Baldwin's criticisms in "Everybody's Protest Novel" and "Many Thousands Gone." Later, Baldwin would further dismiss *Native Son* as "afflicted" with "Stalinist garbage" compared with what he saw as the less political and thus more formally inventive and authentic portrait of black life offered in *Lawd, Today!*.[7] Irving Howe, contrasting Wright's work with the postwar efforts of Baldwin and Ellison in his 1963 essay "Black Boys and Native Sons," praises Wright for the "clenched militancy" of his writing, for not sacrificing political urgency to "aesthetic distance." After all, he concludes, "plight and protest are inseparable from [African American] experience" and thus intrinsic to any authentic representation of black life.[8] Howe's and Baldwin's positions are two sides of a familiar coin. Political commitment or artistic complexity, epistemological curiosity or rigid didacticism, intellectual sophistication or Stalinist garbage—these are the binaries that have inflected discussions of Wright and still often shape conversations about the intersections of politics and black writing. *Ragged Revolutionaries* complicates this legacy by revealing Wright's Marxism to be at once politically committed, intellectually and aesthetically sophisticated, and attuned to the social and psychological complexities of black life.

While this study examines the Depression-era work of each of these three writers, the lumpenproletariat continued to assert itself, albeit in more muted ways, in Wright, Ellison, and Walker's writing following the Depression. While each writer moved away from the institutional Communist left, none of them fully abandoned the spirit of their 1930s Marxism, which involved seeking new resources for revolutionary consciousness and action in the experiences of those on the margins of social and economic structures. The African American leftist poet Frank Marshall Davis's verdict on Wright's post-Communist career could apply, to varying extents, to Ellison and Walker as well: "despite his continued Redbaiting during his final years, his writing showed that basically he was still a Marxist. When you get down to the nitty gritty, he had merely quit the organization and dumped his former comrades, not the ideology."[9]

Invisible Man's reputation as an anticommunist novel has been reified by numerous critics who, as Foley states, "accepted the premise that the invisible man's negative experiences with the Brotherhood faithfully replicate typical features of U.S. Communism."[10] But, as I've argued elsewhere, if the novel advances critiques of the institutional failures of the left, it makes those critiques from a vantage point informed in part by Ellison's earlier interests in Marxist theory and left-wing literary strategies.[11] For one, Ellison's most famous novel is driven by an effort to examine political institutions according to similar criteria he developed as part of his 1930s Marxism. The ability and willingness of self-proclaimed revolutionary institutions to actually enact transformative change, their ability to recognize and implement the resources of African American culture in the name of achieving such change, and the extent to which their theoretical and political methods are free from dogmatic stasis, are all concerns advanced in *Invisible Man*'s representation of the Brotherhood.

Lumpenproletarian figures continue, in *Invisible Man,* to inspire political innovation. Before he gives his first speech for the Brotherhood at a rally, invisible man recalls a syphilitic outcast from his youth who lived near a "Hooverville shanty" by the railroad tracks and who, "sprouting rags," would "beg money for food and disinfectant with which to soak his rags." The memory of this Depression-era member of the ragged proletariat, whose rags signal his desperation and deprivation, prompts invisible man to reject the doctrinaire formulations of the Brotherhood and, in his speech, rely on African American oral "tradition" to rally the crowd. He does so successfully, but is rebuked by Brotherhood leaders who sense, in his innovation, a threat to their ultimate interest in preserving their organization and the status quo of which it forms a part. In this episode, the major themes of Ellison's earlier Marxism—the role of the lumpenproletariat in catalyzing pragmatic revolutionary creativity, the need to interrogate the radical commitment of institutions, and a faith in the transformative power of black culture—continue to shape Ellison's sense of the political. Despite Ellison's skepticism of the Brotherhood, the group's leader, Brother Jack, nonetheless at one point acknowledges the proximity of the lumpenproletarian practice of crime to revolution. After invisible man defies the law by helping a crowd break up an eviction in Harlem, Jack tells him: "sometimes the difference between individual and organized indignation is the difference between criminal and political action."[12] Back in the 1930s, characters like Hymie, Tillman, and Slick had revealed that proximity in Ellison's work.

As noted in the introduction to this book, Walker's major work of her post-Depression career, *Jubilee* (1966), draws its influences from Marxist historiography: not only Georg Lukács's efforts to apply historical materialist categories to historical fiction, but also W. E. B. Du Bois's work, in *Black Reconstruction* (1935), to tell the history of the Civil War and Reconstruction according to classical Marxist principles of historical change.[13] Both Lukács and Du Bois provided rhetorics of historical representation, heavily influenced by Marxist historiography, that enabled Walker to rewrite Southern US history with the African American people as its protagonist. *Jubilee* may tell the story of the emergence of a black nation endowed with a rich folk culture and collective well of empowering experience, but its narrative of that emergence relies on materialist understandings of historical form. In this synthesis of nationalist and Marxist elements, *Jubilee* bears a trace of the 1930s Communist left's combination of black nationalist sensibilities, folk culture, and Marxist theory.

Walker had in fact begun work on *Jubilee* in the 1930s, recalling decades later that she had put it on hold in order to write *Goose Island*.[14] Her sociological interest in the lumpenproletariat from that period makes it into an episode in *Jubilee*. In Alabama during Reconstruction, protagonist Vyry and her partner Innis aim to earn enough money to buy a farm and build a house of their own. At one point, Innis proposes working in a sawmill to make money, but Vyry objects: the proletarianization of African Americans after slavery has resulted in the formation of a black lumpenproletariat that Vyry sees as a threat. "You ain't got no business working with them low-class folks in them sawmills and turpentine camps," she tells Innis. "Them is the worstest folks, just nothing but roustabouts" who "do nothing but drink and give they money to them bad womens."[15] Vyry refuses to make a sharp distinction between the working class, which Innis hopes to join, and the disreputable, immoral lumpenproletariat. Walker uses Vyry's moralizing opinion here to enact an ironic revision of Marx's concept of the lumpenproletariat. If Marx thought the lumpenproletariat was defined by a willed refusal to take part in capitalist production, Vyry here inadvertently suggests capitalism's role in producing the lumpenproletariat's material and moral degradation, a suggestion that implies classical Marxism's scorn toward lumpenproletarian figures is more properly directed towards capitalism itself—a point that, as we've seen, runs through much of Walker, Wright, and Ellison's Depression work.

Innis receives confirmation of the moral danger of laboring from their powerful white landowner. Mr. Jacobson employs Vyry as a cook and Innis for occasional work, pays them well, and doesn't charge them rent. Jacobson warns Innis of the "prostitutes" that make sites of collective labor "a bad environment." Wanting to retain the services of both, Jacobson provides Innis and Vyry with their own plot of land, noting that the federal government's promise of "forty acres of land and a mule" is an empty one that could never be fulfilled in Alabama. Vyry and Innis work on building their own house, but "the work took a long time because Vyry was still cooking for the Jacobsons and Innis did many odd jobs, so that any time Mr. Jacobson needed him he put down his saw and hammer and went to town to finish off another job before working again on his house." Their subservience to the Jacobsons, cloaked as property-owning autonomy, is made plain when Vyry, following the completion of their house, tells Mrs. Jacobson she'll be leaving the Jacobsons' employ in order to work their new farm. Mrs. Jacobson was "almost nasty about it": "you colored people don't want to work the way you useta. What's more you won't work the way you useta. You expect everything to come dropping in your laps . . . and you want to leave the white people holding the bag. We've done everything for you, my husband and I."[16] The Jacobsons have reproduced slavery's ideologies of paternalism and dependence in a slightly altered form, and Vyry and Innis have mistakenly assumed that the Jacobsons' intention was to empower them as landowners and private farmers. Not long after this encounter, the Ku Klux Klan burns down Vyry and Innis's house, an act of repression directed against their challenge to postbellum white supremacy.

This sequence of events reveals how an emerging Jim Crow system can use ideological narratives of moral and familial degradation to keep African Americans from joining the working class and to return them to a quasi-feudal state of servitude. The sawmills and turpentine camps, including all of the lumpenproletarian criminal activity that occurs at the margins of their productive relations, stand as a modern and progressive alternative to the neoslavery of the Jacobsons. Vyry's moralistic disdain for the lumpenproletariat—which, in tone, is also that of classical Marxism's—is here appropriated by the white landowning class. It thus blinds Vyry and Innis to both the socioeconomic causation of criminality and the opportunities both proletarian labor and lumpenproletarian practices might provide. In this manner, some of the thematic concerns driving *Goose Island*'s depiction of the slums and the lumpenproletariat recur decades later in Walker's most well-known work.

Wright wrote *The Outsider* (1953) after moving to Paris and immersing himself in the French postwar intellectual milieu. It enacts a shift in the center of gravity of Wright's thought, from Marxist to more squarely existentialist themes, a shift foreshadowed in *Native Son*. While *Invisible Man* may be more associated with literary anticommunism, *The Outsider* offers a much more scathing depiction of the Communist Party—Wright doesn't disguise the target of his critique with a euphemism like the "Brotherhood"—as cynical agents who dehumanize and manipulate its members. But like *Invisible Man*, *The Outsider*'s criticism of the party is its unwillingness to enact historical transformation. When party leaders order Bob Hunter, a black Trinidadian member, to cease his work organizing a cell in the Dining Car Waiters' Union, Hunter can't understand the reason for abandoning a promising political project. He is rebuked for not following the will of the institution: "being a Communist is not easy.

It means negating yourself, blotting out your personal life and listening only to the voice of the Party. The Party wants you to *obey!* . . . If you don't, then the Party will toss you aside, like a broken hammer, and seek another instrument that will obey." The protagonist Cross Damon, a murderous antihero who rejects all codes of Western culture in the name of an existential freedom from moral or social responsibility, later observes that the Communist leaders don't want to change the world. Rather, for them, "the world is perfect just like it is. They just want a chance to rule that world."[17]

Wright's criticism here is not only similar to Ellison's, that the party's commitment to revolution is mere rhetoric that it uses to dominate its members, but it also builds on his own concern, in *Native Son,* with themes of recognition and subject formation. *The Outsider*'s diagnosis of the Communist Party retains both the political and protoexistential dimensions of the earlier novel. If Wright's expectation for the party in *Native Son* was that it recognize the human subject behind the actions performed by black individuals—a recognition nowhere else extended in a racist, capitalist society—then his criticism in *The Outsider* is that these Communists, unlike Jan and Max, fail to realize the need for the party to serve as a counterpublic space of subjective recognition. Wright's sense of the potential of the party to live up to this criterion may have shifted, but not the criterion itself.

As its title suggests, *The Outsider* also preserves some of Wright's 1930s interest in the political resourcefulness of marginality and exteriority. After he falls in with the Communist Party in New York, Cross Damon watches a violent struggle between one of the Communist leaders and that leader's racist and fascist neighbor. Marginalized as a subject from both of the institutional and ideological discourses each combatant represents, Cross watches with "glee": "Which man did he hate more?" Cross enters the fight and kills both men, and the remainder of the novel plays out Cross's attempts to evade detection and wrestle with the ethical implications of his acts. The murder makes a political point as well. A newspaper dubs it a "DOUBLE TOTALITARIAN MURDER." The investigating district attorney, Ely Houston, not yet knowing that Cross is the killer, speculates with him. The only motive for the murder must be "ideological," he concludes. "But, in order to kill the two of them on ideological grounds, this killer would have to have the support of a *third* set of ideas." When Cross asks what that third set of ideas might be, Houston answers:

"That no ideas are necessary to justify his acts."[18] The novel doesn't espouse that form of irresponsibility, but the murder plot nonetheless allegorizes a concrete political problem. The racist and Communist locked in struggle suggest the contours of a Cold War globe divided between the totalitarian systems and ideologies of the racist West and the Communist East. The struggle suggests their ultimate equivalence: both refuse to recognize the human subject in order to reduce subjects to "instruments," and both seek not a better world but mere power over others in the present. Cross, by dramatically negating both East and West, suggests that African Americans and people of color must and can disrupt this Cold War power binary in the name of a new "set of ideas."

This set of ideas isn't given a concrete identity in the novel, though connections with global anticolonial liberation struggles and the Cold War Non-Aligned Movement can be drawn. Wright followed the development of the postcolonial Third World in the 1950s, and his *The Color Curtain: A Report on the Bandung Conference* (1956) documents the 1955 Bandung Conference, a major meeting of Asian and African nations that refused alignment with either the United States or the Soviet Union.[19] The murder plotline echoes Wright's Depression-era fascination with the ways that socioeconomic marginality in the United States could equip African Americans with revolutionary capacities. What has changed, from 1940 to 1953, is less the structure of Wright's theories of politics and subjectivity, and more the place of the actual institutional Communist movement within those theories.

One could certainly find other echoes of the 1930s in the postwar work of these three writers, but these examples should indicate how even though Wright, Ellison, and Walker all made breaks with the Communist left following the period of the Great Depression, all three remained influenced, in their new literary and political directions, by the idiosyncratic brand of Marxism they developed in that period. This was a Marxism that, by putting pressure on the concept of the lumpenproletariat, sought to craft materialist diagnoses of the racial, gender, and economic exploitations of Jim Crow and capitalism and to pose new resources for action against those exploitations. These writers realized what Louis Althusser realized in his philosophical engagement with Marxism and what the leaders of the Black Panther Party realized in their activism: if you want to be a Marxist in any effective or meaningful way, you need to identify how

Marxist thought can be expanded and situationally applied. You need to find out what still needs to be done, what still needs to be explored, where new paths for revolutionary thought and action could be located. For Wright, Ellison, and Walker, the concept and figures of the lumpenproletariat, precisely because it and they were what mattered least to orthodox Marxism, were central. Their Depression-era work furnishes a valuable indication not only of the ways in which Marxism and the left enabled and empowered black cultural production in the twentieth century, but also of how black writers used the institutions, networks, and discourses of the left to craft their own Marxism: a mode of literary and theoretical practice that stands as a sophisticated and versatile entry in the canons of Western Marxism and black radical expression.

NOTES

INTRODUCTION. COMMUNISTS, WRITERS, AND OTHER OUTSIDERS

1. Ralph Ellison, *The Collected Essays of Ralph Ellison,* ed. John F. Callahan (New York: Modern Library, 2003), 670–71.
2. Margaret Walker, *Richard Wright, Daemonic Genius: A Portrait of the Man, a Critical Look at His Work* (New York: Amistad Press, 1988), 201, 237.
3. Michael Hardt and Antonio Negri, *Multitude: War and Democracy in the Age of Empire* (New York: Penguin, 2004), 130.
4. Brent Hayes Edwards, *The Practice of Diaspora: Literature, Translation, and the Rise of Black Internationalism* (Cambridge, MA: Harvard University Press, 2003), 201.
5. Eldridge Cleaver, *On the Ideology of the Black Panther Party (Part 1)* (San Francisco: Ministry of Information of the Black Panther Party, 1970), 7.
6. Amy Abugo Ongiri, *Spectacular Blackness: The Cultural Politics of the Black Power Movement and the Search for a Black Aesthetic* (Charlottesville: University of Virginia Press, 2010), 73–74.
7. For an account of the Lumpen, see Rickey Vincent, *Party Music: The Inside Story of the Black Panthers' Band and How Black Power Transformed Soul Music* (Chicago: Lawrence Hill Books, 2013).
8. Kathleen Cleaver, *On the Vanguard Role of the Black Urban Lumpen Proletariat* (London: Grass Roots Publications, 1975), 11.
9. Lawrence P. Jackson, *The Indignant Generation: A Narrative History of African American Writers and Critics, 1934–1960* (Princeton: Princeton University Press, 2011).
10. Brian Dolinar, *The Black Cultural Front: Black Writers and Artists of the Depression Generation* (Jackson: University Press of Mississippi, 2012), 15, 8–9.
11. Robin D. G. Kelley, *Freedom Dreams: The Black Radical Imagination* (Boston: Beacon Press, 2002), 49–50.
12. Barbara Foley, *Radical Representations: Politics and Form in U.S. Proletarian Fiction, 1929–1941* (Durham: Duke University Press, 1993), 182–83.
13. Kelley, *Freedom Dreams,* 50; Foley, *Radical Representations,* 184.
14. Kelley, *Freedom Dreams,* 50–51.
15. Dolinar, *The Black Cultural Front,* 24, 23.

16. Cheryl Higashida, *Black Internationalist Feminism: Women Writers of the Black Left, 1945–1995* (Urbana: University of Illinois Press, 2011), 38.
17. John Lennon, *Boxcar Politics: The Hobo in U.S. Culture and Literature, 1869–1956* (Amherst: University of Massachusetts Press, 2014), 140.
18. Ibid., 143.
19. Louise Thompson Patterson, "Unpublished Memoirs of Louise Thompson Patterson," in *We Shall Be Free! Black Communist Protests in Seven Voices*, ed. Walter T. Howard (Philadelphia: Temple University Press, 2013), 103–4.
20. See Harold Cruse, *The Crisis of the Negro Intellectual: A Historical Analysis of the* Louise Thompson Patterson, "Unpublished Memoirs of Louise Thompson Patterson," in *We Shall Be Free! Black Communist Protests in Seven Voices*, ed. Walter T. Howard (Philadelphia: Temple University Press, 2013), 103–4. *Failure of Black Leadership* (New York: Morrow, 1967) and Cedric J. Robinson, *Black Marxism: The Making of the Black Radical Tradition* (London: Zed Press, 1983).
21. William J. Maxwell, *New Negro, Old Left: African-American Writing and Communism Between the Wars* (New York: Columbia University Press, 1999), 12, 2.
22. Barbara Foley, *Wrestling with the Left: The Making of Ralph Ellison's "Invisible Man"* (Durham: Duke University Press, 2010).
23. Ellison, *Collected Essays*, 87.
24. Lawrence W. Levine, *Black Culture and Black Consciousness: Afro-American Folk Thought from Slavery to Freedom* (Oxford: Oxford University Press, 1977), 370.
25. Ibid., 419, 420.
26. Lawrence Jackson, *Ralph Ellison: Emergence of Genius* (Athens: University of Georgia Press, 2007), 179.
27. Hazel Rowley, *Richard Wright: The Life and Times* (New York: Henry Holt and Company, 2001), 129–31.
28. Ellison, *Collected Essays*, 813.
29. This distinction between Ellison and Wright is, of course, foundational of the places each writer occupies in the African American canon and in US literary history. Ellison's essay "The World and the Jug," published in two parts in 1963 and 1964, is often read as Ellison's validation of the narrative in which Ellison, because less politically militant than Wright, is held to offer a more sophisticated and varied vision of black art and life.
30. Ellison, *Collected Essays*, 674.
31. Claudia Tate, "Black Women Writers at Work: An Interview with Margaret Walker," in *Fields Watered with Blood: Critical Essays on Margaret Walker*, ed. Maryemma Graham (Athens: University of Georgia Press, 2001), 34.
32. Alan Wald, *Exiles from a Future Time: The Forging of the Mid-Twentieth-Century Literary Left* (Chapel Hill: University of North Carolina Press, 2002), 272.
33. Rowley, *Richard Wright*, 152–53.
34. Walker, *Richard Wright, Daemonic Genius*, 124.
35. Ibid., 126.
36. Tate, "Black Women Writers at Work," 33.
37. Walker, *Richard Wright, Daemonic Genius*, 9, 237.
38. Ibid., 128.
39. Margaret Walker, *How I Wrote Jubilee and Other Essays on Life and Literature*, ed. Maryemma Graham (New York: Feminist Press, 1990), 64.

40. Ellison, *Collected Essays*, 322.
41. C. L. R. James, *At the Rendezvous of Victory: Selected Writings* (London: Allison & Busby, 1984), 196.

1. THE RAGGED PROLETARIAT

1. See Cedric J. Robinson, *Black Marxism: The Making of the Black Radical Tradition* (Chapel Hill: University of North Carolina Press, 2000).
2. Robert L. Bussard, "The 'Dangerous Class' of Marx and Engels: The Rise of the Idea of the *Lumpenproletariat*," *History of European Ideas* 8, no. 6 (1987): 677, 676.
3. Hal Draper, "The Concept of the 'Lumpenproletariat' in Marx and Engels," *Économies et Sociétés* 6, no. 12 (1972): 2309.
4. Dominick LaCapra, "Reading Marx: The Case of *The Eighteenth Brumaire*," in *Rethinking Intellectual History: Texts, Contexts, Language* (Ithaca, NY: Cornell University Press, 1983), 284.
5. Bussard, "The 'Dangerous Class' of Marx and Engels," 679.
6. Gertrude Himmelfarb, *The Idea of Poverty: England in the Early Industrial Age* (New York: Knopf, 1984), 387.
7. Karl Marx and Friedrich Engels, *The Communist Manifesto* (Oxford: Oxford University Press, 1992), 14.
8. Karl Marx, *The Eighteenth Brumaire of Louis Bonaparte* (New York: International Publishers, 1963), 122–24.
9. Frederick Engels, *The Peasant War in Germany* (Moscow: Foreign Languages Publishing House, 1956), 49, 23.
10. Marx and Engels, *Communist Manifesto*, 14; Marx, *Eighteenth Brumaire*, 75.
11. Himmelfarb, *Idea of Poverty*, 392.
12. Karl Marx, *The Class Struggles in France: 1848–1850* (New York: International Publishers, 1964), 36–37.
13. Peter Hayes, "Utopia and the Lumpenproletariat: Marx's Reasoning in 'The Eighteenth Brumaire of Louis Bonaparte,'" *Review of Politics* 50, no. 3 (Summer 1988): 446.
14. Leon Trotsky, *Fascism: What It Is and How to Fight It* (New York: Pathfinder Press, 1969), 6.
15. Marx, *Class Struggles in France*, 50.
16. Peter Stallybrass associates Marx's descriptions of the lumpenproletariat with a Victorian-era bourgeois gaze that saw the urban underclass as racially othered alongside constructions of its heterogeneous unknowability. See "Marx and Heterogeneity: Thinking the Lumpenproletariat," *Representations* 31 (Summer 1990): 74–75.
17. Marx, *Eighteenth Brumaire*, 75.
18. Stallybrass, "Marx and Heterogeneity," 72.
19. Karl Marx, *Capital: A Critique of Political Economy, Volume One* (New York: Vintage, 1977), 797.
20. Karl Marx, "Economic and Philosophical Manuscripts," in *Early Writings* (New York: Penguin, 1992), 335.
21. LaCapra, "Reading Marx," 284–85.

22. Jacques Rancière, *The Philosopher and His Poor* (Durham, NC: Duke University Press, 2003), 90–100.
23. Stallybrass, "Marx and Heterogeneity," 91.
24. Frantz Fanon, *The Wretched of the Earth* (New York: Grove Press, 2004), 5.
25. Ibid., 80–82.
26. Kathleen Cleaver, *On the Vanguard Role of the Black Urban Lumpen Proletariat* (London: Grass Roots Publications, 1975), 3.
27. Eldridge Cleaver, *On the Ideology of the Black Panther Party (Part 1)* (San Francisco: Ministry of Information of the Black Panther Party, 1970), 6–11.
28. Ibid., 8, 7.
29. Eldridge Cleaver, "On Lumpen Ideology," *Black Scholar* 4, no. 3 (1972): 4, 6–7, 8.
30. Ibid., 10.
31. C. J. Munford, "The Fallacy of Lumpen Ideology," *Black Scholar* 4, no. 10 (July–August 1973): 50.
32. Henry Winston, "The Crisis of the Black Panther Party," in *Strategy for a Black Agenda: A Critique of New Theories of Liberation in the United States and Africa* (New York: International Publishers, 1973), 218.
33. Quoted in Charles E. Jones and Judson L. Jeffries, "'Don't Believe the Hype: Debunking the Panther Mythology," in *The Black Panther Party Reconsidered*, ed. Charles E. Jones (Baltimore, MD: Black Classic Press, 1998), 43.
34. Jeffrey O. G. Ogbar, *Black Power: Radical Politics and African American Identity* (Baltimore, MD: Johns Hopkins University Press, 2004), 97; Chris Booker, "Lumpenization: A Critical Error of the Black Panther Party," in *The Black Panther Party Reconsidered*, ed. Charles E. Jones (Baltimore, MD: Black Classic Press, 1998), 357–58.
35. Cecil Brown, *Stagloee Shot Billy* (Cambridge, MA: Harvard University Press, 2003), 213.
36. Bobby Seale, *Seize the Time: The Story of the Black Panther Party and Huey P. Newton* (Baltimore, MD: Black Classic Press, 1991), ix–x.
37. Kathleen Cleaver, *On the Vanguard Role of the Black Urban Lumpen Proletariat*, 3.
38. Louis Althusser, *Philosophy and the Spontaneous Philosophy of the Scientists & Other Essays* (London: Verso, 1990): 59, 225, 230.
39. Dard Hunter, *Papermaking: The History and Technique of an Ancient Craft* (New York: Knopf, 1967), 309–40.
40. Patricia Yaeger, *Dirt and Desire: Reconstructing Southern Women's Writing, 1930–1990* (Chicago: University of Chicago Press, 2000), 82.
41. Walter Benjamin, "The Paris of the Second Empire in Baudelaire," in *The Writer of Modern Life: Essays on Charles Baudelaire* (Cambridge, MA: Harvard University Press, 2006), 108.
42. Michael W. Jennings, introduction to Benjamin, *Writer of Modern Life*, 11.
43. Theodor Adorno, "Letters to Walter Benjamin," in Adorno et al., *Aesthetics and Politics* (London: Verso, 2007), 130.
44. Mark Twain, *The Adventures of Tom Sawyer* (New York: Modern Library, 2001), 49–50.
45. Ibid., 49.
46. Stephen Crane, *Maggie, A Girl of the Streets*, in *Maggie, A Girl of the Streets and Other New York Writings* (New York: Modern Library, 2001), 18–19.

47. Ibid., 62.
48. William J. Maxwell, "Banjo Meets the Dark Princess: Claude McKay, W. E. B. Du Bois, and the Transnational Novel of the Harlem Renaissance," in *The Cambridge Companion to the Harlem Renaissance* (Cambridge, UK: Cambridge University Press, 2007), 170.
49. Claude McKay, *Banjo: A Story without a Plot* (San Diego: Harcourt, Brace, 1957), 6.
50. Brent Hayes Edwards, *The Practice of Diaspora: Literature, Translation, and the Rise of Black Internationalism* (Cambridge, MA: Harvard University Press, 2003), 198, 210.
51. Maxwell, "Banjo Meets the Dark Princess," 174–76.
52. McKay, *Banjo*, 312.
53. Maxwell, "Banjo Meets the Dark Princess," 176.
54. McKay, *Banjo*, 312–14.
55. See Walter Rideout, *The Radical Novel in the United States, 1900–1954: Some Interrelations of Literature and Society* (New York: Columbia University Press, 1992), and Barbara Foley, *Radical Representations: Politics and Form in U.S. Proletarian Fiction, 1929–1941* (Durham, NC: Duke University Press, 1993).
56. Mike Gold, *Jews without Money* (New York: Carroll and Graf, 1996), 308, 309.
57. Ibid., 27, 125, 136, 140, 31.
58. Ibid., 309, 37, 45.
59. Rideout, *Radical Novel in the United States*, 185.
60. Foley, *Radical Representations*, 287.
61. Edward Dahlberg, *The Confessions of Edward Dahlberg* (New York: George Braziller, 1971), 284.
62. Edward Anderson, *Hungry Men* (Norman: University of Oklahoma Press, 1993), 192, 44.
63. Nelson Algren, "A Lumpen," in *Entrapment and Other Writings*, ed. Brooke Horvath and Dan Simon (New York: Seven Stories Press, 2009), 33–35.
64. William Solomon, *Literature, Amusement, and Technology in the Great Depression* (Cambridge, UK: Cambridge University Press, 2002), 124.
65. William J. Maxwell, *New Negro, Old Left: African-American Writing and Communism between the Wars* (New York: Columbia University Press, 1999), 193–96.
66. Nelson Algren, *Somebody in Boots* (New York: Berkley Publishing Corporation, 1965).
67. Paul Gilroy, *The Black Atlantic: Modernity and Double Consciousness* (Cambridge, MA: Harvard University Press, 1993), 40.
68. Stuart Hall, Chas Critcher, Tony Jefferson, John Clarke, and Brian Roberts, *Policing the Crisis: Mugging, the State, and Law and Order* (London: Macmillan, 1978), 351–52.
69. Michel de Certeau, *The Practice of Everyday Life* (Berkeley: University of California Press, 1984), 37.
70. Houston Baker, *Blues, Ideology, and Afro-American Literature* (Chicago: University of Chicago Press, 1984), 8.
71. Louis Althusser, *The Future Lasts Forever: A Memoir*, trans. Richard Vesey (New York: New Press, 1992), 217.
72. Brown, *Stagolee Shot Billy*, 219, 226.

73. Ibid., 17.
74. De Certeau, *Practice of Everyday Life,* 39.

2. RICHARD WRIGHT AND THE LUMPENPROLETARIAN DESIRE FOR REVOLUTION

1. Karl Marx, *The Class Struggles in France, 1848–1850* (New York: International Publishers, 1964), 50.
2. Richard Wright, "How 'Bigger' Was Born," in *Native Son: The Original 1940 Text* (New York: Harper Perennial, 1968), xx; Karl Marx and Friedrich Engels, *The Communist Manifesto* (Oxford: Oxford University Press, 1992), 14.
3. James Smethurst, "After Modernism: Richard Wright Interprets the Black Belt," in *Richard Wright in a Post-Racial Imaginary,* ed. Alice Mikal Craven and William E. Dow (New York: Bloomsbury, 2014), 15.
4. Of the three writers of this study, Wright was the one most publicly associated with the Communist Party. Wright entered the Communist orbit in 1933, when he joined the party-backed Chicago John Reed Club, and joined the party itself shortly after. Wright was then active in the Communist movement in both Chicago and New York until he broke from the party during World War II, over its unilateral support for the US war effort and attendant deprioritization of antiracist and anticapitalist activism. For accounts of Wright's transactions with the left and formative influence by Communism, see Michel Fabre, *The Unfinished Quest of Richard Wright* (Urbana: University of Illinois Press, 1993) and Hazel Rowley, *Richard Wright: The Life and Times* (New York: Henry Holt, 2001).
5. James Baldwin "Many Thousands Gone," in *Notes of a Native Son* (Boston: Beacon Press, 1984), 34.
6. William Solomon, *Literature, Amusement, and Technology in the Great Depression* (Cambridge, UK: Cambridge University Press, 2002), 123–24.
7. William J. Maxwell, *New Negro, Old Left: African-American Writing and Communism between the Wars* (New York: Columbia University Press, 1999), 191, 184.
8. The novel's approach to subjectivity has been analyzed through various conceptual lenses that both complement and diverge from my reading. In a sophisticated consideration of Wright's corpus, Abdul JanMohamed offers a psychoanalytic reading of Bigger's actions as constituting an instrumental misrecognition and appropriation of death, Mary's as well as his eventual own, to demonstrate the black individual's subjectivity and freedom and thus protest the social death imposed on African Americans. See Abdul JanMohamed, *The Death-Bound-Subject: Richard Wright's Archaeology of Death* (Durham: Duke University Press, 2005). The social and political significances of subjectivity in *Native Son* are analyzed in a host of diverse readings, such as Anthony Dawahare's *Nationalism, Marxism, and African American Literature between the Wars: A New Pandora's Box* (Jackson: University Press of Mississippi, 2003); Kimberly S. Drake's *Subjectivity in the American Protest Novel* (New York: Palgrave Macmillan, 2011); Matthew Elder's "Social Demarcation and the Forms of Psychological Fracture in Book One of Richard Wright's *Native Son,*" *Texas Studies in Literature and Language* 52, no. 1 (Spring 2010): 31–47; Stephen George's "The Horror of Bigger Thomas: The Perception of Form without Face in Richard Wright's *Native Son,*" *African American Review* 31, no. 3 (Autumn

1997): 497–504; and Cynthia Tolentino's "The Road Out of the Black Belt: Sociology's Fictions and Black Subjectivity in *Native Son*," *Novel: A Forum on Fiction* 33, no. 3 (Summer 2000): 377–405.
9. Richard Wright to Mike Gold, c. 1940, box 98, folder 1354, Richard Wright Papers, Yale Collection of American Literature, Beinecke Rare Book and Manuscript Library, New Haven, CT (hereafter RWP).
10. Samuel Sillen, "The Meaning of Bigger Thomas," *New Masses* (April 30, 1940): 26, 28.
11. Donald Gibson, "Wright's Invisible Native Son," *American Quarterly* 21, no. 4 (Winter 1969): 728.
12. Cedric Robinson, *Black Marxism: The Making of the Black Radical Tradition* (Chapel Hill: University of North Carolina Press, 2000), 298.
13. Wright, "How 'Bigger' Was Born," xxiv.
14. Nicholas Thoburn, *Deleuze, Marx, and Politics* (New York: Routledge, 2003), 54, 49, 64.
15. Eldridge Cleaver, "On Lumpen Ideology," *Black Scholar* 4, no. 3 (1972): 4, 7.
16. Rowley, *Richard Wright*, 143.
17. Margaret Walker, *Richard Wright, Daemonic Genius: A Portrait of the Man, A Critical Look at His Work* (New York: Amistad Press, 1988), 126.
18. Rowley, *Richard Wright*, 40.
19. Richard Wright, "Big Boy Leaves Home," in *Uncle Tom's Children* (New York: Harper-Perennial, 2004), 28.
20. Richard Wright, "Almos' A Man," *Harper's Bazaar* (January 1940): 40, 107.
21. Ibid., 107.
22. Houston Baker, *Blues, Ideology, and Afro-American Literature* (Chicago: University of Chicago Press, 1984), 8.
23. Morris Dickstein, *Dancing in the Dark: A Cultural History of the Great Depression* (New York: Norton, 2009), 54–55.
24. Richard Wright, *12 Million Black Voices* (New York: Basic Books, 2008), 87–88.
25. Richard Wright, "Transcontinental," *International Literature*, January 1936, 52.
26. Ibid., 52, 54.
27. Rowley, *Richard Wright*, 103.
28. Ibid., 55.
29. Richard Wright, *Lawd, Today!* (Boston: Northeastern University Press, 1991), 51, 89, 116, 143–44.
30. Ibid., 149.
31. Dawahare, *Nationalism, Marxism, and African American Literature*, 112.
32. Drake, *Subjectivity in the American Protest Novel*, 64, 65.
33. Wright, *Lawd, Today!*, 19–20.
34. Brannon Costello, "Richard Wright's *Lawd, Today!* and the Political Uses of Modernism," *African American Review* 37, no. 1 (Spring 2003): 47–48.
35. Wright, *Lawd, Today!*, 152–53.
36. Marx and Engels, *Communist Manifesto*, 14.
37. Wright, *Lawd, Today!*, 31, 151, 150.
38. Ibid., 175–76.
39. Wright, "How 'Bigger' Was Born," xi, xiii.
40. Ibid., xiv–xv, xvii.

41. Ibid., xx.
42. Wright, *Native Son*, 109–10.
43. Ibid., 7.
44. Ibid., 10–11.
45. Ibid., 12–13, 307, 16.
46. Ibid., 61.
47. Susan Edmunds, "'Just Like Home': Richard Wright, Harriet Beecher Stowe, and the New Deal," *American Literature* 86, no. 1 (March 2014): 78, 76.
48. Wright, *Native Son*, 20.
49. Richard Wright, introduction to *Black Metropolis: A Study of Negro Life in a Northern City*, by St. Clair Drake and Horace Cayton (New York: Harcourt, Brace, 1945): xxxii–xxxiii.
50. Wright, *Native Son*, 21–23.
51. Louis Althusser, *On the Reproduction of Capitalism: Ideology and Ideological State Apparatuses* (London: Verso, 2014), 264.
52. Warren Montag, *Althusser and His Contemporaries: Philosophy's Perpetual War* (Durham, NC: Duke University Press, 2013), 151.
53. Althusser, *On the Reproduction of Capitalism*, 264.
54. Wright, *Native Son*, 32.
55. Ibid., 33.
56. Ibid., 36.
57. Hannah Arendt, *The Human Condition* (Chicago: University of Chicago Press, 1998), 101.
58. Ibid., 180, 41, 190.
59. Hannah Arendt, *On Revolution* (New York: Penguin, 2006), 54, 24, 241, 238.
60. Richard Wright, *12 Million Black Voices*, 75, 136, 145.
61. Jean-Paul Sartre, *Search for a Method* (New York: Vintage, 1968), 43.
62. Fredric Jameson, *Marxism and Form: Twentieth-Century Dialectical Theories of Literature* (Princeton, NJ: Princeton University Press, 1971), 219, 223.
63. Sartre, *Search for a Method*, 97, 109.
64. Wright met both Arendt and Sartre at the New York apartment of his friend Dorothy Norman, the editor of the journal *Twice a Year*, in 1946. Wright became close to both Sartre and Simone de Beauvoir following his permanent relocation to Paris in 1947. Wright discussed existentialism with Arendt in 1946, and would later read the English edition of her 1951 study *The Origins of Totalitarianism*. See Rowley, *Richard Wright*, 326; and Fabre, *Unfinished Quest*, 434. Wright's engagement with existentialist philosophy has been most frequently discussed in analyses of his Paris period and his 1953 novel *The Outsider*, most recently by Konstantina M. Karageorgos in "Deep Marxism: Richard Wright's *The Outsider* and the Making of a Postwar Aesthetic," *Mediations* 28, no. 2 (2015): 109–27.
65. Karl Marx and Friedrich Engels, *The German Ideology*, in *The Marx-Engels Reader*, ed. Robert C. Tucker (New York: Norton, 1978), 160.
66. Michael Warner, *Publics and Counterpublics* (New York: Zone Books, 2002), 59.
67. Wright, *Native Son*, 16–17.
68. Ibid., 17–18, 40–41.
69. Ibid., 34–35.
70. Mikhail Bakunin, *Statism and Anarchy*, in *Bakunin on Anarchy: Selected Works*

by the Activist-Founder of World Anarchism (New York: Knopf, 1972), 334.
71. Wright, Native Son, 86–90.
72. Ibid., 101, 24, 101.
73. Ibid., 100, 334–35.
74. Ibid., 102, 166–67.
75. Ibid., 101, 123.
76. JanMohamed, Death-Bound-Subject, 109.
77. Joseph Entin notes Wright's enthusiasm for mysteries and detective fiction, and argues Native Son uses "the narrative drama and racial formulas of pulp fiction to challenge stereotypes about African Americans." See Joseph B. Entin, Sensational Modernism: Experimental Fiction and Photography in Thirties America (Chapel Hill: University of North Carolina Press, 2007), 241. Incorporating the detective plot's implications for the public revelation of Bigger's subjectivity should be read as a further politicization of pulp fiction on Wright's part.
78. Wright, Native Son, 108, 123, 213.
79. Ibid., 214.
80. Drake, Subjectivity in the American Protest Novel, 59–61.
81. Wright, Native Son, 228–30.
82. Ibid., 215, 219, 222, 305–6.
83. JanMohamed, Death-Bound-Subject, 110.
84. Wright, Native Son, 131–32, 226.
85. Ibid., 235–36.
86. Ibid., 231, 233.
87. Ibid., 248.
88. Jameson, Marxism and Form, 297.
89. Mikko Tuhkanen, "Queer Guerrillas: On Richard Wright's and Frantz Fanon's Dissembling Revolutionaries," Mississippi Quarterly 61, no. 4 (September 2008): 617.
90. Wright, Native Son, 260–61, 374–75.
91. Warner, Publics and Counterpublics, 56–57.
92. Sondra Guttman, "What Bigger Killed For: Rereading Violence against Women in Native Son," Texas Studies in Literature and Language 43, no. 2 (Summer 2001): 173–74.
93. Wright, Native Son, 53, 66.
94. Ibid., 70.
95. Ibid., 268–69, 333.
96. Arendt, On Revolution, 61.
97. Wright, Native Son, 359, 362–63, 366, 364.
98. Ibid., 391–92.
99. Maria K. Mootry, "Bitches, Whores, and Woman Haters: Archetypes and Typologies in the Art of Richard Wright," in Richard Wright: A Collection of Critical Essays, ed. Richard Macksey and Frank E. Moorer (Englewood Cliffs, NJ: Prentice-Hall, 1984), 119, 122, 118, 117.
100. Trudier Harris, "Native Sons and Foreign Daughters," in New Essays on Native Son, ed. Keneth Kinnamon (Cambridge, UK: Cambridge University Press, 1990), 77, 63.
101. See Dawahare, Nationalism, Marxism, and African American Literature, and

Cheryl Higashida, "Aunt Sue's Children: Re-viewing the Gender(ed) Politics of Richard Wright's Radicalism," *American Literature* 75, no. 2 (June 2003): 395–425.

102. Adrienne Rich, *On Lies, Secrets, and Silence: Selected Prose* (New York: Norton, 1995), 212.
103. Bonnie Honig, "Toward an Agonistic Feminism: Hannah Arendt and the Politics of Identity," in *Feminist Interpretations of Hannah Arendt*, ed. Bonnie Honig (University Park: Pennsylvania State University Press, 1995), 143.
104. Arendt, *Human Condition*, 48n39, 30.
105. Hannah Arendt, "Reflections on Little Rock," in *The Portable Hannah Arendt* (New York: Penguin: 2000), 242, 236.
106. Robert Penn Warren, *Who Speaks for the Negro?* (New York: Random House, 1965), 343–44.
107. Danielle Allen, "Law's Necessary Forcefulness: Ralph Ellison vs. Hannah Arendt on the Battle of Little Rock," *Oklahoma City University Law Review* 26 (2001): 861.
108. Ralph Ellison, *The Collected Essays of Ralph Ellison*, ed. John F. Callahan (New York: Modern Library, 2003), 79–80.
109. Anne Norton, "Heart of Darkness: Africa and African Americans in the Writings of Hannah Arendt," in *Feminist Interpretations of Hannah Arendt*, 257.
110. Bonnie Honig, "Toward an Agonistic Feminism," 143.
111. Barbara Foley, "'A Dramatic Picture ... of Woman from Feudalism to Fascism': Richard Wright's *Black Hope*," in *Richard Wright in a Post-Racial Imaginary*, ed. Alice Mikal Craven and William E. Dow (New York: Bloomsbury, 2014), 113.
112. Richard Wright, *Black Hope*, box 18, folder 292, RWP, 960–61.
113. Julieann Veronica Ulin, "Talking to Bessie: Richard Wright's Domestic Servants," *American Literature* 85, no. 1 (March 2013): 161.

3. FROM OKLAHOMA CITY TO TUSKEGEE, FROM HARLEM TO DAYTON

1. Stanley Edgar Hyman to Ralph Ellison, July 19, 1942, box 1:51, folder 15, Ralph Ellison Papers, Manuscript Division, Library of Congress, Washington, DC (REP).
2. Ralph Ellison to Stanley Edgar Hyman, c. July 1942, box 6, Stanley Edgar Hyman Papers, Manuscript Division, Library of Congress, Washington, DC.
3. Ralph Ellison, *The Collected Essays of Ralph Ellison*, ed. John F. Callahan (New York: Modern Library, 2003), 58, 746.
4. Larry Neal, "Ellison's Zoot Suit," in *Ralph Ellison: A Collection of Critical Essays*, ed. John Hersey (Englewood Cliffs, NJ: Prentice-Hall 1974): 60.
5. Barbara Foley, *Wrestling with the Left: The Making of Ralph Ellison's "Invisible Man"* (Durham: Duke University Press, 2010), 5. For other critics who have examined Ellison's radicalism in productive ways, see Frederick T. Griffiths, "Ralph Ellison, Richard Wright, and the Case of Angelo Herndon," *African American Review* 35, no. 4 (Winter 2001): 615–36; William J. Maxwell, "'Creative and Cultural Lag': The Radical Education of Ralph Ellison," in *A Historical Guide to Ralph Ellison*, ed. Steven C. Tracy (Oxford: Oxford University Press, 2004): 59–83; Christopher Z. Hobson, "Invisible Man and African American

Radicalism in World War II," *African American Review* 39, no. 3 (Fall 2005): 355–76; and Robin Lucy, "'Flying Home': Ralph Ellison, Richard Wright, and the Black Folk During World War II," *Journal of American Folklore* 120, no. 477 (Summer 2007): 257–83.
6. For a biographical account of Ellison's trip, see Arnold Rampersad, *Ralph Ellison: A Biography* (New York: Vintage, 2008), 44–51.
7. Jesse Wolfe, "Ambivalent Man: Ellison's Rejection of Communism," *African American Review* 34, no. 4 (Winter 2000): 626.
8. Louis Althusser, "On the Materialist Dialectic," in *For Marx*, trans. Ben Brewster (London: Verso, 1996), 198–99.
9. Rampersad, *Ralph Ellison*, 313; Foley, *Wrestling with the Left*, 6.
10. Ellison, *Collected Essays*, 154.
11. John F. Callahan, "Chaos, Complexity, and Possibility: The Historical Frequencies of Ralph Waldo Ellison," in *Speaking for You: The Vision of Ralph Ellison*, ed. Kimberly W. Benston (Washington, DC: Howard University Press, 1987), 128.
12. Ellison, *Collected Essays*, 51–52.
13. Ibid., 200–202.
14. Althusser, "On the Materialist Dialectic," 209–10.
15. Alain Badiou, *Metapolitics* (London: Verso, 2006), 65.
16. Ellison, *Collected Essays*, 64.
17. John S. Wright, *Shadowing Ralph Ellison* (Jackson: University Press of Mississippi, 2006), 147, 150.
18. Rayvon Fouché, *Black Inventors in the Age of Segregation: Granville T. Woods, Lewis H. Latimer, and Shelby J. Davidson* (Baltimore: Johns Hopkins University Press, 2003), 3.
19. Ralph Ellison, "A Party Down at the Square," in *Flying Home and Other Stories* (New York: Vintage, 1998), 11.
20. Antonio Gramsci, *Selections from the Prison Notebooks of Antonio Gramsci* (New York: International Publishers, 1971), 177–78, 365–66.
21. Ibid., 366–67; Norberto Bobbio, "Gramsci and the Conception of Civil Society," in *Gramsci and Marxist Theory*, ed. Chantal Mouffe (London: Routledge, 1979), 34.
22. Ellison, *Collected Essays*, 773.
23. Rampersad, *Ralph Ellison*, 51.
24. Ellison, *Collected Essays*, 773.
25. Ralph Ellison, *Slick* Novel, box 1:159, folder 13, REP. The pages of notes in this folder are not numbered.
26. Stuart Hall, "Race, Articulation, and Societies Structured in Dominance," in *Black British Cultural Studies: A Reader*, ed. Houston A Baker Jr., Manthia Diawara, and Ruth H. Lindeborg (Chicago: University of Chicago Press, 1996), 55.
27. Ralph Ellison, *Memoirs*, box 1:110, folder 2, REP, 66, 68. Ellison's typescript includes revisions added by hand. When quoting from this and subsequent typed documents in Ellison's archive, I have included these handwritten revisions in my quotations. Throughout this chapter, I have been conservative in correcting any apparent spelling errors in Ellison's manuscripts.
28. Ralph Ellison, "I Did Not Learn Their Names," in *Flying Home and Other Stories* (New York: Vintage, 1998), 89, 91, 93.
29. Ibid., 95–96.

30. Raymond Williams, *Keywords: A Vocabulary of Culture and Society* (New York: Oxford University Press, 1985), 136–37.
31. See J. Martin Favor, *Authentic Blackness: The Folk in the New Negro Renaissance* (Durham, NC: Duke University Press, 1999), and David G. Nicholls, *Conjuring the Folk: Forms of Modernity in African America* (Ann Arbor: University of Michigan Press, 2000).
32. Anthony Dawahare, *Nationalism, Marxism, and African-American Literature between the Wars: A New Pandora's Box* (Jackson: University Press of Mississippi, 2003), 74–76; Barbara Foley, *Radical Representations: Politics and Form in U.S. Proletarian Fiction, 1929–1941* (Durham, NC: Duke University Press, 1993), 184.
33. Lucy, "'Flying Home,'" 263.
34. Ibid., 274.
35. Richard Wright, "Blueprint for Negro Writing," *New Challenge* 2, no. 2 (1937): 53–65.
36. Marian Minus, "Present Trends of Negro Literature," *Challenge* 2, no. 1 (1937): 10–11.
37. Richard Wright, "Joe Louis Uncovers Dynamite," *New Masses*, October 8, 1935, 19.
38. My use of the term "lumpen-folk" to name the presence of the lumpenproletariat as an operative figure in Ellison's work is intended, on one level, to dialogue with Robin Lucy's "working-folk," which she introduces in her reading of Ellison to name the modernized refiguration of cultures of resistance in the urban black proletariat. See Lucy, "'Flying Home,'" 263.
39. Ralph Ellison, "Hymie's Bull," in *Flying Home and Other Stories* (New York: Vintage, 1998), 82, 83, 88.
40. Rampersad, *Ralph Ellison*, 99.
41. Robert Penn Warren, *Who Speaks for the Negro?* (New York: Random House, 1965), 332.
42. Ellison, *Collected Essays*, 53.
43. Minus, "Present Trends of Negro Literature," 11.
44. Gramsci, *Selections from the Prison Notebooks of Antonio Gramsci*, 332–33.
45. Ibid., 418.
46. Ellison, *Collected Essays*, 16–17.
47. Ralph Ellison to Richard Wright, May 11, 1940, box 97, folder 1314, Richard Wright Papers, Yale Collection of American Literature, Beinecke Rare Book and Manuscript Library, New Haven, CT. All Ellison–Wright correspondence cited is contained in this box and folder.
48. Ellison to Wright, April 22, 1940.
49. Ralph Ellison, "Recent Negro Fiction," *New Masses*, August 5, 1941, 22.
50. Ellison to Wright, April 14, 1940.
51. Richard Wright, "How 'Bigger' Was Born," in *Native Son: The Original 1940 Text* (New York: Perennial, 2003), xxvii.
52. Ben Davis Jr., "Richard Wright's 'Native Son' a Notable Achievement," *Sunday Worker*, April 14, 1940, 4, 6.
53. Ellison to Wright, April 14, 1940.
54. Davis Jr., "Richard Wright's 'Native Son' a Notable Achievement," 4.
55. Lillian Johnson, "'Native Son' Is Personal Triumph, but No Value to a Nation," *Baltimore Afro-American*, April 13, 1940, 13.
56. Ellison to Wright, April 14, 1940.
57. Ellison to Wright, April 22, 1940.

58. Ellison to Wright, April 14, 1940.
59. See James Baldwin's 1949 essay "Everybody's Protest Novel" and his 1951 "Many Thousands Gone," in *Notes of a Native Son* (Boston: Beacon Press, 1984), 13–23, 24–45.
60. Rampersad, *Ralph Ellison*, 101–4.
61. Ibid., 104.
62. Quoted in Rampersad, *Ralph Ellison*, 105.
63. Ellison to Wright, November 8, 1937.
64. Rampersad, *Ralph Ellison*, 103. Many of Ellison's writings from this period are composed on the back of letterhead from the Montgomery County Republican Executive Committee and from Sutton's office.
65. Ellison to Wright, November 8, 1937.
66. Quoted in Rampersad, *Ralph Ellison*, 109.
67. Hazel Rowley, *Richard Wright: The Life and Times* (New York: Henry Holt, 2001), 150.
68. Ralph Ellison, *Tillman and Tackhead*, box 1:165, folder 11, REP, 1. This folder contains the most complete draft of *Tillman and Tackhead*, and the page numbers in the following citations refer to the manuscript pages numbered by Ellison in this draft.
69. Natalie Spassky, "Winslow Homer: At the Metropolitan Museum of Art," *Metropolitan Museum of Art Bulletin* 39, no. 4 (Spring 1982): 37.
70. Ellison, *Tillman and Tackhead*, 3.
71. Ibid., 4–6.
72. Peter H. Wood, *Weathering the Storm: Inside Winslow Homer's* Gulf Stream (Athens: University of Georgia Press, 2004), 16–21, 33–60.
73. Ellison, *Tillman and Tackhead*, 11, 7, 11.
74. Ibid., 7.
75. Ibid., 8–10.
76. Ibid., 10–11.
77. Ibid., 20–21.
78. Ibid., 15.
79. Ibid., 27–28. Ellison here draws on his own recollections of witnessing the devastation of Tulsa in 1921. See Rampersad, *Ralph Ellison*, 21–22.
80. Ellison, *Tillman and Tackhead*, 30, 32.
81. Ibid., 38–40, 62.
82. Ibid., 45.
83. Ibid., 61, 64, 67.
84. Ralph Ellison, "Slick Gonna Learn," *Direction* 2 (September 1939): 10–11, 14, 16.
85. Ellison, *Slick*, folder 10, 10.
86. Ibid., 16.
87. Ibid., 19, 22–23.
88. Ibid., 33.
89. Ibid., 42–46.
90. Ibid., 46.
91. Ibid., folder 11, 2.
92. Ibid., folder 10, 49–50.
93. Ibid., 52. For an account of the involuntary sterilization of African American

women and women from other racial and ethnic groups in the twentieth century, see Angela Davis, *Women, Race, and Class* (New York: Vintage, 1983), 215–21.
94. Ellison, *Slick,* folder 13.
95. Ibid., folder 9. The drafts of the Snodgrass episode in this folder are not paginated.
96. Ibid., folder 13.
97. William H. Sheldon, *Psychology and the Promethean Will: A Constructive Study of the Acute Common Problem of Education, Medicine and Religion* (New York: Harper, 1936), 76.
98. Foley, *Wrestling with the Left,* 131.
99. Ellison, *Slick,* folder 10, 65–67.
100. Ibid., folder 11, 18.
101. Ibid., 24, 27–29.
102. Ibid., 39, 41; Karl Marx, *The Eighteenth Brumaire of Louis Bonaparte* (New York: International Publishers, 1963), 15.
103. Ellison, *Slick,* folder 11, 41–44.
104. Ibid., 46–47.
105. Ibid., 48.

4. PROSTITUTES, DELINQUENTS, AND FOLK HEROES

1. Margaret Walker and Kay Bonetti, "An Interview with Margaret Walker," *The Missouri Review* 15, no. 1 (Winter 1992): 117.
2. Carolyn J. Brown, *Song of My Life: A Biography of Margaret Walker* (Jackson: University Press of Mississippi, 2014). The fullest overview of Walker's activity on the Communist left is a brief three-page discussion provided by Alan M. Wald. See *Exiles from a Future Time: The Forging of the Mid-Twentieth-Century Literary Left* (Chapel Hill: University of North Carolina Press, 2002), 271–73. Nancy Berke is the scholar who has most thoroughly examined Walker's work in the context of her leftism. As Berke explains, Walker criticism otherwise "focuses almost exclusively on her evocations of southern life," and discussions of *For My People,* her only published work of Depression-era poetry, generally revolve around the text's depiction of black life in the South and neglect its left-wing political orientations. See *Women Poets on the Left: Lola Ridge, Genevieve Taggard, Margaret Walker* (Gainesville: University Press of Florida, 2001), 124.
3. Wald, *Exiles from a Future Time,* 272; Margaret Walker to Richard Wright, October 9, 1937, and June 1, 1938, box 107, folder 1667, RWP. All Walker–Wright correspondence cited is contained in this box and folder.
4. Wald, *Exiles from a Future Time,* 272; Walker to Wright, August 30, 1938.
5. Her journal entry for September 4, 1939, describes how she attended events marking the party's twentieth anniversary. See Margaret Walker, September 4, 1939, Journal entry, series II, box 3, folder 16, Margaret Walker Alexander Personal Papers, Margaret Walker Center, Jackson State University, Jackson, MS (hereafter MWAP). Walker to Wright, June 30 and March 19, 1938.
6. Walker to Wright, September 29, 1937.
7. Walker to Wright, June 1, 1938.

8. Walker to Wright, November 24, 1937.
9. Margaret Walker, "Radical Revolutionary," subseries III.A, box 1, Poetry Manuscript Perpetual Date Book (hereafter Poetry Date Book) Part 2, MWAP, 194. Page numbers of this and following manuscript poems are those printed on one of the two date books in which Walker drafted poems during the 1930s. The first book covers the period 1929–1934, the second 1936–1940. The poems in the date books are handwritten and, as drafts, reflect Walker's writing process, often containing revisions, additions, and deletions. In this chapter, I have generally included these changes when quoting from her poetry manuscripts. In instances when a revision seems thematically significant, or when alternate versions of a part of a poem are available on the manuscript page, I have signaled the nature and status of the revision in the chapter text or notes.
10. Walker to Wright, April 7, 1938.
11. Cecil Brown, *Stagolee Shot Billy* (Cambridge, MA: Harvard University Press, 2003), 193, 13, 198.
12. Karl Marx, *Karl Marx: Early Writings* (New York: Penguin, 1992), 350.
13. Roderick Ferguson, *Aberrations in Black: Toward a Queer of Color Critique* (Minneapolis: University of Minnesota Press, 2004), 7–8, 10.
14. Frederick Engels, *Socialism: Utopian and Scientific* (New York: Pathfinder Press, 1989), 83–84.
15. I here allude to the utopian sense of queerness theorized by José Esteban Muñoz, in which the nonalignment of queerness with the normative and restrictive structures of present social life enables queer culture to gesture negatively toward futurity, toward an order of reality organized beyond and outside those structures. See *Cruising Utopia: The Then and There of Queer Futurity* (New York: NYU Press, 2009).
16. Karl Marx, *Capital: A Critique of Political Economy, Volume One* (New York: Vintage, 1977), 797.
17. Karl Marx and Friedrich Engels, *The Communist Manifesto* (Oxford: Oxford University Press, 1992), 16.
18. Eldridge Cleaver, "On Lumpen Ideology," *Black Scholar* 4, no. 3 (1972): 10.
19. Margaret Walker, *Richard Wright, Daemonic Genius: A Portrait of the Man, a Critical Look at His Work* (New York: Amistad Press, 1988), 70–71.
20. Margaret Walker, "Factory-hand," Poetry Date Book Part 1, 347.
21. Margaret Walker, "Rich Fokes Worl," Poetry Date Book Part 2, 40–41. Revisions to the manuscript indicate that Walker considered the title "Monologue" as well, and a version of the poem was eventually published as "Monologue" in Walker's 1989 volume of collected poems. Perhaps an indication of Walker's tendency to efface her 1930s Marxist investments by attributing primacy to racial over economic factors, "Monologue" attributes the speaker's struggles to a "white folks world." See Walker, *This Is My Century: New and Collected Poems* (Athens: University of Georgia Press, 1989), 161–62. This decision does not cancel the clear intersectional workings of race and class in the body of the speaker's monologue, however.
22. Peter Stallybrass, "Marx and Heterogeneity: Thinking the Lumpenproletariat," *Representations* 31 (Summer 1990): 71.
23. Margaret Walker, "Men at Work," Poetry Date Book Part 2, 150–51.
24. André Gorz, *Farewell to the Working Class: An Essay on Post-Industrial Socialism* (Boston: South End Press, 1982), 16.

25. St. Clair Drake and Horace R. Cayton, *Black Metropolis: A Study of Negro Life in a Northern City* (New York: Harcourt, Brace, 1945), 598.
26. Cleaver, "On Lumpen Ideology," 10.
27. Margaret Walker, "Gun Moll," Poetry Date Book Part 2, 142–44.
28. Margaret Walker, "Prostitute," Poetry Date Book Part 1, 302.
29. Margaret Walker, *For My People* (New Haven, CT: Yale University Press, 1942), 54.
30. Berke, *Women Poets on the Left*, 151.
31. Walker, *For My People*, 54; Berke, *Women Poets on the Left*, 155.
32. Walker, "Prostitute," 302.
33. Jane Addams, *A New Conscience and an Ancient Evil* (New York: Macmillan, 1923), 59.
34. Walker, "Prostitute," 302–3.
35. Madhu Dubey, *Signs and Cities: Black Literary Postmodernism* (Chicago: University of Chicago Press, 2003), 8.
36. Margaret Walker, "The Red Satin Dress," *The New Anvil*, December 1939, 19–20.
37. Carolyn J. Brown, *Song of My Life*, 25; Walker, *Richard Wright, Daemonic Genius*, 125–26.
38. Solomon Kobrin, "The Chicago Area Project—A 25-Year Assessment," *Annals of the American Academy of Political and Social Science* 322, no. 1 (March 1959): 21, 28.
39. Walker, *Richard Wright, Daemonic Genius*, 126.
40. Margaret Walker, *Goose Island*, subseries III.B, MWAP, ii.
41. Marx and Engels, *Communist Manifesto*, 14.
42. Walker, *Goose Island*, 78–79.
43. Ibid., 96.
44. Ibid., 96–97, 78, 97.
45. Ibid., 128–32.
46. Ibid., 132–34.
47. Ibid., 136.
48. The line is from Dunbar's poem "Life," which appears in his 1893 volume *Oak and Ivy*.
49. Walker, *Goose Island*, 134.
50. Ibid., 183.
51. Ibid., 271.
52. Ibid., 272, 274.
53. Walker, *For My People*, 13–14.
54. Ibid., 25.
55. Derek Furr, "Re-Sounding Folk Voice, Remaking the Ballad: Alan Lomax, Margaret Walker, and the New Criticism," *Twentieth-Century Literature* 59, no. 2 (Summer 2013): 250–51.
56. Berke, *Women Poets on the Left*, 144.
57. Walker, *For My People*, 33–34.
58. Berke, *Women Poets on the Left*, 145–47.
59. William Scott, "Belonging to History: Margaret Walker's *For My People*," *MLN* 121, no. 5 (December 2006): 1095.
60. Robert Penn Warren, *Who Speaks for the Negro?* (New York: Random House, 1965), 332.

61. Walker, *For My People*, 35.
62. Ibid., 38, 35.
63. Ibid., 38–39.
64. Keith Gilyard, *John Oliver Killens: A Life of Black Literary Activism* (Athens: University of Georgia Press, 2010), 286–88.
65. Walker, *For My People*, 49.
66. Furr, "Re-Sounding Folk Voice," 252.
67. Walker, *For My People*, 49.
68. Furr, "Re-Sounding Folk Voice," 252.
69. Walker, *For My People*, 42–43.

CONCLUSION. AFTERLIVES OF THE DEPRESSION LUMPENPROLETARIAT

1. Ralph Ellison, *The Collected Essays of Ralph Ellison*, ed. John F. Callahan (New York: Modern Library, 2003), 167.
2. Lawrence P. Jackson, *The Indignant Generation: A Narrative History of African American Writers and Critics* (Princeton, NJ: Princeton University Press, 2011), 359–60.
3. Barbara Foley, *Wrestling with the Left: The Making of Ralph Ellison's "Invisible Man"* (Durham, NC: Duke University Press, 2010), 4–5.
4. Margaret Walker, *Conversations with Margaret Walker*, ed. Maryemma Graham (Jackson: University Press of Mississippi, 2002), 124.
5. Anthony Dawahare, *Nationalism, Marxism, and African American Literature between the Wars: A New Pandora's Box* (Jackson: University Press of Mississippi, 2003), 135, xviii.
6. Hazel Rowley, *Richard Wright: The Life and Times* (New York: Henry Holt, 2001), 293.
7. James Baldwin, *Conversations with James Baldwin*, ed. Fred L. Standley and Louis H. Pratt (Jackson: University Press of Mississippi, 1989), 204.
8. Irving Howe, *Selected Writings: 1950–1990* (New York: Harcourt Brace Jovanovich, 1990), 127, 131.
9. Quoted in Bill V. Mullen, *Popular Fronts: Chicago and African-American Cultural Politics, 1935–46* (Urbana: University of Illinois Press, 1999), 43.
10. Foley, *Wrestling with the Left*, 1.
11. Nathaniel Mills, "Writing Brotherhood: The Utopian Politics of Ralph Ellison's *Invisible Man*," in *Lineages of the Literary Left: Essays in Honor of Alan M. Wald*, ed. Howard Brick, Robbie Lieberman, and Paula Rabinowitz (Ann Arbor: Michigan Publishing, 2015), 195–210.
12. Ralph Ellison, *Invisible Man* (New York: Vintage, 1995), 336–37, 342, 293.
13. Margaret Walker, *How I Wrote Jubilee and Other Essays on Life and Literature*, ed. Maryemma Graham (New York: Feminist Press, 1990), 64, 57.
14. Ibid., 51.
15. Margaret Walker, *Jubilee* (Boston: Mariner Books, 1999), 367.
16. Ibid., 367–69, 373.
17. Richard Wright, *The Outsider* (New York: Perennial, 2003), 248, 448.
18. Ibid., 300, 436, 376.

19. For an illuminating discussion of *The Outsider* in the context of Wright's criticisms of the Communist Party and European existentialist philosophy, and his perception of the possibilities inherent in the global emergence of a postcolonial "outside" of the West, see Jeffrey Atteberry, "Entering the Politics of the Outside: Richard Wright's Critique of Marxism and Existentialism," *Modern Fiction Studies* 51, no. 4 (Winter 2005): 873–95.

INDEX

action, 70, 72, 90–91; and crime/criminality, 174
Adams, John, 71
Addams, Jane, *A New Conscience and an Ancient Evil*, 150
Adorno, Theodor, 36
African American literature: Bigger Thomas (*Native Son*) as most lumpenproletarian character, 17, 49–51; bottom dogs fiction, 12, 40, 42–45, 55, 107; and Marxism, 170
African American studies, 9
African Americans: Arendt on, 91; black folk, 5, 34, 97, 108–9, 111, 113, 139–40, 160, 164–65, 169; black manhood, 53; black Marseilles lumpenproletariat, 38; black masculinity, 54, 76, 123; black vagabond, 39; blackness and criminality, 123–24; and blues music, 94; and Communist Party, 5–7, 9, 83–84, 112–13, 172; and dislocation, 17; Ellison cautions application of Marxist concept to, 94–95; folklore of, 11, 18, 160; and Homer, 119; invisibility of, 52, 66, 91; and labor, 161, 168; and lumpenproletariat, 3, 48, 163; and marginality, 47; and Marxism, 1–2, 4, 9, 19, 33, 52, 95, 117, 138, 170–72; oral traditions and music, 47; outside of social order, 3–4; and paper, 39; and philosophical method, 15–16; and revolutionary change, 3–4, 6, 33–34, 84, 169; and sterilization, 193n93; and technology, 102; transience as survival, 54; urban experience, 47; vernacular culture, 140; working class, 53. *See also* black culture; black lumpenproletariat; black Marxism; folk; recognition; subjectivity
African diaspora, 38–39
Agee, James, *Let Us Now Praise Famous Men*, 35
Algren, Nelson, 12, 44–45, 55–56, 137; "A Lumpen," 44; and Marx, 44–45; *Somebody in Boots*, 45
Allen, Danielle, 91
Althusser, Louis, 15, 34, 47–48, 51–52, 82, 98, 100, 103, 178; on subjectivity, 67, 70
The American Progress, 44

INDEX

American Revolution, 70–71, 87
anarchism, 75
Anderson, Edward, *Hungry Men*, 43
antihero, 140, 177
Arendt, Hannah, 15–16, 51, 73, 78, 84, 89–92, 188n64; on African Americans, 91; *The Human Condition*, 69–70, 90; on labor, 69–70, 90–91; *On Revolution*, 70–71, 87; "Reflections on Little Rock," 90–91; on women, 90
Armstrong, Arnold, *Parched Earth*, 41
Atteberry, Jeffrey, 198n19

Badiou, Alain, 101
Baker, Houston, 12, 47, 55
Bakunin, Mikhail, 75; *Statism and Anarchy*, 75
Baldwin, James, 50, 116, 172; "Everybody's Protest Novel," 172; "Many Thousands Gone," 172
Baltimore Afro-American (periodical), 115
Basset, Theodore, 115
Bates, Ruby, 7–8
Baudelaire, Charles, 36
Beauvoir, Simone de, 188n64
Benjamin, Walter, 36, 47; on ragpicker, 36
Berke, Nancy, 149–50, 163–64, 194n2
Berry, Abner, 115
black culture, 5–6, 9, 15, 46–48, 140, 169, 172, 174; and labor, 161; and literature, 48; and lumpenproletariat, 48
black folk. *See* folk
Black Lives Matter, 19
black lumpenproletariat, 19, 134, 163, 175; defined by *Native Son* as agent of revolutionary change, 17; and identity, 53; and marginality, 52; in Marseilles, 38; and recognition of subjectivity, 63; revolutionary potential of, 30–31, 53
black Marseilles lumpenproletariat, 38
black Marxism, 1–2, 4–5, 9–10, 19–20, 48, 53, 139, 159, 169; Ellison and Wright as coarticulators of, 118
Black Panther Party, 3, 15; dress style of, 3; and lumpenproletariat, 3–4, 9, 17, 20, 28–34; and Marx and Engels, 33–34; and Marxism, 4, 17, 28, 34, 178; Wright anticipates, 53
black vagabond, 39
blacks, transatlantic, and labor, 46
blues music, 47–48, 55, 94–95, 134; and African Americans, 94
Bobbio, Norberto, 104
Bonaparte, Louis-Napoléon, 22, 25
Booker, Chris, 33
bottom dogs fiction, 12, 40, 42–45, 55, 107
bourgeois political economy, 27
Brown, Carolyn J., 137
Brown, Cecil, 12, 33, 47–48, 140
bureaucratization, and revolutionary change, 112–13
Bussard, Robert, 21

Callahan, John F., 98
Cantwell, Robert, *The Land of Plenty*, 41
capitalism, 7, 31–32, 43, 45; and Bigger Thomas (*Native Son*), 51–52; and catharsis, 104; and crime, 157; and Jim Crow, 62, 102, 104–5, 120, 126–27, 126–28, 135; and labor, 84; and lumpenproletariat, 138, 158, 160, 175; and nationalism, 58; and prostitution, 141; and racism, 144; and slavery, 11; and slums, 158; and technology, 101; and workers, 60, 168; and working class, 30. *See also* financiers; social order, economic determination of
Carmichael, Stokely, 33
catharsis, 103–4
Catholicism, 128–29
Cayton, Horace, *Black Metropolis*, 66, 147
Certeau, Michel de, 46–48
chaos, 98–99
children, 90
cinema, 57; in *Native Son*, 67–69

[200]

city, 99; urban life, 26, 47. *See also* polis
class rule, 56–57, 104–5, 120
class struggle, 72, 103
Cleaver, Eldridge, 3, 45, 58; criticism of, 32–33; on lumpenproletariat, 29–30, 143; Marxism repurposed by, 29–33; on proletariat, 53; "ultimate revolutionary demand," 148; Walker anticipates, 142
Cleaver, Kathleen, 3–4, 29, 34
colonial context, 28–29. *See also* imperialism
communism, 43–45, 106; and crime/criminality, 74–75; Depression writers drawn to, 55; and racism, 178
Communist Party, 34; and African Americans, 5–7, 9, 83–84, 112–13, 172; "Black Belt" thesis, 5–6, 108; on black folk identity, 97, 108; criticism of, 176–77; and Ellison, 96, 112; literary inadequacy of, 113–15; and lumpenproletariat, 43; and racism, 5; and Scottsboro incident, 6–7, 104; and Walker, 136–37, 171, 194n2; Workers' Alliance, 160; and Wright, 1–2, 50, 56, 63, 172, 176–77, 186n4, 198n19; in Wright's *Native Son*, 83–88
Conroy, Jack, 137
Costello, Brannon, 60
Crane, Stephen, *Maggie: A Girl of the Streets*, 11, 37–38
crime/criminality, 73–82; and action, 174; and blackness, 123–24; and capitalism, 157; and gender, 167; glamorization of, 164; and Jim Crow, 165; juvenile delinquency, 138, 157; and labor, 158, 169; and lumpenproletariat, 140, 176; Marx and Engels on, 138; in *Native Son* (Wright), 76–79, 85–88; and recognition of subjectivity, 75–80; redefined in African American folklore, 18; and revolutionary change, 73–75, 160; in *Tillman and Tackhead* (Ellison), 121–24
Crisis (journal), 136

Cruse, Harold, 9

Dahlberg, Edward, 12, 43, 45; *Bottom Dogs*, 42
Daily Worker (periodical), 117
Davis, Angela, *Women, Race, and Class*, 194n93
Davis, Ben, Jr., 115
Davis, Frank Marshall, 173
Dawahare, Anthony, 58, 89, 171; *Nationalism, Marxism, and African American Literature between the Wars*, 186n8
deconstruction, 20–21, 24, 27, 47, 92, 143. *See also* philosophy
desire: beyond proletarian organization, 5; and revolutionary change, 62, 121; for subjective visibility, 52, 63, 73, 78; for subjectivity, in *Native Son*, 63–72
diaspora, 38–39
Dickstein, Morris, 55–56
dislocation, 17
Dolinar, Brian, 5–6
domestic/domesticity, 59–60, 65, 70–71, 81–82, 88, 90, 92–93. *See also* labor; workers
double consciousness, 121, 163
Douglass, Frederick, and Marx, 133–34
Drake, Kimberly, 58–59, 79; *Subjectivity in the American Protest Novel*, 186n8
Drake, St. Clair, *Black Metropolis*, 66, 147
Draper, Hal, 21, 24
Dubey, Madhu, 151
Du Bois, W. E. B., 38, 52; *Black Reconstruction*, 174; *The Souls of Black Folk*, 52, 163
Dunbar, Paul Laurence, 158

Edmunds, Susan, 65
Edwards, Brent Hayes, 3, 38–39
Elder, Matthew, 186n8
Ellison, Ralph, 165; on chaos, 98–99; and Communist Party, 96, 112; in Dayton, 116–17; in Decatur, 104–5; on fluidity of American society, 18,

[201]

Ellison, Ralph (*continued*)
97–100; on folk, 108–9; "Harlem is Nowhere," 16; "Hidden Name and Complex Fate," 99; "Hymie's Bull," 13, 110–11; "I Did Not Learn Their Names," 106–8, 110; and institutional critique, 111–16, 173–74; on integration, 90–91; *Invisible Man*, 98, 170–71, 173; on Jim Crow, 104–5; and lumpenproletarian black Marxism, 118; and lumpenproletariat, 2, 94–97, 103, 105–6, 125–26, 174; and Marxism, 10, 12–13, 96–97, 99, 102–3, 105, 108, 110, 132, 135, 171, 173–74; "A Party Down at the Square," 102, 104; and possibility, 135; psychological interest of, 16, 130; "Remembering Richard Wright" (lecture), 1, 13; *Shadow and Act*, 99; trip from Oklahoma to Tuskegee, 96–97, 99–101, 111; "Twentieth-Century Fiction and the Black Mask of Humanity," 10; and Walker, 14; "The World and the Jug," 182n29; on Wright, 1, 13, 170; and Wright, 12–13, 113, 117; on Wright's *Native Son*, 13, 114–16

—*Slick*, 4, 18, 97, 104, 125–35; Douglass and Marx in, 133–34; hunting in, 132–34; resembles *Native Son*, 117, 126; writing of, 116–17

—"Slick Gonna Learn," 125; on technology, 101–3, 127

—*Tillman and Tackhead*, 4, 13, 18, 97, 116–25; painting slashed in, 121–22; person slashed in, 123–24; writing of, 116–17

Engels, Friedrich: and Black Panther Party, 33–34; *The Communist Manifesto*, 22–24, 31, 40–41, 45; on criminality, 138; on lumpenproletariat, 2, 21–28, 41, 50, 141; *The Peasant War in Germany*, 22

Entin, Joseph, 189n77

equality, 32

Evans, Walker, *Let Us Now Praise Famous Men*, 35

everyday tactic, 46–48
existentialism, 72, 98, 176; and Marxism, 72

Fabre, Michel, *The Unfinished Quest of Richard Wright*, 186n4, 188n64
Fanon, Frantz, 3, 28–29, 31; on lumpenproletariat, 29; Marx revised by, 29; *The Wretched of the Earth*, 28
fascism, 6, 24, 49, 51, 63
Favor, J. Martin, 108
feminization, tropes of, 89
Ferguson (Missouri), uprising in, 19
financiers, 23–24
fluidity, 97–100, 110, 120; and lumpenproletariat, 125; and overdetermination, 101
Foley, Barbara, 6, 43, 92, 96, 98, 131, 171, 173; *Radical Representations*, 40; *Wrestling with the Left: The Making of Ralph Ellison's "Invisible Man,"* 10, 190n5
folk, 103, 108–11, 120; ballads, 138–40; black folk, 5, 34, 97, 108–9, 111, 113, 139–40, 160, 164–65, 169; lumpenfolk, 18, 97, 110–11. See also Du Bois, W. E. B.
Fouché, Rayvon, 102
free indirect discourse, 155
freight trains. *See* trains
French Revolution, 70–71
Freud, Sigmund, 16
Furr, Derek, 162, 168

gangsters, vs. workers, 60
gender: and crime/criminality, 167; in Walker, 141, 148, 154, 167; in Wright, 53–54, 59, 81, 88–90, 92–93. *See also* intersectionality; masculinity; patriarchy; prostitution; women
George, Stephen, 186n8
Gibson, Donald, 52
Gilroy, Paul, 46
Gilyard, Keith, 167
Gold, Mike, 51; *Jews Without Money*, 41–42

Goose Island (Chicago, IL), 15, 153–60. *See also* Walker, Margaret
Gorky, Maxim, 62
Gorz, André, 145
Gramsci, Antonio, 15, 98, 103, 105, 110, 112, 131
Great Migration, 56, 71, 108, 161
Griffiths, Frederick T., 190n5
Guttman, Sandra, 84

Hall, Stuart, 105; *Policing the Crisis: Mugging, the State, and Law and Order,* 46
happiness, 70–71
Hardt, Michael, 2
Harlem Renaissance, 11, 38, 109
Harris, Trudier, 89
Hayes, Peter, 23
Henry, John, 140, 144, 163, 167–68
Higashida, Cheryl, 7–8, 89
Himmelfarb, Gertrude, 23
history, 82
hobos, 13, 45–47, 60, 104–5; as archetypal figure of lumpenproletariat, 7
Hobson, Christopher Z., 190n5
Homer, Winslow: and African Americans, 119; *The Gulf Stream,* 118–25, 129
Honig, Bonnie, 90–91
hospitals, 128–29, 132
housing, 82
Howe, Irving, "Black Boys and Native Sons," 172
Huckleberry Finn, 10–11, 36–38; as lumpenproletariat, 36; and rags, 36–37
Hugo, Victor, *Les Misérables,* 145
hunting, 117, 127–28, 132–34
Hyman, Stanley Edgar, 94–95

identity: black folk, 97, 108–9; and recognition, 64, 77; transnational, 39; Wright challenges Marxist sense of, 52–53. *See also* recognition; subjectivity
ideology, 67, 69

imperialism, 38–39, 62–63, 108. *See also* colonial context
institutional critique, 111–16, 173–74; literary inadequacy, 114
integration, 90–91
intellectuals, 112
internationalism, 5–6, 11, 38–39, 42, 113, 133
interpellation, negative, 67
intersectionality, 7, 17–18, 40, 45, 53–54, 139, 149, 162. *See also* domestic/domesticity; gender; prostitution; women

Jackson, Lawrence, 5, 12, 170–71
James, C. L. R., 16
James, William, *The Principles of Psychology,* 66
Jameson, Fredric, 15, 51, 72, 82–83, 88
JanMohamed, Abdul, 78, 80; *The Death-Bound Subject: Richard Wright's Archaeology of Death,* 186n8
jazz, 1, 99
Jennings, Michael, 36
Jim Crow, 18, 107; and capitalism, 62, 102, 104–5, 120, 126–28, 135; and crime/criminality, 165; and desire for revolutionary change, 121; Ellison on, 104–5; and *The Gulf Stream* (Homer), 119–25; and Marxism, 8; and masculinity, 55; Oklahoma City, 99; and overdetermination, 102; and social order, 105; in *Tillman and Tackhead* (Ellison), 119–25; and transience, 54, 56; and working class, 176
juvenile delinquency, 138, 153–54, 156–57

Kafka, Franz, 16
Karageorgos, Konstantina M., 188n64
Kelley, Robin D. G., 6
Kierkegaard, Soren, 16
Killens, John Oliver, *A Man Ain't Nothing But a Man,* 167
Kobrin, Solomon, 153

labor, 32, 57, 59; and African Americans, 161, 168; Arendt on, 69–70, 90–91; and black culture, 161; and capitalism, 84; and crime, 158, 169; Huckleberry Finn avoids, 36; and John Henry, 168; and lumpenproletariat, 48, 145–46, 158; Marx on, 142; and Marxism, 46, 83–84; in *Native Son,* 64–65; postal work, 58; and prostitution, 146, 150; transatlantic blacks don't see emancipation in, 46. *See also* domestic/domesticity; prostitution; workers; working class

LaCapra, Dominick, 22, 28

leadership, 111–14, 134; literary inadequacy of, 114

Lenin, Vladimir, 33, 61–63

Lennon, John, 7–8

Levine, Lawrence, 11

literary analysis, 26–27

literature: African American, 17, 49–51, 170; and black culture, 48; bottom dogs fiction, 12, 40, 42–45, 55, 107; free indirect discourse, 155; literary inadequacy, 114; proletarian, 40–43, 57. *See also* names of individual authors

Long, Huey, 44

Louis, Joe, 109–10, 113, 126, 131

Lucy, Robin, 108–9

Lukács, Georg, 174; *The Historical Novel,* 16

lumpen, 22, 181n7

lumpen-folk, 18, 97, 110–11

lumpenproletariat: and African Americans, 3, 48, 163; against every organized structure in the world, 32; Bigger Thomas (*Native Son*) as archetype of, 17, 49–51; and black culture, 48; and black Marxism, 10; and Black Panther Party, 3–4, 9, 17, 20, 28–34; and capitalism, 175; Cleaver on, 29–30, 143; and crime/criminality, 140, 176; as de-classed, 94–95; definition of, 2, 21; and Ellison, 2, 94–97, 103, 105–6, 125–26, 174; Fanon on, 29; and fluidity, 125; focus on, 12; hobo as archetypal figure of, 7; and labor, 48, 145–46, 158; Marx and Engels on, 2, 21–28, 41–42, 50, 52, 60, 63, 75, 83–84, 95, 105, 138, 141, 148–49, 153–55, 163, 169, 175, 183n16; and Marxism, 2–3, 7–8, 17–18, 20, 27–28, 33, 40, 43, 138; misery, 156; and potential, 40; as precursor to post-class society, 32, 107; and proletariat, 21–23, 26, 30–31, 53, 57, 80–82, 142, 144–45, 168; and raggedness, 35, 40; rags as figures of, 17; resistance to revisions of, 32–33; and revolutionary change, 33, 46, 50, 55–56, 62, 105–7, 138, 173, 178–79; in *Slick* (Ellison), 132–33; in *Tillman and Tackhead* (Ellison), 121; and transience, 54–56; vagabondage, 39; and Walker, 2, 18, 54, 138–40, 142–45, 142–46, 142–47, 149–50, 149–51, 158, 160, 167; and women, 11, 54, 139; and Wright, 1, 14, 17, 52–53, 56–57, 61, 63, 80–82; writing about, 45. *See also* black lumpenproletariat; proletariat

lynching, 8

Malraux, André, 16

marginality, 35; and African Americans, 47; and black lumpenproletariat, 52; and potential, 38; and raggedness, 35, 37, 40; and revolutionary change, 53, 57, 139, 178; and Wright, 177. *See also* social order; society

Marx, Karl: and Algren, 44–45; and Black Panther Party, 33–34; *Capital,* 26, 142; *The Class Struggles in France,* 49; *The Communist Manifesto,* 22–24, 31, 40–41, 45; *A Contribution to the Critique of Political Economy,* 103; on criminality, 138; and Douglass, 133–34; *Economic and Philosophical Manuscripts,* 27, 141, 149; *The Eighteenth Brumaire of Louis Napoleon,* 25, 31, 95, 133–34, 154; Fanon revises, 29; "first as tragedy, then as farce," 133; "gens sans feu," 24–25, 29, 49; *The*

German Ideology, 73; on labor, 142; on lumpenproletariat, 2, 21–28, 41–42, 50, 52, 60, 63, 75, 83–84, 95, 105, 138, 141, 148–49, 153–55, 163, 169, 175, 183n16; on prostitution, 141–42; on revolution of 1848, 22, 27; on urban life, 26

Marx, Karl, 16, 44

Marxism: and African American literature, 170; and African Americans, 1–2, 4, 9, 19, 33, 52, 95, 117, 138, 170–72; and Black Panther Party, 4, 17, 28, 34, 178; Cleaver repurposes, 29–33; deconstruction of, 20–21, 27; and desire for recognition, 72; and Ellison, 10, 12–13, 96–97, 99, 102–3, 105, 108, 110, 132, 135, 171, 173–74; and existentialism, 72; and Jim Crow, 8; and labor, 46, 83–84; limitations of, 26–28; and lumpenproletariat, 2–3, 7–8, 17–18, 20, 27–28, 33, 40, 43, 138; *Native Son* on, 114; objective/subjective determinations of, 82, 88; and proletariat, 145; revisionary, 2, 9, 17, 20, 29–34, 50–52, 57, 97, 109, 125, 134, 138–41, 143, 145, 169, 178–79; and subjectivity, 114; on wages, 167; and Walker, 10, 14–15, 136–38, 143; and Wright, 10, 12–14, 17, 49–52, 172–73. *See also* black Marxism

masculinity, 48, 54–55, 59–60, 76, 89; black, 54–55, 76, 123; and Jim Crow, 55

mass culture, 56, 60, 62, 69, 71, 74

masses, 112–13

Maxwell, William, 9, 39, 45, 50, 190n5

McKay, Claude: *Banjo,* 11, 38–39; *Home to Harlem,* 38

Miller, Charlie, 97, 106

Mills, Nathaniel, 197n11

Minus, Marian, 109, 111, 117; "Present Trends in Negro Literature," 109

mobility/transience, 54–56; and lumpenproletariat, 56; and revolutionary change, 55, 106

Montag, Warren, 67

Mootry, Maria, 89

Morgan, J. P., 66

movies, 57; in *Native Son,* 67–69

Munford, C. J., 32

Napoléon III, emperor of France, 22, 25

National Negro Conference, 112–13, 143

nationalism, 5–6, 9, 39, 58, 89, 108–9, 126, 171–72, 174; and capitalism, 58; and racism, 58

Neal, Larry, 96

Negri, Antonio, 2

Negro Quarterly (journal), 94

The New Anvil (magazine), 136–37, 151

New Challenge (journal), 137

New Masses (magazine), 51, 109, 112, 114, 117

Newton, Huey, 3, 29

Nicholls, David G., 108

Non-Aligned Movement, 178

Norman, Dorothy, 188n64

Norton, Anne, 91

Occupy Wall Street, 19

Ogbar, Jeffrey O. G., 33

Oklahoma City, 99, 103, 111

Ongiri, Amy, 3

outlaw. *See* crime/criminality

overdetermination, 100–102; and fluidity, 101; and Jim Crow, 102; and possibility, 101

paper: and African Americans, 39; and rags, 17, 35–36, 35–37, 39–40, 44, 151, 157

patriarchy, 38, 53, 166–67

permanent revolution, 61

philosophy, 15–16, 198n19; deconstruction, 20–21, 24, 27, 47, 92, 143; knowledge and truth, 34; *Native Son* as philosophical novel, 114. *See also* identity; possibility; potential; subjectivity

poet, 36

polis, 70–73, 77, 84, 88, 91, 93

Political Affairs (journal), 32

political economy, 27

[205]

politics, 90–91
poor/poverty, 2, 25–26, 43
possibility: and Ellison, 135; and overdetermination, 101; and raggedness, 37–38, 44
postal work, 58
potential: and lumpenproletariat, 40; and marginality, 38
proletariat, 40–41; Cleaver on, 53; literature, 40–43, 57; and lumpenproletariat, 21–23, 26, 30–31, 53, 57, 80–82, 142, 144–45, 168; and Marxism, 145; ragged, 35, 49, 174; revolution, 141; Walker on, 143–45; Wright on, 60
prostitution, 23, 37, 42, 141–43, 146–47, 149–51; and labor, 146, 150

race, Hall on, 105
racial divisions, 28–31, 33, 45, 58; and double consciousness, 121; and subjective in/visibility, 52; and subjectivity, 68
racism: and capitalism, 144; and communism, 178; and Communist Party, 5; and nationalism, 58; sterilization, 193n93; subjectivity of blackness/whiteness, 66–67; and trains, 107; and working class movement, 6. *See also* colonial context; Jim Crow; recognition; subjectivity
radios, 101, 127
ragged, 26
ragged proletariat, 35, 49, 174
raggedness, 17; and lumpenproletariat, 35, 40; and marginality, 35, 37, 40; and possibility, 37–38, 44
ragpicker, 36, 47
rags: and Huckleberry Finn, 36–37; and paper, 17, 35–36, 35–37, 39–40, 44, 151, 157; and revolutionary change, 152; in *Tillman and Tackhead* (Ellison), 122; in Walker, 151–52, 156–57
ragtime music, 48
Rampersad, Arnold, 98, 111, 117
Rancière, Jacques, 28

rap music, 47
rape, 79; and recognition, 79–80
reality, challenge apparent forms of, 98
recognition: and crime/criminality, 75–80; desire for, 63, 66; and identity, 64, 77; in *Native Son*, 85–87; nothing worse than being completely unnoticed, 66; and rape, 79–80; as revolutionary change, 63, 69, 72–73, 77, 84; and society, 78. *See also* identity; marginality; subjectivity
revolutionary change: and African Americans, 3–4, 6, 33–34, 84, 169; American Revolution, 70–71, 87; and black lumpenproletariat, 30–31, 53; and bureaucratization, 112–13; and crime/criminality, 73–75, 160; and desire, 62, 121; French Revolution, 70–71; and lumpenproletariat, 33, 46, 50, 55–56, 62, 105–7, 138, 173, 178–79; and marginality, 53, 57, 139, 178; and *Native Son*, 17, 51–52; origination of, 62; and overdetermination of social order, 100–102; permanent revolution, 61; philosophical background of, 15–16; and rags, 152; recognition of subjectivity as, 63, 69, 72–73, 77, 84; reconceived as outsider tactic, 12; Russian Revolution, 71; Soviet-style, 56–57, 61; and subjectivity, 51; and transience/mobility, 55, 106; ultimate demand of, 32; vanguard of, 3, 8, 12, 30, 32–33, 57; Walker on, 138, 162; and Wright, 53–57, 61
Rich, Adrienne, 90
Rideout, Walter, 42; *The Radical Novel in the United States*, 40
Robinson, Cedric, 9, 20, 52
Rollins, William, *The Shadow Before*, 41
Rowley, Hazel, 13, 53–54, 57; *Richard Wright: The Life and Times*, 186n4, 188n64
Russian Revolution, 71; Soviet-style revolution, 56–57, 61

Sartre, Jean-Paul, 15–16, 51, 72, 74, 76, 83, 188n64; *Search for a Method*, 72
school integration, 90
Scott, William, 165
Scottsboro case, 6–9, 61, 72, 104, 107, 110; and Communist Party, 6–7
Seale, Bobby, 33–34
Shaw, Clifford, 153; *The Jack-roller*, 153
Sheldon, William H., *Psychology and the Promethean Will*, 16, 130
Sillen, Samuel, 51
slavery, 87; and capitalism, 11; and imperialism, 39
slums, and capitalism, 158
Smethurst, James, 50
social order: African Americans outside of, 3–4; and crime/criminality, 74–75; economic determination of, 98, 103; Huckleberry Finn refuses, 10–11, 36–37; and Jim Crow, 105; overdetermination of, and revolutionary change, 100–102; and technology, 102. *See also* marginality
society: and Bigger Thomas (*Native Son*), 51; Ellison on fluidity of, 18, 97–100; lumpenproletariat as precursor to post-class, 32, 107; and recognition, 78; those who fall out of, 21, 23, 27, 31, 46, 50, 125. *See also* marginality
Solomon, William, 45, 50
Soviet-style revolution, 56–57, 61; Russian Revolution, 71
Soviet Union, 106, 178
Spassky, Natalie, 193n69
Stagolee, 11, 33, 47–48, 140, 164–69; as early antihero, 140
Stallybrass, Peter, 25, 28, 145, 183n16
sterilization, 193n93
subjectivity: Althusser on, 67; and blackness/whiteness, 66–68; and crime/criminality, 75–80; desire for, in *Native Son*, 63–72, 186n8; Ellison on lumpenproletarian, 105; and in/visibility of black subject, 52, 63; and Marxism, 114; *Native Son* as portrait of lumpenproletarian, 50;

and racial divisions, 68; and revolutionary change, 51. *See also* identity; recognition
Sunday Worker (periodical), 115
Sutton, Frank, 117

technology, 101–3, 127; and African Americans, 102
Third World, 178
Thoburn, Nicholas, 52–53
Thompson, Louise, 8
Tolentino, Cynthia, 187n8
Trader Horn (film), 67–69
trains, 6, 13, 45–47, 46–47, 54–56, 97, 104, 106–7, 110–11, 125, 165; and racism, 107; revolutionary implications of, 106
transience/mobility, 54–56; and lumpenproletariat, 56; and revolutionary change, 55, 106
Trotsky, Leon, 24, 61
truth, 34
Tuhkanen, Mikko, 83
Twain, Mark: *Adventures of Huckleberry Finn*, 37; *The Adventures of Tom Sawyer*, 36–37; Huckleberry Finn, 10–11, 36–38

urban life, 26, 47; city, 99. *See also* polis

Vincent, Ricky, 181n7

Wald, Alan, *Exiles from a Future Time: The Forging of the Mid-Twentieth-Century Literary Left*, 182n32, 194nn2–3
Walker, Margaret, 1, 12, 136–69; "Bad-Man Stagolee," 164–66; "Big John Henry," 167–68; and Communist Party, 136–37, 171, 194n2; and Ellison, 14; "Factory-hand," 143, 148; folk ballads, 138–40; *For My People*, 4, 10, 18, 140, 149, 157, 160, 162, 165, 167–68; gender in, 141, 148, 154, 167; *Goose Island*, 5, 14, 18, 138–39, 153–60, 164, 174, 176; "Gun Moll," 145–50; *Jubilee*, 16, 174–76; "Kissie Lee," 166–67;

[207]

Walker, Margaret (*continued*)
"Lineage," 162, 166–67; and Lukács, 16; and lumpenproletariat, 2, 18, 54, 138–40, 142–47, 149–51, 158, 160, 167; and Marxism, 10, 14–15, 136–40, 143; "Men At Work," 144–45; "Molly Means," 163–64; on proletariat, 143–45; "Prostitute," 150; prostitution in, 141–43, 146–47, 149–51; "Radical Revolutionary," 138–39; on rags, 151–52, 156–57; "The Red Satin Dress," 136, 151–52; on revolutionary change, 138, 162; "Rich Fokes Worl," 144, 148; "Two-Gun Buster and Trigger Slim," 168; "Whores," 149; on women, 18, 146–47, 149, 162; on working class, 143, 148, 151; and Wright, 13–14, 137–38, 143

Warner, Michael, 73, 84

Weatherwax, Clara, *Marching! Marching!*, 41

welfare, 31

Wertham, Fredric, 16

white supremacy, 44–45, 54, 99, 102

white trash, 8

Williams, Raymond, 108

Winston, Henry, 32

Wolfe, Jesse, 97

women, 7–8, 38; in Arendt, 90; and lumpenproletariat, 11, 54, 139; undercover as male hobos, 104; Walker on, 18, 146–47, 149, 162; in Wright, 59, 88–89, 92–93. *See also* gender; intersectionality; prostitution

Wood, Peter H., 119

work. *See* labor

workers, 7–8, 27, 32; and capitalism, 60, 168; vs. gangsters, 60; and prostitution, 141

working class, 30–31; African Americans, 53; and Jim Crow, 176; and proletariat literature, 40; and racism, 6; in Walker, 143, 148, 151; in Wright, 59–60, 64, 81

WPA, 137, 152

Wright, John S., 101–2

Wright, Richard, 137; "Almos' a Man," 55; anticipates Black Panthers, 53; "Big Boy Leaves Home," 54; *Black Hope*, 92–93, 146; "Blueprint for Negro Writing," 109; in Chicago, 1, 62; *The Color Curtain: A Report on the Bandung Conference*, 178; and Communist Party, 1–2, 50, 56, 63, 172, 176–77, 186n4, 198n19; crime/criminality in, 73–82, 87–88; domesticity in, 59–60, 65, 70–71, 81–82, 88, 90, 92–93; and Ellison, 12–13, 113; Ellison on, 170; and Ellison, rift with, 117; and folk, 108–9; gender in, 53–54, 59, 81, 85, 88–90, 92–93; "How 'Bigger' Was Born," 49, 61, 63, 114; "Joe Louis Uncovers Dynamite," 109–10, 126; *Lawd, Today!*, 4, 53, 57–62, 81, 89, 126, 144, 172; and lumpenproletarian black Marxism, 118; and lumpenproletariat, 1, 14, 17, 52–53, 56–57, 61, 63, 80–82; and marginality, 177; and Marxism, 10, 12–14, 17, 49–52, 172–73; *12 Million Black Voices*, 56, 71

—*Native Son*, 4, 49–53, 59, 63–67, 70–73, 89, 126, 130, 144, 160, 176–77; Baldwin on, 172; Bigger Thomas as lumpenproletarian, 17, 49–51; and capitalism, 51–52; communism in, 83–88; desire for subjectivity, 63–72; Ellison on, 13, 114–16; Marx clouds reading of, 50–51; movie scene, 67–69; murder in, 76–79, 85–88; and pulp fiction, 189n77; rape in, 79; recognition in, 85–87; reviews of, 51, 114–16; and revolutionary change, 17, 51–52; Walker influence on, 14

—*The Outsider*, 176–77; patriarchal tendencies of, 53; and philosophy, 16; on proletariat, 60; and revolutionary change, 53–57, 61; "Transcontinental," 4, 56–57, 62; and Walker, friendship, 13–14, 137–38, 143; women in, 59, 88–89, 92–93; on working class, 59–60, 64, 81

—*Writing Red* (anthology), 136

Yaeger, Patricia, 35

www.ingramcontent.com/pod-product-compliance
Lightning Source LLC
Chambersburg PA
CBHW030137240426
43672CB00005B/161